JON POLITO

Jon Polito:

Unicycling at the Edge of the Abyss—An Actor's Autobiography

By Jon Polito
As told to Scott Voisin

JON POLITO: *Unicycling at the Edge of the Abyss—An Actor's Autobiography*

© 2022 By Jon Polito As told to Scott Voisin

Published in the United States of America by:

BearManor Media
1317 Edgewater Dr #110
Orlando FL 32804
bearmanormedia.com

Printed in the United States.

All photos used with permission.

Typesetting and layout by DataSmith Solutions

Cover by DataSmith Solutions

ISBN — 978-1-62933-891-0

Acknowledgments

Scott Voisin would like to thank the following people for their contributions:

James Pippi, for collecting and sharing many of the photos of Jon's friends and family used to illustrate this book.

Charlie Peters and Stephen Rivele, for taking time off from writing their own novels and screenplays in order to proofread the manuscript and offer important feedback.

My wife Alysia Voisin, and my daughters, Trinity and Hallie, for their continued love, patience and understanding as I endlessly toil away on my laptop in the basement.

Tim Ferrante, for spending a few years of his life poring over Jon's autobiography page by page, word for word, over and over (and over) again. This book wouldn't have been nearly as good without your eagle eyes, keen insight and masterful editorial suggestions, for which I'm forever in your debt.

And Darryl Armbruster… Jon and I worked on this book together, but you were the inspiration in seeing it through to the end. That wouldn't have been possible without your encouraging words and endless support.

Foreword

"OH, MY GAWD! CAN WE PLEASE JUST DO IT OVER AGAIN? I SUCKED IN THAT ONE! PLEASE DEAR GOD IN HOLY HELL!!!"

Those, ladies and gentlemen, were the first words I heard out of Jon Polito's mouth. I fell in love with him immediately.

We were in New Orleans on the set of *Miller's Crossing*. I'd already completed my first day of shooting which, in my opinion, had gone horribly. I was green, awkward, self-conscious and nervous as hell. This was my first movie, directed by the funny, kind and genius Coen brothers. Delighted? Yes, of course! Who wouldn't be? But this was the BIG time; an A-list film. I was a theater actor just out of grad school and didn't want to blow it! I took myself SOOOO seriously, and insecurity threatened to cripple anything creative that was going on in my head or body.

Did they notice that I didn't hit my mark? What does "next set-up" mean? What does "turning around" mean? How do I know the size of the shot? How come nothing happens when a scene ends? How come no one claps? The AD (what IS an AD?) just says, "Moving on," and it's over. That moment is gone forever!

This was all new for a theater gal, so I decided to visit the set and learn from the legends: Albert Finney, John Turturro, Gabriel Byrne and Jon Polito.

The stage was dark, I crossed over cables and equipment and shrank into the shadows, a fly on the wall. Yep, there was John Turturro crying on cue, making Joel and Ethan laugh. (*Shit, I hope I'll be able to do that!*) And there was Gabriel Byrne – not a bad angle on his beautiful, chiseled face – mumbling in his sexy accent. (*I hope the camera likes MY face!*) There's Albert Finney punching his way downstairs, the stunt man falling backwards. But wait! What's he doing before they say action? Is he actually punching air? And huffing and puffing? (*It looks really embarrassing. I wonder what the crew thinks?*) Albert later told me he was creating, "The moment before, daaahlinng. One has to be private in public, my dear." (*Shit. I don't know anything! I'm going to be laughed at!*)

Then there was Jon Polito... He was literally sweating buckets; rivulets of perspiration running off his bald head down to his pencil-thin mustache. He was playing mob boss Johnny Caspar as a lovable, morally conflicted, funny and fierce gangster who had his own ideas about ethics. Take after take, Jon tried something new. He listened. He was brave. And most importantly, he laughed at himself when he screwed up. In fact, he announced it! "I SUCK. PLEASE, CAN WE GO AGAIN?!" (*So THIS is how it's done!*) Later that evening, we met at the bar for a vodka. "Oh Marcia, stop taking yourself so seriously! Take the work seriously but not yourself. They can't laugh *at* you if you can laugh at yourself. They laugh *with* you." This is perhaps the best life advice I've ever received.

Jon quickly became my good friend. We partied together, gossiped together, ate together, drank together and jumped on the bed together. But my favorite times with Jon were talking about the craft of acting and listening to his critiques. He was generous – with his emotions, his own insecurities, his struggles and his opinions. He was loud and ballsy, and very soon held a special place in my heart.

At my wedding several years later, Jon arrived in Texas after a long flight, and I learned he'd held the newborn baby of our manager, Mary-ellen Mulcahy, for most of the trip. Jon Polito... baby whisperer? Yes, he was! When he finally made it to the ranch, he quickly realized we were in a dry county and would have none of it. Within minutes, he rallied several other fun cohorts and was off to the package store, returning with beer, wine and copious amounts of vodka.

Later that night under a dark Texas sky, Jon held our party spellbound while he played the piano, thrilling us with his own soft composition. It was intimate and melancholy, a side of Jon not often shared, but it filled the night with romance. I was again struck by his many remarkable and varied talents.

Watching Jon work was like a master class in acting. No matter the project, he created little windows for his characters; a moment when you could see behind the presented self, behind the words and recognize the frailty of the human being. Jon understood that being human is a struggle and he wanted audiences to recognize themselves in his characters.

Jon battled an addiction to alcohol and drugs, aided and abetted by a large group of fellow partiers. Eventually, this group turned into people who simply wanted to use him. And although he had an enormous capacity to give love, Jon never really believed anyone would truly love him for who he was. When he met Darryl Armbruster sometime after 2000, the new century presented him with the best gift of his life. Jon became sober and he inspired others to do the same. Most importantly, he finally learned that he was *worthy* of love.

During the latter years of Jon's life, he worked with Scott Voisin writing this autobiography. Thank goodness! It's full of old Hollywood stories, self-deprecating humor and the kind of smart, humane and sassy insights that defined Jon as an actor, a friend and a simply marvelous human being.

— Marcia Gay Harden

The September 1990 premiere of Miller's Crossing *with Marcia Gay Harden, Joel Coen, John Turturro, Ethan Coen and Gabriel Byrne*

"Unicycling at the edge of the abyss… That's how I describe surviving many of the events in my life. There've been times I've come dangerously close to falling into that dark, bottomless pit, but through luck or fate or divine intervention, I found myself able to pedal away."

— *Jon Polito*

Contents

Prologue

I arrived in New York in 1974 – big suitcase in hand, fully packed with clothes and dreams – and was about to enter the Actors' Equity Building on 46th Street and 7th Avenue to officially register with the union. I walked in the door and a rather attractive guy turned to me and asked, "Do you want to be on television?" *This has to be fate*, I thought. I was already on my way to fame and hadn't even reached the elevators yet.

"Absolutely!" I replied, at which point he gave me a little card and said to call the phone number printed on it.

It turned out this guy was a shill who was hoping to entice people to try out for *The $10,000 Pyramid*, hosted by Dick Clark. You had to go for an interview, and if you did well and passed a practice round, you *might* get on the program. Truth be told, I'd never actually seen the show, but ten thousand dollars in 1974 was like half a million to me. I took it as a sign I was at the right place at the right time, something I'd heard repeatedly was the key to success in show business.

With my potentially life-changing *Pyramid* audition card in hand, I went up to the Equity office to register my name. After waiting in line for about forty-five minutes – the first of many lines I'd be waiting in for auditions over the years – I finally got to speak with a rather officious woman. She said, "Oh, your name is Polito... You don't want to keep that, do you?"

"Why wouldn't I?"

"Well, Philip Polito is very famous right now for the play *1776* and it would be too much of a conflict," she explained.

"Polito is my father's given name and I'm going to keep it, but I'll tell you what I'll do... I'll take the 'h' out of John and make it Jon Polito."

"Have it your way," she uttered dismissively.

I was officially JON POLITO, union actor!

With that business taken care of, I hopped on the subway and went down to the Chelsea district to stay with my buddy Michael Morin, a fellow actor from my college theater company. He'd made the move from Philadelphia just months before and generously offered to share his little ground floor apartment. Aside from Michael, I had no other connections and spent the next week looking around and wondering where I could get a job.

At this point in the '70s, painted denim clothing was the "in" thing and being a hippie at heart, I'd gone with the artistic fey and fashionable look. I couldn't afford much except what I could piece together and paint myself. One day, I walked into a store around the corner from Michael's apartment and there was a bearded, Serpico-looking guy who loved what I was wearing. He said, "I'm starting up a clothing factory and we're going to do painted tee shirts. You're obviously an artist so why don't you work with me? Can you use an airbrush?"

"Of course," I answered, not having any idea how to airbrush anything. "I can do whatever you need but it'll cost you $200 a week." Shockingly, the man agreed! I thought, *Wow, if I can fake my way through this for at least four weeks, that's $800. I'll be able to live for months!*

In the meantime, I was filling out all the forms to get on *The $10,000 Pyramid.* I wasn't very good at the game… As a matter of fact, I watched the show twice and it didn't make much sense. It was kind of like Charades except you gave words as clues, and I practiced by watching it in the afternoon while trying to figure out how in the hell I was going to paint shirts when I didn't know the first thing about an airbrush. I thought if I actually had one maybe I could learn how to use it, so I borrowed $150 from my parents to buy the equipment.

On a Tuesday, I got the call saying I'd been chosen to be a contestant and was told to report the next morning. That same day, I took the subway down to the arts district in Soho to purchase an airbrush and compressor. After spending an hour-and-a-half searching for the best, low-cost devices, I hailed a taxi because I had to get back to Michael's apartment to watch the show one more time. A beautiful blue-eyed cab driver stopped, smiled and said, "How ya doing, sir? Where are we going?"

"Get me to 21st and 8th Avenue," I replied hastily. "I've got to see *The $10,000 Pyramid!*"

"21st and 8th, you've got it." And off we went. He turned to me and said, "You know, sir, you're the very first person I've had in this cab."

And BAM! We smashed into another car.

My face violently slammed into the partition, crushing my glasses into the bridge of my nose. The cab driver looked and said, "Oh my God, mister, oh my God!"

"What's wrong?" I asked.

"You don't look so good. We've got to get you to the hospital."

"Forget the hospital!" I said defiantly. "Get me to 21st and 8th! I've got to see *The $10,000 Pyramid!*" After arriving at Michael's place, the driver kept insisting I seek medical attention. Swearing everything was fine, I got out and in my dazed condition, I not only paid the fare but included a generous tip, too.

I rushed into the apartment and turned on the show – which was now almost over – but I couldn't watch in front of the TV because I was literally covered in blood. There was a huge chunk of flesh missing from between my eyes and the area was beginning to swell. Knowing that look wouldn't play for daytime television, I went to St. Vincent's emergency room around 5 p.m. A doctor and nurse drugged me, stitched up the wound and put a huge brace on the top of my nose to protect the damage. Even though they said not to remove any of it, I told them, "I *have* to remove it. I'm going to be on *The $10,000 Pyramid* tomorrow morning!"

In a bit of a haze, I made it back to Michael's apartment around midnight. He walked into his place, saw blood splashed all over the sink and floor, and started to panic. Looking like Marlon Brando in *On the Waterfront*, I explained the situation and he wisely suggested canceling my appearance on the show. "I'm going in at six and see what happens," I said. He was being realistic. I was being loopy.

After a few hours of painkiller-induced sleep, I woke up at five, selected two outfits – I was told to bring two in case I made it through the first show, at which point I could change clothes and pretend it was another day – and packed up my makeup kit. When I arrived at the Ed Sullivan Theater, the producer took one look and said, "Oh, honey, we can't put you on."

"There's no problem," I replied. "Wait'll you see what I can do." I went into the bathroom, pulled off the brace, placed a tiny bandage over the stitches on my swollen nose, used a little makeup to smooth the rough edges and put on my denim outfit. I came out and declared triumphantly, "I can do it!"

On the set of The $10,000 Pyramid

She said, "Well, I don't really think you should but we'll keep you in the lineup." I took a seat with the other contestants in the audience and waited for the first group of people to go through the show. I didn't know when – or more importantly, *if* – I was even going to be on. The announcer warmed up the audience and when Dick Clark came out, we were cued by bright, blinking "Applause" signs, which we enthusiastically obliged. The two guest celebrities were Jo Ann Pflug – a very pretty, smart and shapely woman from the movie *M*A*S*H* who had the longest eyelashes I'd ever seen – and Nipsey Russell, who was very popular on *Pyramid* because he was one of the best players. By this time, the medication and lack of sleep were beginning to take their toll. I was disoriented, my head was spinning and odd thoughts started racing through my mind: *What is Nipsey Russell famous for? Should I tell Dick Clark that I'm from Philadelphia and my brother and sister were on* American Bandstand? *How the hell can Pflug see through those ten-foot eyelashes?*

The game began and as soon as one of the players lost, someone approached me and barked, "Okay, you're next." I was whisked up on stage and partnered with Jo Ann Pflug. Although I was physically sitting beside her, my mind was in another world.

Dick Clark walked to his podium, having been told that the person in denim has a bandage on his nose and he should comment on it. "Our next contestant is Jon Polito," he began. "I understand you had an accident."

I responded with, "Yeah, these New York cab drivers…" And the audience started to laugh! Through bleary eyes and hearing that reaction, I thought I was the best thing in the world even though I had no idea what I was doing there.

Mr. Clark asked, "Which category would you like to start with?"

"You choose, Jo Ann," I said confidently, stoned out of my gourd.

The first clue appeared. She turned to me and said, "A Mexican hat."

I looked at her and she blinked. All I saw were those huge fans of hairy eyelashes.

Tick. Tick. Tick.

Say WHAT? I don't know what the hell she means…

She tried again. "A *MEXICAN* hat."

Blink. Blink.

"I… I… wha…?"

BUZZ! My time was up.

Nipsey Russell and his partner chose a category and got every one of the answers right, winning the round and – eventually – the game.

It was over… So much for a cushy financial beginning to my career! As a consolation gift, I received an electric blanket. Later on, I thought about that good-looking fellow who asked if I wanted to be on TV. Well, I was on TV and I blew it. It wasn't the first time I squandered a huge opportunity, nor would it be the last.

How to Become a Star

I was fourteen or fifteen when I realized I wanted to be an actor, but as a fat, pimply and awkward kid, I couldn't even get into the plays being staged at my high school, West Philadelphia Catholic High School for Boys. Brother William, the head of the theater department, wasn't very fond of me and made it clear I wouldn't be participating in any of the upcoming productions.

About four blocks away was our counterpart institution, West Philadelphia Catholic Girls. One day, I heard auditions were being held there for a musical called *Carnival*, and with no other options available, I tried out for it. I was depressed as a young man and I remember riding a trolley to school the morning they were going to announce who would be in *Carnival*'s chorus. I thought, *If I don't get into this, I'm going to kill myself*. I was THAT kind of dramatic person; everything was life or death. I *had* to be an actor and if I didn't make it, I was going to give up... permanently. When I got there, I found out I'd been chosen to be part of the chorus and was finally going to achieve my dream!

Things really began to change with the arrival of Brother Dominic Garvey at West as the new head of the theater department, taking over from Brother William. He was kind of a genius and was studying for his third PhD at Villanova University. When I met Dominic, he immediately began to engage me and I, in turn, tried my best to impress him. I think I reminded him of himself when

he was younger, and he cast me in my first theatrical role in *The Man Who Came to Dinner*. I played a very flamboyant character and got my first laugh from an audience, which was intoxicating.

Dominic was determined to shake things up and began to change the way theater was thought of at West Catholic. He was organizing the drama students into a professional troupe and when Villanova needed projects mounted, he offered to have us perform in them. Thanks to Dominic's relationship with people at the school, I was getting noticed. Unfortunately, I never stood a snowball's chance in hell of getting in because I only took the college boards once and didn't do well. Besides, I wanted to go straight to New York City to be a "star" even though my parents believed continuing my education would be best. At their insistence, I applied to community college where I was certain to be accepted. Unbeknownst to them, however, I was planning on instantly flunking out so I'd have an excuse to go to New York.

The summer after high school graduation, I got involved in a production of *110 in the Shade* at one of the local theaters, and Dominic was the musical director. He shared the news that for the first time in history, Villanova would be offering undergraduate scholarships and he was going to submit me as a candidate. I told him about my difficulties with the entrance exams, to which he replied, "Let me see what I can do." A few weeks before I was scheduled to start community college, he said, "You've been given a fully paid scholarship to Villanova University." My parents were ecstatic!

When I got there, the theater people figured out pretty quickly I was a character guy and started casting me in a variety of roles. Even though I wasn't a good student and basically ignored all of my classes, I was certainly making an impression on the stage. At the end of the first year, I had a "D" average and was told I'd be losing the scholarship because I didn't meet the academic requirements. My mother went to see the head of the arts department and had a meeting. I don't know how she did it but at the end of that ninety-minute sit-down, she convinced him to let me *repeat* my freshman term! Not only would the school wipe out the first year and let me do it all over again, if I received at least a "B" in all of the classes the scholarship would be reinstated.

My parents made it crystal clear I'd have to concentrate solely on my studies and could no longer be distracted by the theater. I was also told it was time to start paying my own way. They'd spent $1,000 of their savings to cover me thus far and it was now my responsibility to take out a loan for the next round of classes. I did all of the paperwork and got the money, but I hated having such immense debt. However, since I was now assuming financial responsibility for my education, I decided to allow myself some real time for the arts.

Dominic Garvey left West Catholic and went into professional theater. *Hair* had opened on Broadway and was a huge success, so I pitched the idea of a similarly themed musical to Dominic's replacement, a wonderful man named Brian Morgan. "It's called *Groove On!*" I began. "I want to put together a group of kids – not just actors, but regular kids off the street – and have an interracial cast. Give me six weeks and I'll give you a play." And Brian said yes! I called a couple of old high school friends for help, and as promised, in six weeks I wrote the script, chose thirty-six teenagers for roles and rehearsed the two-hour production.

Being an Orson Welles fan, one of the first things I thought about was how to publicize the show to attract audiences. We knew friends and family of the actors would come and see it, but how could I get other people in there to make it a full house? One of my buddies was a great photographer and I had him take a series of somewhat suggestive pictures of the cast. The kids lined up in a "V" shape with the wonderful Rick Piccinino front and center, whose character was vital to the story about a young man going from adolescence to realization. Also in a "V" shape was a black hand and a white hand coming together to block out Rick's crotch, implying that he was naked. We put that image and several others on display outside of West Catholic's auditorium, which caused quite a stir. Everybody heard about them, everybody was looking at them and everybody wanted to know if there was nudity in this high school musical! The principal demanded the photos be taken down immediately, but channeling my inner Orson, I simply replaced them with shots that were blanked out by text that read, "These pictures from *Groove On!* have been CENSORED by the school. Come see this play!" The gimmick worked and every performance played to capacity crowds, becoming a bona fide hit. It was a wonderful experience, and through it all I managed to keep my grades up. I ended the year with a "B" average and my scholarship was reinstated. However, I still had to pay back that $1,000 for the student loan.

In 1969, the Villanova Theatre Company was being formed at the school. The head of this newly-created group was Robert Hedley, a powerful and talented Canadian export who worked tirelessly behind the scenes to get our plays moved to theaters in Philadelphia and New York. Those are the dreams of every university theater department, but Hedley had more connections than most and he was a force who could make things happen.

One of those connections was Ellen Stewart, affectionately known as "La MaMa" because she was the founder of the La MaMa Experimental Theatre Club in Manhattan's East Village. As her moniker implied, she was a motherly umbrella for such up-and-coming playwrights as Sam Shepard, Lanford Wilson and Harvey Fierstein. Thanks to Hedley, Ellen came to Villanova to talk to our group. She gave a wonderful speech about what was happening in the theater scene, and people were asking very profound and pertinent questions about the arts. When my turn came, I raised my chubby hand and said, "Miss Stewart, Miss Stewart... How do you become a star?"

Everyone let out audible moans and groans while looking at me like I was the biggest asshole in the world. I suppose I was, making such a shallow and superficial inquiry. Nonetheless, I *really* wanted to know the answer. She turned and looked at me very deeply and said, "You have to want it very badly." That was the extent of our communication... I was rather intimidated by her and remained silent for the rest of the afternoon's gathering, feeling as though I'd made a fool of myself.

Five years after my embarrassing brush with her, I was desperate to break into the New York theater scene and pleaded with Robert Hedley to give me the contact numbers for Ellen Stewart, which he eventually did. I'd randomly call at all hours trying to reach her to no avail. One Saturday night around 1 a.m after an evening of

Ellen Stewart

heavy drinking, I thought, *I'm gonna try her now.* I dialed the number and was shocked when she actually answered the phone. "Miss Stewart? Hello... My name is Jon Polito. I don't think you'll remember me. I'm a—"

"—You are a heavyset boy from Villanova who wants to be a star," she interrupted.

"Well, I'm not heavyset anymore. I've—"

"—You will come tomorrow to the Truck and Warehouse Theatre," she continued. "We have just lost the lead of our play and you will come in and audition for it. I believe you will get the part and it will start your career." I don't know what made her say those things but I went in the next day, did the audition and got the part! It was a leading role in a play called *Language*, one of those wonderful three-and-a-half hour epics that used to get respectable reviews in the early '70s.

In 1980, I was presented with an OBIE award for my work in Off-Broadway theater. Ellen was there, winning another one of her numerous accolades. When I saw her, I ran up and said, "Miss Stewart, Miss Stewart... I'm Jon Polito. Do you remember me?"

She looked at me coldly. "I have no idea who you are," she replied, quickly walking away. What began as kismet ended with a forgotten relationship.

Fast-forward to 2004, thirty years after my drunken phone call led to a starring role in *Language*... I was in New York working on a TV show and a great friend of mine named Theodora Skipitares was assisting Ellen, who was now about eighty-four years old and in the middle of directing yet another production at La MaMa. Theodora asked, "Would you like to come and say hello to her?" Even though I figured Ellen would never remember me, I agreed to go along. When we arrived at her studio, she was managing all of these young people – there must've been about twenty-five of them building sets and rehearsing in the corner with her coordinating it all – and it was truly exciting to see, taking me back to my early days in the theater.

As I approached Ellen, Theodora said to her, "This is Jon Polito." She stared at me intently. "Do I know you?"

"Yes, you do." I turned to the group and said, "Will you guys listen up for a minute?" I began to tell everyone the story of our first meeting at Villanova when I asked her how to become a star, including when I auditioned for the part she claimed would start my career. I ended by turning back to her and saying, "You were right, it *did* begin my career. Miss Stewart, I want to thank you for that."

She looked at me and asked, "Baby, is that true?" I told her it was and she pointed to her cheek and said, "Give me some sugar." I leaned over and kissed her, which was just a small expression of gratitude for the important role she played in my circle of life.

And that loan I took out to pay for my second chance at Villanova? After getting my nose broken in the taxi the day before my *Pyramid* appearance, I sued the cab company and settled for $1,700. That accident officially made me debt-free.

It was the last time I could say that for the next few decades.

2

Doorways in Time

You have to do a lot of things to survive when you're working in the theater. Although *Language* had opened and wasn't a hit, I was mentioned in *The New York Times* review, which was a very important milestone for any young actor. I was now thinking of myself as a pro, but what would I do next?

I made a point every day of keeping myself active, which included taking the subway to the Actors' Equity office to find out what new plays were holding auditions. I went to a few of these "open calls" and noticed there was always somebody at the front desk to greet you when you came in. That person would take your name and Equity card, and I thought, *I wonder how you get that job?* After asking around, I went back to the office that week and found the man who scheduled those tasks. To be honest, I flirted with him disgracefully, telling him how wonderful he was and how I'd love to be on the list to take the cards. Sitting behind that desk paid $15 a day and if I could get enough of those assignments – combined with the $60 a week of unemployment I was making from a job in Philadelphia – I could pay my rent and stay alive while waiting for the next acting opportunity.

Well, God bless him, he started hiring me for those gigs. Not only did I collect the cards, I was meeting wonderful people, some of whom I'm still friends with now. I went out of my way to be extremely nice because I remembered the unpleasant jerks who made it very difficult when I was in line waiting for hours to audition. I was the perkiest thing in the world, flirting with everyone who came my way. In turn, I was receiving good feedback, which led to getting more and more of those jobs.

One of the great gifts that came from taking those Equity cards happened about two years later. I was manning the desk for an audition when a girl came up to me and screamed, "Jon Polito! Oh my God!"

I stared at her blankly. "I'm Anne DeSalvo. I was Gertie Cummings in the production of *Oklahoma!* at West Catholic High School." I *still* had no idea who this woman was, but she was so effusive and wonderful and crazy that I was eager to get to know her. After her audition, Anne came up to me and said, "Give me your phone number and if I ever hear of anything for you, I'll let you know." She called two nights later. "Jon, I'm doing this production of *The Transfiguration of Benno Blimpie*. It's by Albert Innaurato and the lead guy walked out, so I recommended you to read for the part."

The Transfiguration of Benno Blimpie

It was an amazing one-act play about a morbidly obese man who was eating himself to death. He sat on a stool and ate through the whole show while all around him portions of his life were depicted on stage. Benno was a boy with major problems who is at the point of suicide, and the show ends horrifically with him doing a very long monologue that describes why he's so disturbed. It was Grand Guignol… a dark and troubling speech but powerful as all hell. I got the lead, we staged the production and the critics loved it. *The New York Times* gave *Benno Blimpie* a wonderful review and it quickly became the play to see. James Coco, a terrific actor whom I admired, was in the audience one night. After the show, I was able to meet him and he was very complimentary.

The following year, another up-and-coming theater group called Playwrights Horizons was presenting "An Evening of Albert Innaurato" starting with his new play, *Gemini*, followed by *Benno Blimpie*. I was asked to read for a character in *Gemini* and ended up landing the lead role, which was a very different type of part for me. I was playing a man questioning my sexuality, Sigourney Weaver was the leading lady and my old friend Anne DeSalvo was cast as the neighbor. While we were in rehearsals, word came down that *Benno Blimpie* wasn't going to be performed that night because James Coco had optioned it and was going to present it at another venue.

Gemini opened to wonderful reviews and good box office, and for once I was actually making a decent salary. Sigourney was quite amazing to be around in those days and I was kind of in awe of her. We all knew she was the daughter of Sylvester 'Pat' Weaver – the head of NBC – and that she had come from money, but there was a chip on her shoulder as though she had something to prove. We were told a producer was interested in bringing the play to his Off-Broadway theater, which was exciting news. That's when I learned he was going to recast my part. I was devastated... Sigourney decided not to go because she was moving on to bigger and better things, but everyone else got their contracts except me.

I no longer had a job.

Gemini *with Reed Birney*

Gemini was an even bigger hit with its revamped cast and garnered a lot of press, which I had to read about while looking for work. Not only that, a show called *Monsters* was going to open in New York featuring two one-act plays back-to-back, and one of them was James Coco starring as Benno Blimpie! I thought I might be able to get a standby job because he'd seen me in the play and its producers knew my history with the character. I was desperate for work and tried my damnedest but I learned Mr. Coco didn't want me involved in any aspect of the production. Both of the plays I originated were drawing raves and I had no part in either of them. What should've been my successes were instead stabbing me as failures.

Several years later, I was hired for a small role on an episode of a soap opera called *The Doctors*. The cast included a young actor causing quite a stir named Alec Baldwin, and an up-and-coming actress by the name of Kathleen Turner. The guest star appearing that same week was none other than James Coco. I was sitting in the makeup room when he walked in and took a seat next to me. The tension was thick and the silence was deafening. Finally, I turned and asked, "Do you know who I am?"

"I know who you are," he replied, staring straight ahead.

"Why didn't you just let me read for your standby? I really needed the job back then."

He looked at me and said, "I saw you in the play. You were very good in it and I didn't want you anywhere near me. If I couldn't go on, I didn't want you to take my place. You'll understand as you get older... Sometimes you have to protect yourself."

I found that statement distressing and decided to let him know it. "You know something, Mr. Coco? I did learn a lesson here. For the rest of my life I'll never do to anyone else what you did to me." And I walked out. I know he was a good actor and everybody else loved him, but I didn't. I thought what he did was cruel, and it felt good to finally confront him and say my piece.

* * *

In case you didn't know, actors are *crazy*. For God's sake, Richard Belzer, for all of his intelligence and wit, believes in flying saucers, aliens and all that stuff.

Me? I believe in psychic powers.

My aunt Julie was born with a caul over her face, which is a skin covering that has to be removed from an infant when the amniotic sac doesn't break during birth. The old Europeans would save that piece of skin because they believed it to be a sign of psychic ability. Aunt

Julie was an important woman to me. As a kid when I would visit Atlantic City for our family reunions, she would teach me the piano and tell me I would be in show business. Some people considered her a bit of a psychic, and when I was a child, she said she felt I had similar powers.

In the early '70s, Philadelphia was an out-of-town tryout for plays bound for Broadway, and the Public Theater was testing out a production of Strindberg's *The Dance of Death* starring Robert Shaw and Zoe Caldwell. As I sat in the Annenberg Center waiting for the show to begin, I read the program cover to cover and noticed the director had a very strange name: A.J. Antoon. It was the first time I'd ever seen his name and I knew absolutely nothing about him, but for some reason that name stayed in my head.

Flash-forward a few years and I'd moved to Chelsea from 50th Street. The neighborhood at the time was a wonderful mixture of whites, Hispanics, blacks, straights and gays. One night I was walking to my apartment around ten-thirty and noticed a timid-looking man cruising me. As I passed him he started to follow, which was the standard procedure in those days. I stopped and very politely said hello, and I could see he was terribly nervous. I started talking with him and figured maybe we could fool around a little. I'd try anything – and anyone – at least once! I gave him the okay that he could come back to my place, and as we started walking he asked, "What do you do?"

"I'm an actor," I replied. An odd look immediately washed over his face as I continued chatting. "Are you in the business?"

"Yes," he answered hesitantly.

I don't know what compelled me to ask but I turned to him and said, "Are you a director?"

He looked frightened. "Do you know me?"

"No, I don't, but are you… are you… A.J. Antoon?"

Panic immediately set in. "You know all about me!"

"I know nothing about you and I don't care. I remembered your name from the program for *The Dance of Death*." I somehow intuitively knew he was the man whose name I'd seen several years ago that had stayed in my brain for some reason. In my mind there's always a series of running pictures, which I refer to as "Polaroids." Those snapshots fly by, and most of them are memories. I'll see something and it'll remind me of an event in the past, but once in a while, there'd be a Polaroid I didn't recognize. I'd think, *Wait a minute, what is this? Look at it. Record it. Maybe it's a picture from the future and not the past.*

Jon (left) in Wait Until Dark

I was cast in a dinner theater production of *Wait Until Dark* in Ohio. One day during a dress rehearsal, I turned to look out into the theater and a Polaroid came up. Instead of seeing the nondescript interior of this auditorium, I saw endless rows of elegant red velvet seats, a large balcony and a chandelier hanging from the ceiling. I thought, *What is this place?* I couldn't explain it and put it aside and finished rehearsal, but it was an image that kept nagging at me.

In 1977, *American Buffalo* had opened at the Ethel Barrymore Theatre in Manhattan and was causing some controversy. It was a three-character play with Robert Duvall, the great character actor Ken McMillan and a young, spaced-out John Savage. Word on the street was that it was magnificent, but the rough language was kind of an issue for some people. Also, theater at that time was still running three hours. You went in at eight and got out at eleven. With *Buffalo*, you were out at ten even though the ticket prices were the same. Audiences were having a hard time adjusting but its writer – David Mamet – was establishing himself. Everyone knew he would become a force to be reckoned with.

Back then, the opinion of *The New York Times* was the final word on the ultimate success or failure of a show, and its review was good enough to keep *Buffalo* running. As such, the production started to look for standbys as opposed to understudies. A standby is a better position because instead of someone learning lines for everybody, you're there to step in for a specific character if needed. I wanted to read for Robert Duvall's standby. Ever since I'd first seen him in *To Kill a Mockingbird* when I was eleven, I loved his work and intently followed everything he did. I went to my agent and asked, "Can you try to get me in for the standby role?"

She said, "Jon, they're looking for somebody in their forties. There's no way you're going to get it."

"Please just get me in to read," I begged.

As much as I loved Duvall's work, I was even more in love with his character's nemesis Donny, played by Ken McMillan. That role, however, was *way* out of my range. Donny was at least in his fifties and I was only twenty-six. Being the little Lon Chaney character guy that I was, I tried to make myself look older and went in the next day to read for the Duvall part. When I finished, one of the producers walked up to the front of the stage and said, "Don't leave yet. I want to see what you can do with Donny."

Nothing was ever in my way as an actor, so I told him, "Oh, I've got a full performance prepared for you," which I didn't. "Give me twenty minutes and I'll be ready." I went to the bathroom and started making instant makeup changes. I took my flat hair and curled it, and I put a little cigarette ash on my face to give the illusion of being unshaven. With that done, I worked very quickly on memorizing one of the first scenes. The lines went into my brain easily because the brilliance of Mamet is that his dialogue is like learning music. If you really pay attention, you'll remember the notes. A half hour later, I was back on the stage reading for the part of Donny.

Two days later, I got a call saying that I'd been cast as Ken McMillan's standby in *American Buffalo* on Broadway. My first day there, I walked onto the stage and as the curtain lifted, I was met with a sea of red velvet seats, a large balcony and a chandelier hanging from the ceiling. My Polaroid had come to life right before my eyes!

Whatever psychic ability I possess, there are pictures that are like doorways in time. This instance happened to be a doorway to the future, but I've found there's also a doorway to the past, and it's a very dangerous one. As much as those Polaroids could foretell the good that would happen in my life, they could also remind me of the bad.

When I was thirty-one, I went home to Philadelphia during the holidays to visit my family. Our Italian Thanksgiving dinners were huge and this particular one had about twenty people there. Everybody was reminiscing about one funny thing or another, and there was a lot of laughter as we took turns telling stories. "Do you remember this?" and "Do you remember that?"

Out of the blue I said, "Do you remember the sailor?" The table went quiet… It was like the moment in *The Producers* where everybody just sat there with their mouths hanging open.

"What sailor?" someone asked.

"Oh, nothing," I meekly replied. "Forget about it." I got incredibly frightened, excused myself from the table and went upstairs to my room. Sweaty and shaking, I sat on the bed and thought to myself, *Jon, what sailor?* In my mind was the image of a man's butt in very tight white pants. One of the things that always kind of excited me on the streets of New York was to see the Navy men wearing their uniforms, but at the same time, I was always leery and avoided them. As I was trying to figure out this strange situation, the Polaroid suddenly opened up.

I was a kid – about five years old – walking up the steps behind a strange man in my Aunt Julie's hotel in Atlantic City. I'd seen him several times in the lobby during our stay and he was always nice to me. He took me very quickly down the hallway to his room where I was instructed to do things to him, which I did. I couldn't figure out how

Jon (left) and family in Atlantic City

it was possible I could've been abused because my family was around all of the time, but as those doors opened in my mind, I remembered everybody went to church on Sunday and I was left in my aunt's care. Somehow on this day, she wasn't there looking after me and I went up those steps with him. It was shocking I was able to suppress this traumatic event, and even more surprising that it would suddenly pop out in the middle of dinner twenty-six years later.

Being a gay man, I've been asked questions like, "Were you born gay?" and "Did you become gay because of something that happened to you?" As a child I had no concept of what sexuality was, but I do know that I had a sexual encounter at five years old. It stayed with me and made me explore things that I don't think I would've been aware of otherwise. I can't speak for people's sexual development in general or why some people are gay and others straight, but I believe that when there's abuse involved – especially when someone older is taking advantage of someone much, much younger – it does somehow set your preferences because it's the first thing you experience.

American Buffalo was a joy and I loved being there every night. I was in awe of Mr. Duvall – his work was brilliant – but I was equally impressed with Ken McMillan. Ken sat in a rolling chair for most of the play, and when he got out it was like watching a lion attack. His power was amazing and he became my inspiration. Everything Ken did, I did. Unfortunately, he was a cokehead and a drinker, and I naturally followed his lead.

Just like him, I was becoming a drug addict.

* * *

There was a man I knew from the Villanova days named Jonathan Sand who was now working in the acting division of the Writers & Artists Agency. Although I didn't know him very well, I called and asked to audition. In those days they'd let you come in and read, and if they liked what they saw, they'd consider representing you. It was a simpler time when agents would actually work with you even though you weren't a star, unlike today where you already have to be on a series before you get signed.

Jonathan liked what I did which meant I had to meet with Joan Scott, the head of the agency and a beautiful, powerhouse blonde. I don't think she was as taken with me as Jonathan was but she was willing to give me a shot. Young actors often used theater as a stepping-stone to television and film, but I never thought I had what it took to work well on the screen. I explained to Joan I had no desire to leave the stage, and she was okay with this approach.

I now had a good agency and my name and rep were getting around New York. I was invited to read for director David Jones, a Brit who came to town to form a repertory company. It had an incredible group of character people like Joe Morton, Roxanne Hart and Stephen Lang, and we all gathered together in a wonderful Brooklyn theater to do four plays in a year.

As the season was coming to an end, I got a call from David inviting me to go with him to the OBIE awards. When I asked why, he played coy and just insisted I come, which led me to think I might actually be nominated. That was a huge deal, so I got dressed up in a weird outfit and asked my friends Anne DeSalvo and Michael Morin to join us. Michael wouldn't go – he flat-out refused, which I thought was rather odd and a little hurtful – but Anne was at my side. It was a surreal night as I sat there trying to take it all in. I watched Ellen Stewart win her eighth OBIE and then Nancy Marchand, the great actress who played Tony Soprano's mother in *The Sopranos*, walked up to the podium. "This next actor performed in six incredibly different roles this season," she said. "The OBIE award for Best Actor goes to Jon Polito."

As I approached the stage to accept the honor, I went blank... Absolutely *blank*! I stuttered, I stammered and I don't think I made a bit of sense. I finally managed to say, "Thank you," and walked off.

Despite my giving one of the worst acceptance speeches in the history of anything, David Jones proudly paraded me around, showing me off to everyone who came into the building. While basking in all the attention, I couldn't stop thinking about what plays – and opportunities for more accolades – the upcoming season would bring. Two days later, he called me into a meeting and said, "Jon, we won't be using you next year."

"What are you talking about?" I asked, dumbfounded.

"Well, I don't really see a play that I think you're right for and the rep company has to be able to alternate actors." And just like that, I was let go from the theater where I did some of my best work.

It was around this time that a casting person was in New York looking for actors for a new TV series called *The Gangster Chronicles*. NBC's Brandon Tartikoff, then working under Fred Silverman, had come up with the idea for an organized crime show after watching *The Godfather Saga*, an ambitious seven-hour miniseries re-edit of the first two *Godfather* movies. Two of *Chronicles'* main characters were real-life Mafia figures "Lucky" Luciano and "Bugsy" Siegel, and a third was a Meyer Lansky-inspired character cleverly named Michael Lasker. Lansky was still living at the time and the last thing the production company wanted was a lawsuit. I was up for the small part of Thomas "Three Finger Brown" Lucchese.

After meeting with the director, I got a call from my agent, Joan. "They liked you, Jon, but the fact is they're going to cast this part from L.A. We suggest you go there and re-read for the role."

I'd never been to L.A. and honestly had never even *thought* about going, so I sought out my parents' opinion. My mother said, "Can't you think about going back to college to get your master's?" God love her, she was still trying to back me up with a second career.

My father, on the other hand, was more supportive. "Do you have the money to do this?" he asked. When I told him I didn't, he said, "I'll give you $2,000. It's time you go out and try it."

The Gangster Chronicles

And that's what I did… I flew out to L.A. and at eleven o'clock on a Monday morning, I went to Universal Studios for the audition. Less than an hour later I got a call saying that I'd been cast in *The Gangster Chronicles*. Michael Nouri, Joe Penny and Brian Benben were the leading men and they were wonderful. I was nervous as hell and eager to learn, and they taught me a lot of technical things about working in front of the cameras. It was a pretty spectacular time, and while I wasn't very good in a show that wasn't very good, I was making what I thought was unbelievable money – $5,000 a week! Joan was furious that I wouldn't even negotiate; I just took the first offer, not realizing after taxes and agency fees there was very little left over.

Being in Los Angeles was great but ultimately I decided it wasn't for me. I was a theater guy and my brief dalliance with television only served to reinforce that mindset. After paying back Dad with my first check, I also got my parents a place to stay in Atlantic City for the summer. I took the rest of the money back to my apartment in New York and started looking for stage work. Two weeks later, I was hired for a movie called *The Killing Hour* co-starring my favorite drug buddy, Ken McMillan.

3

Agony of a *Salesman*

In the early 1980s, there was a lot of buzz coming from Chicago's Steppenwolf Theatre Company. One of its productions was a 1982 revival of Sam Shepard's drama, *True West*. It co-starred Gary Sinise – who also directed – and John Malkovich, two remarkable actors whose careers were just beginning to take off.

One day, my agent called and said, "Jon, they're considering you to replace Malkovich in *True West*. I want to go with you to see it and then you can decide whether or not you want the role."

The play started with Sinise sitting at a desk and this insane, marvelous-looking man – Malkovich – standing there looking around the room with nothing being said. Malkovich made a little noise and then he adjusted his crotch. The audience began to chuckle… He moved around and made little Brando-esque noises, went to get coffee, came back in and fondled his crotch again. The audience chuckle turned into a laugh. I thought, *Holy Jesus, who is this*? Then he did a little more action with his crotch and said in a weird voice, "So Mom took off for Alaska, huh?"

I remember when I heard that voice and saw that man, I turned to my agent and said, "I'm not going near this thing. I can't do any of this. Let me just sit back and watch." I spent an incredible two hours watching Sinise and Malkovich make magic on that stage.

About two years later in 1984, I read a blurb on the catty Page Six of the *New York Post*: "Get this… Dustin Hoffman is considering coming to New York for a production of *Death of a Salesman*. Who's he going to play, the son?" It was a really snide remark and I remember thinking, *Why are they being so bitchy*? Admittedly, Hoffman – who was in his late forties at the time – didn't exactly fit the image of Willy Loman, but playwright Arthur Miller released a statement saying he'd always imagined the character as a small figure, not the large, powerful man who had been portrayed by actors like Lee J. Cobb. This was going to be a completely different interpretation.

Arthur Miller and Dustin Hoffman

With Hoffman in, speculation ensued about who else was going to be cast. Several names were being tossed around until the news broke that Malkovich was considering the role of Biff and committing to *Salesman*'s intended one-year Broadway run. I thought, *This is going to be amazing!* I hadn't seen him since *True West* and I was excited to see what he would do with the part. Word then started to spread that Malkovich was reluctant to sign on for the whole year. I had *nothing* to do with this production; this was just me as an actor always trying to keep my ears open to what was happening in the local theater scene.

In those days, I made an annual trek to Atlantic City to visit my family for two weeks. It was a big deal because leaving New York to go on vacation was a lot of work, having to lug around a bunch of suitcases and spending over two hours on an uncomfortable bus. All of my relatives were gathered at my aunt's hotel and when I arrived, my mother and father were waiting. I had an urgent phone call from my agent.

"Jon, they want you to come in tomorrow morning to read for Biff in *Death of a Salesman*."

"Malkovich is doing—"

"—Malkovich isn't committing to the year," he interrupted. "They want to cover themselves and your name came up."

"Well, I have a problem…" I said hesitantly.

From college onward, every time an actor goes to a class they'll have to do the scene from *Salesman* of the two brothers – Biff and Happy – in the bedroom discussing what's happening with their dad. It's a lovely and important exchange where Biff describes what it was like escaping the hellish big city and moving to the beautiful country, leaving his sad father behind. It's a wonderfully written scene, but in all my attempts to play Biff there was a series of lines I couldn't get through. Miller writes that Biff turns to Happy and says, "There's nothing more beautiful than the sight of a mare and a new colt." Every time I got to that part – for some unknown reason – I'd hit a mental block on that line and completely lose the character. I couldn't do it then and knew I still couldn't do it now.

My agent said, "You're coming in tomorrow morning to read for Biff."

"I can't do it," I responded. "I can't say, 'There's nothing more beautiful than the sight of a mare and a new colt.'"

"What the hell are you talking about?" he asked.

"It's one of the lines. I've tried it and I can't play Biff."

"Jon, you're being requested by the company to come in. You *have* to meet with them!"

Telling him I'd call back with a decision, I hung up the phone. My father asked if everything was okay. After explaining my dilemma, he looked me squarely in the eyes and calmly said, "I've got a feeling about this, Jon. Get back on the bus." And that's exactly what I did. I packed up everything, returned to New York, and at nine-thirty that night, I pulled out my copy of *Salesman* and started to do the scene. Although I was bald, I had an assortment of hairpieces to choose from. Finding the perfect one, I moved on to picking an outfit while saying the dialogue over and over and over. I was a nervous wreck, but at eight o'clock the next morning I got dressed, put on my hair and went to the Edison Theatre, knowing deep down in my heart I wasn't going to be able to get that line out.

Every time I read *Death of a Salesman* and every time I saw it – both movie versions and one theater production in Philadelphia – the *only* role I really wanted to get a stab at was the boss, Howard Wagner. I always felt the character was unfairly portrayed as a mustache-twirling villain instead of someone having to deal with an employee who might have mental issues, which is heavily implied. In fact, one of Howard's lines is, "You didn't crack up again did you, Willy?" I felt it was too easy to just play Howard as a flat-out bad guy but everybody always did. That thought was in the back of my mind as I walked into the theater.

The lobby was overflowing with people waiting for their turn to audition. I spotted Michael Tucker – a wonderful actor who would later be on *L.A. Law* with his wife, Jill Eikenberry – and I approached him, visibly trembling. "What's wrong?" he asked.

"Michael, I can't do this. I can't read for Biff. I can't say, 'There's nothing more beautiful than the sight of a mare and a new colt.'"

He looked at me rather oddly but before I could start to explain, I noticed Sylvia Fay, a casting director I'd known for years. I ran up to her and said, "Sylvia, I'm going to have a problem here. I don't think I can read for this role."

"But they heard about your Off-Broadway work and want to see you," she responded.

"Sylvia, I have to go." I started to walk away but she grabbed my arm.

"What is it you want to do?" she asked.

Without thinking, I blurted out, "I want to read for Howard. It's the only part I've ever wanted to play."

"You mean Howard in the second act, that one scene? I think we already cast that."

"Then I have to go," I told her.

"Wait, wait, wait," she said. "Let me see what I can do."

As she disappeared into the darkened theater, I walked to a corner of the lobby, ripped off my hairpiece and started furiously flipping through the script. Although I had strong feelings about the character, I wasn't that familiar with the actual scene. Sylvia came over and said, "They're in the mid-

dle of something so I couldn't ask about it, but when you go in just tell them what you want to do." When Michael Tucker went in to read, I ducked into the bathroom. While cleaning myself up and getting the glue from the hairpiece off my head, I was prepping and reading the words out loud. I had about eight minutes to pull together a performance I hadn't prepared for at all.

Through the closed doors, the sounds of a heated argument could be heard coming from the theater. When it was my turn to audition, Sylvia led me inside to the war zone. Dustin Hoffman briskly walked past me toward the lobby, and I could see a small group of men bickering in the dim light. From what I could piece together, it sounded like Hoffman had some kind of disagreement with Michael Rudman, the director. I recognized a gray-haired man as producer Robert Whitehead, but there was a third, older gentleman sitting there whose identity eluded me. As they talked, Hoffman came back in and stood behind me, instantly silencing the group. One of them said, "Who's this handsome young man?"

I turned to Hoffman and asked, "Is he talking to you or me?"

"He's talking to you. Get in there and do your thing."

As Hoffman walked back to his seat, I made my way to the stage, thinking I'd better tell them my intention right away because they were expecting a Biff performance that I didn't have. I tried to get their attention but they were engaged in another discussion, oblivious to the bundle of nerves standing in front of them. Finally, I raised my voice and said, "Excuse me, excuse me... I'm not going to be able to read for Biff."

The theater became dead silent. Hoffman looked at Whitehead and said, "What did he just say?"

"He said he's not reading for Biff," answered Whitehead, who then turned to me. "What do you mean you're not reading for Biff?"

"I can't read for Biff," I explained. "I can't say, 'There's nothing more beautiful than the sight of a mare and a new colt.'"

Hoffman was perplexed. "What did he just say?"

"He said he can't say, 'There's nothing more beautiful than the sight of a mare and a new colt,'" responded the mysterious fourth man, who I then recognized as Arthur Miller, the playwright. I'd just criticized the man's dialogue right in front of him!

Hoffman looked at me and said, "If you're not going to read for the part then what are you doing here?"

"I want to read for Howard," I declared proudly.

"Uhhhh, I think we've got a Howard already," Hoffman said, still confused by the situation unfolding in front of him. "Wait a minute, hold on…" and the group started to murmur. He then turned and said, "I'm gonna read with ya, kid." This was *not* what I expected! The stage manager brought out two folding chairs and Hoffman sat down, opened up the script and said, "I'm gonna do this cold," meaning he hadn't prepared.

"So am I," I replied.

We began to read the scene and it was incredible. He would run the lines and occasionally throw a little improv at me, which I happily threw right back. We had great chemistry and were feeding off each other's energy, getting into the kind of back-and-forth rhythm all serious actors aspire to. At the end of the scene, he thanked me and then said, "Hold on, we might have a problem." I thought, *What??? This was amazing, there can't be a problem.* He stood in front of me, looked me up and down and then turned to Miller, Whitehead and Rudman. "We might need someone taller."

A couple of years earlier, I'd seen the movie *Tootsie* where Hoffman played an actor who kept getting rejected during auditions. One of the reasons given was, "We need someone taller," and he replies, "I can *be* taller!" My initial reaction was to stare at him and repeat that line but I thought, *Wait a minute. We just made theater magic here and he wants somebody taller? Who does he think he is?*

I was pissed off and said, "Really? Well, *thank you* very much!"

I stormed out of the building, went back to my apartment, packed up my stuff and headed back to Atlantic City. About ten days later, I got a call from Sylvia Fay. "Well, Jon, they're offering you the part. It's a year's commitment."

I was in complete shock. "They're offering me the part?"

"After you left, their feeling was that if you could walk out on Dustin Hoffman at the audition then you could certainly fire him on stage for a year," she explained.

And so, I'd finally achieved my dream of playing Howard in *Death of a Salesman*… on Broadway, no less! Besides Hoffman and Malkovich – who finally did make a deal and committed to the run – the rest of the cast was just as amazing. The role of younger brother Happy was played by Steve Lang, who I'd worked with at the Brooklyn Academy of Music. People know him now because of *Avatar*, but decades before that film he was impressing audiences with his incredible performances. As good of an actor as he is, he's an even more wonderful man who became an important part of my life. A terrific guy named David Chandler played the neighbor, and there were a couple of actresses who made an impression on me. One was Kate Reid and the other was Linda Kozlowski, who later became famous for her work in *Crocodile Dundee* and its sequels. Both of them were lovely and we all became instant friends.

The Death of a Salesman *company*

We started rehearsing in New York in November and the plan was to open in Chicago in January. Instead of being a villain who twirled his mustache, I turned the character into an officious prick. I was thirty-four at the time but played him with a higher voice so he'd be thirty-one, just this side of snot-nosed. I really emphasized the lines and tried to show that he was dealing with a man with mental problems. I thought the rehearsals went well, with Hoffman going through his very sad speech until the end of the scene when I fire him. I'm the iceberg and he's the Titanic, and after I cut him loose, the rest of the play is about his demise. After rehearsing for weeks, we took the holidays off before trekking to Chicago.

The play was going to be presented in the historic Blackstone Theatre, which was a beautiful, acoustical dream of a building. You could say something from the middle of the stage and be heard in the top row. The Thursday night opening performance was briefly jeopardized due to a major snowstorm, but considering the bad weather, we still drew a respectable crowd. Afterward, we waited anxiously for the reviews to come out. Malkovich and Kate Reid earned some positive words but there was a negative edge to what was said about Hoffman in this new interpretation of the classic tragedy.

Friday night's show was kind of mediocre, and at 6 a.m. Saturday morning, my phone rang. I'd only been asleep for two hours – this was the '80s, so I was partying quite a bit – but I was able to answer it. The stage manager said, "Jon, we've got a problem. You have to come to the theater at eight o'clock."

"What are you talking about?" I mumbled in a groggy daze.

"You have to come for a meeting," he responded. "You'd better get in here, it's important." I was really angry and *really* hungover, but he sounded serious so off I went to the Blackstone.

The stage manager was there waiting for me and I had no problem letting him know how pissed I was. "This isn't right, we've got two shows today," I grumbled. "What the hell is going on?" As if on cue, Arthur Miller, Michael Rudman and Hoffman entered from the back of the theater and stormed onto the stage in mid-conversation.

Rudman approached and said, "I have to be honest, Jon, there's something I haven't been telling you." He began to explain that while he supported my decision to play Howard in a less aggressively angry way, there were certain points during rehearsals when Hoffman had asked him to direct me to be more hateful. I didn't know any of this, and Rudman admitted, "I didn't give him that note, Dustin."

Hoffman looked at him and then looked at me. I could tell he hadn't slept at all, and instead of talking, he rambled: "I've got a problem, I've gotta do this but I can't. You've gotta do this, it's not gonna work."

"What's happening here?" I asked, confused.

"You've got to be meaner," he replied.

Michael Rudman added, "You've got to come down on him more," and Arthur Miller shook his head in agreement.

"Wait a minute," I said. "That's the way it's *always* been played. You could've hired *anyone* to do that. Are you telling me that now you don't want to go with the way I'm doing it? This is crazy!"

Hoffman looked at me and kept repeating, "I can't, I can't."

I turned to him and said, "What's the problem?"

"I can't finish the play!" he shouted, appearing on the verge of a breakdown. "I can't... finish... the play. I look at you and I can see that you know who I am, and I get *sad*. And then you fire me and I get *sadder*. I'm crying from the time I leave you until the end. I can't do it! I can't finish the play!"

Basically, by me portraying Howard as a guy who knows Willy has mental problems instead of just being this mean prick, I was holding back the rest of Hoffman's performance. I looked at this man – this wonderful actor – and asked, "What do you need from me?"

"You've got to be meaner. I've got to see something that I can use in my mind."

"Let's do it... But can we *try* to get my performance back in before we go to New York?"

"I'll let you know when you can lighten up," he answered, looking instantly relieved and rejuvenated.

Death of a Salesman *with Dustin Hoffman*

We spent the next two hours rehearsing and I acted like the biggest asshole that had ever set foot on stage, giving him hateful looks and snapping at him every time he said something. He wanted me to be a dick and I played it that way for the rest of the Chicago run. Even though I wasn't happy about my performance, I was thrilled to watch what was happening to Hoffman. He was changing from that point on, becoming something like a desperate soldier by the time I fired him; crushed but ready for a fight. Because of that single adjustment in tone, the whole play was evolving.

The production then moved to the Kennedy Center in Washington. Since I didn't come in until the second act, I was like a mother hen running all over the place and checking with everyone to make sure they were okay. Hoffman came up to me and said, "You can ease up a bit tonight." Little by little, I was starting to get my original performance back into the play. When those reviews came out, they were much more positive than the ones from Chicago. The show was really becoming something special. By the time we got to Broadway for our first series of previews, Hoffman told me, "I'll give you a week, do whatever you want. Get back to your performance for opening night." From that point on, the critics loved us.

There were many great experiences during *Salesman*. For instance, I was pleased to see that the way Malkovich and Hoffman worked was similar to my own approach. I wasn't a Method actor… I thought I could get into character at the last minute, and I watched as they would do the exact same thing. They were offstage goofing around between scenes and when the moment came, they got right back into the thick of the drama. Acting is a game where you have to jump from one fantasy to another at a moment's notice, like a kid playing cops and robbers and then deciding to play *Star Wars*. Hoffman and Malkovich could effortlessly move into whatever was required and it was wonderfully reassuring to see such respected actors using the same technique as mine.

One of the odder moments came during our opening weekend in New York. Before each performance, I'd always go up to speak to the understudies and standbys because I've been in that position and respect their roles. One of those understudies was Bruce Kirby, a wonderful character man who was the father of the late Bruno Kirby, another terrific actor who passed way too soon. I went up to Bruce before the show and he said, "You know something, Jon? I always wondered when you tell Willy to get out of your office, why don't you give him his hat?"

"What?" I asked, somewhat confused.

"Willy puts his hat on your desk and I always wondered why you never give it back to him. It would be like a way of saying goodbye."

I stumbled and stammered, not having a clue as to how to respond to this suggestion. I simply replied, "That's interesting, thanks a lot. Have a good show, Bruce."

During my scene – to this day I don't know how or why it happened – I said, "Willy, I'm busy now," and I grabbed his hat off the desk and held it in front of him. Hoffman looked at me and then he looked at the hat... and he was completely silent.

His line was supposed to be, "Howard, the kids are all grown up," but he was frozen and staring at me like he had no idea what to do next. Time seemed to come to a halt and all I could think about was, *I'm going to kill Bruce Kirby!* Instead, Hoffman grabbed the hat very tentatively and put it back on the desk. It was spellbinding! That simple gesture with the hat added electricity you could feel, and when he said his line, "Howard, the kids are all grown up," we began a brand new dance to end that scene. It truly was an exhilarating piece of theater.

However, I was pretty sure I was going be fired... again. I found out later from the stage manager that had I not agreed to change my performance in Chicago, they were going to let me go. I was already on shaky ground and I'd just pulled a stunt that literally froze the leading man! Hoffman's makeup person came up to me backstage and said, "Dustin wants to talk to you." I thought, *Oh, Christ, I'm in a hit show and I'm going to be out of work tomorrow.*

When I got to his dressing room, Hoffman was absolutely glowing. "Polito, that was *great*! *That's* what I wanna do for the whole rest of the run. Anything you throw at me, I'll throw back at ya." The next day, a review from a London critic was published which devoted almost a full paragraph to our scene and the use of the hat. Bruce Kirby's suggestion got a friggin' rave! I thanked Bruce – even though I wanted to wring his neck – for inspiring a moment of captivating acting that I'll never forget.

4
A Life in *Crime* (Story)

I don't remember the circumstances of being cast in *Digby* in 1985, but I know I wanted to be in the play because I'd seen an actor named Anthony Heald on the stage. He was the new "hot thing" in town and was *very* good. The story's premise focused on the title character – played by Heald – and his efforts to win over a woman portrayed by Roxanne Hart, who I'd worked with at the Brooklyn Academy of Music. John Glover, Tony Goldwyn and I were cast as three of her other suitors, and in a time when theater was dealing with serious topics like AIDS and drugs, this was a simple, well-written romantic comedy.

However, as much as I loved watching Heald, I didn't like working with him. He was the kind of actor who was somehow able to draw attention to himself – or draw attention *away* from you – in a very strange way. When I first saw him perform I couldn't take my eyes off him, and it was only when we shared a stage that I figured out how he accomplished that. While we were in previews, I found a lovely moment during one of the scenes and got a nice laugh from the audience. During the next show as we were approaching the same moment, he moved on my line and overreacted. I lost the laugh and he got it instead.

I realized this was war, and the other actors were starting to notice it, too. I think we came to the conclusion that you had to fight to keep anything because if you didn't, it would be gone. I'd worked with very generous actors like Dustin Hoffman and Faye Dunaway, and in most of my theater experiences, I felt like everybody was always working toward the same goal. That wasn't the case with *Digby*. I believe all actors think of themselves as being important but Heald took it to a level of extreme selfishness by getting recognition at the expense of everyone else. It was another experience in which I learned what I didn't want to do and who I didn't want to be.

Despite the behind-the-scenes drama, *Digby* was a successful play that had a nice run. I'd portrayed a kind of buffoonish cop and someone saw me who thought I might be right for a similar role in a movie called *Highlander*. We shot the film in England, and London in the '80s was an absolute blast. I was partying like crazy… There was coke, there was booze, there was everything! Our leading man, Christopher Lambert, took us out one night to the newest and biggest club in town where we were promptly escorted past the immense line of people waiting to get in. Mel Brooks and his entourage were there, which I found terribly exciting. At that point, Mel had produced *The Elephant Man* and was being taken seriously as a dramatic filmmaker. He'd just bought the rights to do a remake of *The Fly* and he came over to our table to speak with Christopher about the lead role. I, of course, was obnoxiously pushing my face up front and saying, "I could be in that movie," but I don't think Brooks even looked my way except to politely acknowledge me.

Highlander

The *Highlander* shoot was wonderful, as was its crew. We worked at the historic Pinewood Studios on some beautiful sets that stood in for New York. Unfortunately, I never got to meet Sean Connery. All of his scenes were shot separately because his story took place in the past and my character was in the present, but I did get to hang out with Clancy Brown, who played the bad guy. I love Clancy – I've always been a fan of his work – and he and I got along well. Director Russell Mulcahy was a lovely man who was one of the first to make the transition from MTV music videos to large-scale films. I was cute and in my mid-thirties but still lacked the ability to act well on camera, so I didn't make much of an impression.

My next job hinged on a meeting with a director in California named Duncan Gibbins. He was a new filmmaker who, like Russell, had also cut his teeth making rock videos. Duncan's movie was called *Fire with Fire* and I was reading for the antagonist who ran a detention center for boys. I liked the part – we've seen that type of villain a million times before – but I thought I had an interesting take on it. The way the script was written, I couldn't quite understand the character's obsession with the lead teen played by Craig Sheffer. Since I'm gay, I thought maybe it was due to some sexual frustration, and that's how I decided to play it. During the audition, Duncan kept saying how wonderful I was, which was usually followed by questions of what it was like to work with Mulcahy. I don't know if the two had some kind of rivalry but it really felt like I got the job because he wanted to have the same actor who worked with Russell. Duncan was very generous and very good to me, and he was an interesting and sweet director… to a point.

In addition to Craig Sheffer, the cast was filled with up-and-coming talent such as Virginia Madsen – a truly beautiful woman – and D.B Sweeney, a great young actor. Because it was kind of a variation on *Romeo & Juliet*, the other half of the story takes place in a Catholic girls' school that's run by Kate Reid, who had played the mother in *Death of a Salesman*. I loved and adored Kate and couldn't wait to spend two-and-a-half months with her in Vancouver. The producer was Gary Nardino, a guy who'd been around a long time at Paramount. He was a very large man who reminded me of Jabba the Hutt but he was also very charming, a trait which he used to his advantage whenever possible.

Although the shoot was fairly smooth, it wasn't without its problems. Kate was drinking an awful lot of booze, I was doing drugs and both of us were a mess when we got on the set. The biggest issue for me, though, was when I showed up for my first day of filming. Duncan suddenly decided my character should have a Southern accent as an homage to *Cool Hand Luke*. It didn't make sense because the movie takes place in Oregon, but that's what he wanted so I literally had to pull the accent out of my ass on the spot. I knew it was going to be terrible, and it was.

I had a portable video camera and was recording everything on the set including the night they filmed the big finale, which involved blow-

Fire with Fire *with Craig Sheffer*

ing up a cabin. I got a lot of footage of all the cast and crew standing around wrapped in their coats in the cold mountain air watching this beautifully built structure explode. As flames poured from the building, for some reason I kept focusing on Duncan. He was standing in front of the raging inferno looking quite excited and proud. I always felt sorry that *Fire with Fire* wasn't a success because Duncan didn't have much luck finding work afterward.

If I cut ahead as films do – as life does, in memory – I was in my California apartment in the early '90s in the middle of a serious coke binge. I was going through my home movies when I came across the tape I shot during *Fire*. I started to watch it and when I got to the end, I began to slow-motion the footage of Duncan being backlit by the flames emanating from the cabin. I spent hours doing this and watching it in a stupor, thinking there was a reason why but having no idea what it was.

At the end of my two-day binge, I finally turned on the television to see what was happening in the world. The hills of Malibu were ablaze but most of the people in the area were able to evacuate. It looked like everyone had gotten out safely except for one person. That man was staying at a friend's house and after initially leaving, he decided to go back in and search for a missing cat. He was the only one to die in the Malibu fires, and that person was Duncan Gibbins... It was one of those moments when I cried because, after several years, I suddenly felt connected to him and then found out he was gone.

* * *

Although my career was now on the rise, I knew something had to change about my style of screen acting because it wasn't nearly as effective as my performances on the stage.

I got a call from Steve Lang, the wonderful actor who was back in my life after playing Happy in *Salesman*, and he told me about a project he was doing with Michael Mann. We'd all heard a lot about Mann because of his film *Thief* with James Caan, and his TV series *Miami Vice*. He was a director with style who was using new sounds, music and interesting cinema techniques, and people were excited to work with him. Lang said he'd been cast in a show called *Crime Story* that was going to be filmed in Chicago, and he'd recommended me for a role as a gangster. Even though I didn't have a good feel for playing that type of character, I figured I'd give it a shot because I wanted to hang out with Lang again.

When I went into the casting office, they were doing something new at the time: video auditions. Mann apparently didn't like being in the room with actors during their tryouts, so he wanted them recorded and had the tapes sent to him. I told the woman that at the end of my performance I'd like to turn to the camera and address Mann personally. It was kind of silly, but I thought, *What the hell? I'll give him a laugh.* After doing my best gangster-esque reading of a very dramatic scene, I looked straight into the lens and said, "Mr. Mann, I'm a fan of yours, but I think very little of you right now because you've made the major mistake of casting Steve Lang, the most frightening actor I've ever worked with!" It was a very funny bit about me hating Steve even though I really loved him. I heard very quickly that I got the part, and while I always assumed it was because of my clever banter, I'm sure Steve's recommendation had something to do with it, too. Somewhere in my memory, I recall being told that he described me to Mann as a "company guy," meaning I'd be a supportive part of the ensemble.

The cast of Crime Story

I arrived in Chicago for the first meeting of the cast. It was a terrific group of people, many of whom weren't well-known at the time but went on to become highly successful: Billy Smitrovich, Dennis Farina, Billy Campbell and Ted Levine. We were all scheduled to leave our hotel on a Saturday morning to meet Mann, and I noticed a very good-looking but strange, dark figure of a man named Anthony Denison. I didn't know him, but I knew he had been cast as Luca – a character I shared scenes with – as a last-minute replacement for Michael Madsen. He sat next to me in the van and as we talked, I felt a great rapport with him. He was young, spirited and very excited to be there.

We were driven to a studio that was being built in an old factory. Mann came in and started to describe the show, which was based on a true story about a police officer in a Major Crimes Unit obsessed with catching a criminal. As Mann was explaining this, he had to leave the room occasionally to take phone calls. We later learned that on the set of *Miami Vice*, Don Johnson was threatening not to shoot another scene unless his television antenna was fixed. It was diva drama and Mann was trying to make a joke out of it by saying, "Actors... I hope nobody in this group pulls that kind of bullshit."

Of course, everybody at the table was agreeing with him about how strange and terrible it was, and I sort of quietly said, "Well, if he negotiated the antenna it really should be working." The room suddenly got quiet and the group was staring at me like I was an elephant who just made a mess on the floor. Mann gave me a look that said, *Oh, brother, here comes a challenge*, but he laughed it off.

That evening, we all went to dinner at an Italian restaurant and sat at a big, long table. It was like a re-creation of da Vinci's *The Last Supper* and everybody was hanging on Mann's every word. As the night went on, I was getting a little revved up, drinking freely and doing coke during the bathroom breaks. Mann said something that made me sigh loudly in exasperation, and Billy Smitrovich scolded, "Jon, be quiet. Michael is talking."

I said "Ohhhhh, Michael is talking. Ohhhhh, big deal!" It once again silenced the room and Mann gave me another one of those looks.

With the party moving back to the hotel, Mann insisted that I ride with him. As soon as we got in the car, he looked at me and asked, "Do we have a problem here?"

"No, we don't have a problem," I replied. "I was half-joking with you. It's just with all of the 'Michael Mann-this and Michael Mann-that,' I couldn't take much more of the Michael Mann stuff." And he laughed! He saw that I wasn't going to be a major problem, but he also took notice that I wasn't going to be someone who would just bow down, and I think he appreciated that.

Production on *Crime Story* was about to begin and the person who usually handled the deals at my agency wasn't in town, so they left the negotiating to an up-and-coming agent named Perri Kipperman, a sweet and fun girl. In the contract, my character – Phil Bartoli – was conceived as a limited role and would only appear in four or five episodes, with the possibility of more. The salary was $5,000 per show, which in fact wasn't very good money, but it sounded great to me. There was a clause that stated if I was still on the series beyond thirteen episodes, the same salary would be in effect. I told Perri, "Let's cross that part out. If they still want me after thirteen, we'll renegotiate."

Being young and inexperienced, she asked, "Can we do that?"

I said, "I don't know if we can but let's do it and see if they sign." We crossed out that paragraph, submitted the paperwork and it was formally approved.

Crime Story

I had a wonderful time doing that first episode of *Crime Story*, which was going to be presented as a two-hour pilot. We were allowed to watch the dailies and what I was seeing on the screen was gorgeous. It was unlike anything being done in those days, and truth be told, it barely looked like it was in color. This early 1960s cop drama had a blue/ green quality to it, and I later heard that Mann instructed the designers and wardrobe people not to use the color red, or use it only sparingly. The whole show had the look of an old black-and-white movie; a film noir quality which worked in strange juxtaposition to the '60s, which were bright and perky. It made Chicago and these men look harsher and tougher and cooler.

I enjoyed the style, but more importantly, I was looking forward to acting on film and *finally* being successful at it. My brother, Jack, made stop-motion animated movies which inspired me to make my own films as a kid. I never thought I was any good in them but I knew where the camera was and I played to it. That was the problem with my early film work because instead of being "in the moment" as an actor, I had an awareness of the camera. I was determined to fix that problem on *Crime Story*, and the first thing I did was become acquainted with the crew. I made sure everybody knew who I was, and in turn, I knew who they were. When it came time to shoot, I imagined being back on the stage doing theater, and all of these people who I'd engaged – and who were engaged in some ways with me – became my front row audience. I now had something else to play to other than the camera.

In the pilot, there's a major confrontation scene between my character and Anthony Denison's in which I'm basically testing his loyalty to see how far he's willing to go in order to work for me. I tell him that he has to kill someone, and when he blindly agrees, I come in with the big reveal: "You have to kill your best friend." That friend was played by David Caruso. He was an intense Method actor who, on camera, was amazing! However, when those cameras stopped rolling, he wasn't a nice person, and that's putting it mildly. I had no problems with him directly, but I heard everyone else talking about his antics. Acting with him was like going into a sword fight without a weapon, and I thought he gave an incredible performance. Behind the scenes, though, I went out of my way to avoid him.

As the show went on, the chemistry between Anthony and me was very good. People liked it but the story editor, David J. Burke, *loved* it. David enjoyed my work so much that he didn't want the character to die, so I continued to appear week after week. At the end of the thirteenth episode, I got a call from someone in the studio's business department. A young, snooty guy said, "Since you're still on the show, you'll be paid the same amount of money for episodes fourteen and fifteen as stated in the contract."

"Wait a minute," I replied. "That's not correct. We crossed that part out and you guys signed it. I'm to be renegotiated for anything after thirteen, and I want more money."

"If that's the case, they'll probably just write you out," he responded matter-of-factly.

I hung up the phone and immediately got a call from Perri Kipperman, who was panicked. "They don't want to renegotiate. Do you want to take the $5,000 for the next two episodes?"

"I want $7,500 each," I told her. "Wait for half an hour because we're going to get this settled."

I left my hotel room and walked up to the floor that had been taken over by the *Crime Story* production. Mann was sitting in his office, and although he was on the phone, he cut short the call to speak with me. "What's going on, Jon?" he asked.

I said, "I've just been told by a man at the studio that they refuse to renegotiate my next two episodes. Here's his name and I'm sorry I won't be able to do them. Thank you."

And with that, I proceeded to walk out of the office and head back down to my room. I could hear the phone ringing before I even reached the door. Perri was on the other end. "Whatever you just did, they immediately agreed to the $7,500," she said. "And the guy you talked to is probably out of a job."

Working on the show was a rewarding experience all the way around, but since Mann was drawn to the underbelly of society, there were edges to *Crime Story* that were scary. His movie *Thief* begins with an incredible robbery in which James Caan is drilling through a vault door with a monstrous piece of equipment, and in fact, that was a real piece of machinery designed by a scuzzy little crook named John Santucci. Santucci – who was cast in the series as the right-hand man of Anthony Denison's character – was married to a girl named Carol Korda, a vivacious redhead with whom I became great friends. He had given her a three-karat diamond ring and said he was going to take it and have it cleaned. When he gave it back to her, it was no longer a diamond but a cubic zirconia. He put all the bills in her name, skipped town and ruined her, financially and emotionally. He was scum, pure and simple.

And then there was Ray Sharkey… I didn't know much about him, but I knew he'd made something of a name for himself in a movie called *The Idolmaker*. He was also a heroin addict who didn't know his lines and acted like a complete lunatic on the set. I remember we had a huge trial sequence, and everyone was waiting for him to figure out his dialogue. The day was dragging on and on and I couldn't stand it anymore. I pulled him aside and growled, "I don't know who the fuck you think you are but *you're* the reason why we're still here!"

He gave me a look like he was going to punch me, but instead he said meekly, "I know, I know... I need help." I went over his lines with him and we eventually got through the scene. Even though Ray was a train wreck on the verge of collapsing and dying at any given moment, David Burke enjoyed his work and cast him as the villain on the show *Wiseguy*, which led to Ray becoming something of a star.

A few years later, I got a call from a very big producer who asked for a meeting. I had no idea what he wanted to talk about, but when I arrived at the studio, he said, "I'm doing a half-hour comedy with Ray Sharkey and it's not working out. He's having a problem and said the only way the show will work is if I put you in it. He said you were very kind to him on *Crime Story* and he wants you in the cast." All I could think was that I wasn't kind at all; I wanted to kill the guy! I didn't do that series, and it didn't last long. The next year it was revealed that Sharkey had AIDS, but that didn't stop him from fucking and infecting everything in sight. He ended up dying a horrible death, as did his reputation.

Crime Story *with Turk Muller*

My last episode of *Crime Story* was bittersweet. When I did the pilot, there was an extra named Turk Muller who was cast as my body-guard, a character conveniently named "Turk." He was a big old athlete, wannabe gangster, occasional drug dealer and – in his spare time

– an actor. After filming, I told the camera people, "Whenever you see me, I want you to see him." The idea came from a juxtaposition of images. Whenever I sat, Turk stood; he was always behind me. Whether or not they filmed him or cut to him didn't matter. The fact that my character – a person of power – was always surrounded by somebody bigger really emphasized just how small I was. He was put into every scene with me and we became very friendly.

When it came time to film my death scene, I went to the writers and begged them to give Turk a line so he could get his SAG card. After Anthony Denison shoots and kills me, he walks out the door and sees Turk, standing guard and looking happy. Anthony turns to him and says, "Enjoy the house, Turk," to which Turk replies, "Thanks, Mr. Luca." Those three words got Turk into the union, and we stayed in touch until he passed away in 2012. During that last episode I couldn't stop crying because I was so sad to be leaving. David Burke asked if I wanted to stay but I declined, knowing it was time for Phil Bartoli to go.

Crime Story was an invaluable learning experience and a gift in my life. It was the beginning of my new approach to acting on camera, but in some ways, it also signaled the beginning of the end, as my drug addiction started spiraling out of control.

5
Meeting the Nerds

Crime Story was quite a success, getting good reviews and large audiences. My work was already completed when the show began airing in the fall of 1986, and thanks to my association with it, I was starting to get a bit of a name in the business.

After coming back to New York City and partying on the money I made, I was asked to audition for a struggling TV series called *Ohara* starring *The Karate Kid*'s Pat Morita. I thought it was a very thin and boring concept in which Morita – in his uniquely Asian way – would Sherlock Holmes the ending and figure out who did what. It didn't have much panache, it certainly didn't have much style, and the producers were looking to spice it up by adding a new police captain. That was the part I was up for, and I was flown to California to compete against four other actors. One of them was Bobby Costanzo, a great character guy with whom I worked later in my career. I didn't know him at the time but as we were waiting to read for the role, he started talking to me and let it be known that this job was *very* necessary for him. I don't know why he shared that information – maybe it was some kind of a psych out – but I came away from that conversation feeling bad for him.

However, that didn't keep me from trying to get the gig. I was cocky as hell and walked into the audition room armed with what I thought was a brilliant acting choice. During the reading, I decided to throw in a line about Mother Teresa that wasn't in the script. Not only did I think it was the greatest rewrite of dialogue ever, I figured it would make me stand out. After I was finished and about to walk out of the building, the casting woman said, "Don't leave yet, Mr. Polito." I didn't realize it until years later but it's a *very* strange thing when they ask you to stay. Usually, all actors do their auditions, go home and then find out later if they got the job. When the other guys waiting to read heard her say that, they looked at me like I'd just crushed their dreams. Bobby went in and wasn't asked to wait, and the other guys sort of wandered around hoping to hear something before they left. I was brought back into the room and told the part was mine.

Moving out to Los Angeles for *Ohara* wasn't a particularly special experience. I was doing drugs and drinking, but I wasn't the only one indulging. Morita was quite the alcoholic but managed to handle it beautifully, unlike me. I looked terrible and wasn't acting well at all, giving mediocre performances. The writers knew I was usually high or drunk – or both – and they could see it wasn't working. I was brought in to give the show a jolt and ended up dragging it down. Although my contract was guaranteed for seven episodes, I was dropped after five and paid to go away.

Despite my addictions, I continued to get jobs. I won a small part in a comedy called *Critical Condition*, a Richard Pryor vehicle that was going to be directed by Michael Apted. I loved Michael's work, especially his *Seven-Up* documentary series and *Gorillas in the Mist*, which I thought was wonderful. The scene I did for the audition took place in a courtroom and it was by far one of the funniest things I'd ever read – hilarious on the page, hilarious to deliver. I was hired to play the defense lawyer for Pryor's character, who decides the best way to avoid going to jail is to claim insanity and then act completely crazy in front of the judge. It was a really hysterical bit, and I couldn't wait to film it.

Critical Condition *with Richard Pryor*

The first thing I shot was a brief sequence in which we initially meet in jail. Pryor said everything right, I said everything right and it went smoothly. A couple of days later, we moved to the courtroom and it was *very* different than what I expected. Pryor wasn't saying anything from the script... It became obvious he wasn't going to do one line of what was written, and Michael just went along with whatever Pryor wanted to do. No matter how it was played and directed, it was *never* – at any moment – as good as what I had read. Pryor was one of the greats, but in the end, the movie hinged on this scene and his improv never came close to being as funny as the scripted material. Being an old theater actor, I think the film suffered from the lack of respect for the page, and it wound up being a minor movie that could've been so much more.

When I went back to New York, I got a lead on another show called *Alone in the Neon Jungle*. It was a television movie starring Suzanne Pleshette that served as a pilot for a series. I *loved* Suzanne. She was famous for her work on *The Bob Newhart Show,* but I knew her from *The Birds* and a lot of other movies I watched growing up, and I was very excited to be working with her. *Neon Jungle* was based on a true story

Alone in the Neon Jungle *with Suzanne Pleshette*

about a female police captain who was tasked with cleaning up an area of a big city with a high crime rate, and it made for good TV drama. The director was Georg Stanford Brown, who was wonderful, kind and strong. He was the first black director I'd ever worked with, which was kind of exotic for the time.

I played a corrupt cop who was pressuring a new recruit played by Jon Tenney to look out for himself and screw as many people as he could, both literally and financially. My guy was a prick and I was playing it to the hilt! I was really butch and it was the first time I saw myself getting fat and starting to form my vocal patterns, becoming the kind of annoying character I had always loved in the old Warner Bros. films. For that alone, it was an important performance in my repertoire.

However, my behavior was a problem for Suzanne. Having been around the block a time or two, she recognized I was doing drugs. I was sweating a lot and was very anxious while waiting to do the scenes. At one point, she confronted me in our dressing room. I don't remember the exact words she used but it was something along the lines of, "You're not fooling me. Get yourself together!" I could tell she didn't like me, and it was scary.

Something else scary about the shoot was the crew. I thought the key to my success in *Crime Story* was getting to know everyone, and I made the same effort on *Jungle*. I was trying to be cordial but they weren't buying it. My homosexuality was a source of tension for some, but knowing these guys were party people, I decided to host a gathering in my hotel room for the department heads of the crew. I had lots of cocaine in a big plastic bag and there was plenty of booze for everyone. It was crowded and kind of tacky, but I thought the best way to get close to this group was to bribe them with drugs and drinks.

The festivities lasted late into the night and by five o'clock in the morning, it was just me and two of the toughest department heads. "Let me lay this out there," I began. "I know you don't like me because I'm gay, but I want us to get along and do good work together. What can I do to make that happen?"

One of them asked me where I thought my gayness came from. He was a sweet man, so we started to talk openly and honestly about that. The other guy said, "I always wondered what I would do if my son told me he was gay. I think I'd love him just the same, but I'd worry about him." I was blown away. These were two blue-collar men living very different lives than me, and we had a great conversation. It was a wonderful way to end the party.

On Monday morning, news had gotten around that I'd organized a huge drug bash and Suzanne was *pissed*! She and the producers confronted the heads of the crew, and in one of the kindest gestures I've ever witnessed, all of them denied it ever took place. They defended and covered my ass, which meant I'd still have a job. Georg Stanford Brown never had a problem with me, and in fact, when word was coming down from the top – which was Suzanne – that they were going to cut back my part, he said he would keep on filming everything that was written for me. I was finally in trouble because of drugs, and it was the first of many iffy situations due to addiction.

About eight years later, I was at a huge premiere with a lot of big stars when I spotted Suzanne. I still adored her and always felt bad about what happened, so I thought this was the perfect opportunity to apologize. I walked up to her and said, "Suzanne, I'm Jon Polito."

"Yes, I remember you, darling," she replied.

"I just want to apologize for my behavior during *Alone in the Neon Jungle*."

"Don't be silly, darling," she responded. "I loved you then and I still love you and all of your work."

No matter what happens in Hollywood, it doesn't last long. Whatever problems exist are usually swept under the rug, as much of my bad behavior was. Fortunately, my talent was enough to make others overlook my downward spiral.

* * *

In the summer of 1989 – at thirty-eight years old – my career changed. I don't know if it really moved forward but it certainly shifted into a different realm.

I received a script called *Miller's Crossing* and I remember taking it into the tiny bedroom of my New York apartment to read. It was by the Coen brothers – Joel and Ethan – who burst onto the scene with an artistic bang in 1984's *Blood Simple*. I watched that movie several times in the theater and was quite impressed with the strange performance of Frances McDormand. *Raising Arizona* had come out in '87, and I found it to be a fascinating and weird comedy with another appearance by the wonderful Ms. McDormand. *Miller's* was the newest project from the Coens and when I read it, I sensed that my part was going to be Johnny Caspar. From his monologue that starts the film, I knew exactly who he was and how to play him. This was MY role, so I called my agent, Jinny Raymond, and said, "Yes, I'll go in for *Miller's Crossing*. I'm very anxious to read for Johnny Caspar."

"No, no, no," she replied. "That's not the part they want to see you for. They want to see you for the Dane."

"No, no, no. Caspar is what I want. Call casting and tell them that's what I'll read for. There's no one else in the world who can play this character, and if they won't see me for the role then to hell with them!"

Disappointed that I wouldn't be considered for Caspar, I tried out for a play called *Other People's Money*. Having found a small bit of success in film and television, I really had no desire to go back to the theater. However, this was a leading part in a tough and interesting piece, so I took a shot and knocked the audition out of the park. The director, a terrific woman named Gloria Muzio, seemed very happy with me, as did Jerry Sterner, the playwright. I agreed to do the show, and rehearsals began during the first week of October. I no sooner got settled in when the phone rang on a Wednesday evening. "Jon, the Coens want to see you now for *Miller's Crossing*," Jinny said excitedly. "They want you to read on Monday."

"I don't know if I can make it," I responded.

"Look, they're about to go to Chicago and almost have this thing cast. You'd better come in."

Being kind of a petty bitch, I told her, "Tell them to go to Chicago and I'll read for them when they come back."

"You're going to lose this role, Jon."

"Jinny, I already lost it in August."

I rehearsed *Other People's Money* and started to prep for the *Miller's Crossing* audition, which was a long, three-page opening monologue. I went in and the casting woman was sitting with the Coens. I thought right away, *These guys are nerds! How could they have written this?* Well, there ain't no "look" for genius. We began to read, and it was a truly wonderful audition. I remember the brothers' kindness, encouragement and goofy little laughs as I went through the speech. When I finished, I walked out of the room and once again experienced that strange and exciting moment of having the casting woman run after me and say, "Jon, they don't want you to leave yet. Please stay."

Somebody else went in to read for something and I started to run through the screenplay. I hadn't prepared for anything else so I was looking quickly at all the lines and scenes, not really making heads or tails of it. When I was brought back in, Joel said, "We'd like to go through the script."

"The *whole* script?" I asked.

Ethan and Joel Coen

"The whole script," he confirmed. So, we sat in that room and read every one of my scenes from beginning to end. I was reading it cold, but I have to say it was magic. It was kismet. And at the end of it, I was officially offered the role of Johnny Caspar in *Miller's Crossing*.

But I almost didn't do the movie. After the audition, I began the intense process of mounting *Other People's Money*. I played an evil businessman nicknamed "Larry the Liquidator," and I really thought this was going to be a special experience. It was one of the first stories about the greed of the '80s in which a millionaire takes over a company and pretends to offer support, while his true intention is to destroy it and sell off the pieces. However, he's fought every step of the way by the female lead portrayed by Mercedes Ruehl.

Mercedes was quite opinionated about *everything*. She thought it was her play and I thought it was mine, so there was a bit of a war between us, albeit a healthy one because it *was* fun to act with her. We worked pretty well together as enemies and I thought we had an intense and emotionally powerful dynamic. However, she felt the story needed to focus more on her and was determined to get the playwright to script a new scene where she could stand alone in the spotlight. I didn't think it was necessary but Mercedes was adamant, and although I was getting tired of her demands, I kept my mouth shut.

The day before the opening at Hartford Stage in Hartford, Connecticut, the writer presented the new material to her during rehearsal. She read it and then threw it aside. "It's *still* not right," she complained.

That was the last straw for me. I called her a bitch and yelled, "Quit wasting time! We open tomorrow night!" I went absolutely nuts and she burst into tears, which was really strange to see. It was like watching Maleficent cry. In retrospect, though, it was kind of funny and dramatic, perfectly encapsulating the trials and tribulations one often goes through for a play.

Jon and Mercedes Ruehl

Despite the conflicts, the production was a joy; so much of a joy that I wanted nothing more than to go with it forever. It was going to be my greatest theater role! The reviews came out and they were *very* good. Mercedes and I got wonderful notices, it was becoming a buzzed-about show and the run was extended. Two weeks later, a meeting was called by the producers, one of whom was a wealthy woman whose sole contribution was her money. She loved Mercedes and they often had lunch together. This woman gathered the whole cast and said, "I've got news… We're moving the play to New York! It's going within the next six months and we have contracts for those coming with us."

She began to hand out the contracts to every member of the cast, but when she got to me, she motioned towards the hallway and we sat down on the steps of the staircase going down the stage. "Jon, we're not taking you to New York."

"You must be joking. You're bringing everyone but me? What's the problem here?"

"We need a bigger name to open the play," she explained.

I was in shock. I didn't know what to say to this woman when I suddenly remembered the wonderful movie *Broadcast News*. There's a scene of a boss firing a newsroom employee and the boss says, "Now, if there's anything I can do for you…" to which the employee replies, "Well, I certainly hope you'll die soon."

That's the only thing I could think of, so I turned to this woman and said, "Well, I certainly hope you'll die soon," and I went on stage and played that role beautifully for the rest of the run, knowing that I wouldn't be going to New York.

Instead, I went to New Orleans to shoot *Miller's Crossing*. We were scheduled to have a reading of the whole script with the Coens and then start filming the next day, but tragedy struck. Trey Wilson, the wonderful actor who played the father of the babies in *Raising Arizona*, died suddenly of a brain aneurysm. He was supposed to play Leo, the Irish crime boss, which is one of the most important roles in the movie. While we were waiting to see who would be recast, I began to create my character with the wardrobe and makeup people. I worked with an incredible hair stylist named Cydney Cornell and asked her to make me look like a bowling ball with a mustache. I was already swollen and chunky, and she cut my hairline back on each side so my face extended even more.

As I was putting Johnny Caspar together, word came down that Albert Finney was replacing Trey Wilson in the role of Leo. I got scared… Finney was simply one of the greatest actors ever. He was older than Trey and I wondered how in the hell I was going to appear like I was Albert's peer. As it turned out, I didn't really have to worry about it. My swollen condition worked in my favor and I looked an indeterminate age, as heavy people sometimes do. You can't tell if they're old or they're young; all you see is fat. My performance still works not only due to Albert's generosity and the Coens' brilliance, but also because of my obesity. My weight was now the final touch in defining who I was going to be: a big, round actor with a pencil-thin mustache and a gravelly voice. I'd finally become one of the old Warner Bros. character guys I grew up watching and loving.

Miller's Crossing

The first scene of the movie is Johnny Caspar's monologue. The words were music, but I wasn't quite there that first day of shooting and it caused a bit of a problem. I found myself needing to take small breaks between the words, and rhythmically, I don't think the Coens expected those brief pauses. Truth be told, I'm pretty sure it caused a technical problem for them because I believe their initial plan was to film the entire speech in a single dolly shot that would mimic a similar scene in *The Godfather*. We spent the entire day filming the speech, and poor Albert sat off-camera for hours on an apple box reacting to my dialogue. He and I had become very social, and one of the funniest things I remember is that after the fourth or fifth take, he turned to me and said, "Pick it up, just pick it up," meaning I should increase the speed of my line delivery. It was kind of a joke and we laughed about it, but he might have been serious. We filmed that opening scene in one continuous shot, and then two weeks later we went back and filmed it again in a different way.

Marcia Gay Harden was cast as the lead girl, a role that every woman in town wanted. I thought she was fantastic. I'd never seen anyone who looked like her, sounded like her or had her energy. She was excited to be in the movie and we spent hours talking about the business. I told her stories about my experiences and she loved listening to them. One night, we were in my hotel room drinking and being as silly and goofy as could be, and I turned to her and said, "Marcia, you're going to win an Oscar someday, my darling."

Her eyes lit up. "And do you know who I'm going to thank? ME!" She went on to give a very funny speech expressing eternal gratitude to herself for being so fabulous. That's a memory I'll never forget because when she did win that Oscar several years later, I was *praying* for her to get up on the stage and shout to the rafters, "I want to thank ME!" Instead, she was gracious and classy and said what she was supposed to say. Not only is she a great actress, she's an even greater person whom I love dearly.

While enjoying my time on *Miller's*, I couldn't help but think about *Other People's Money*, which had opened in New York. The "bigger name" they chose was Kevin Conway – a very good character guy – but the *New York Times* wasn't impressed with him. The critic thought Conway's performance was like a bad Jackie Mason impersonation, and he pointed out that Kevin was padded to look heavy instead of being naturally heavyset. I was relishing every bit of bad press I could find because I felt the producers had made a big mistake in letting me go. In the end, though, I knew the play would rise above it. The premise was just too good for the Wall Street audience to ignore, and Kevin's work ultimately earned him the Outer Critics Circle Award for Outstanding Actor.

There's an old saying that suggests if you lose something and it doesn't come back, you were never meant to have it. As it turned out, I wasn't done playing with *Other People's Money* just yet...

6

A Character Guy with a Problem

After *Miller's Crossing* wrapped, I read that Marlon Brando was coming back to the screen to play a variation of one of his most iconic characters, Don Corleone from *The Godfather*. The movie was called *The Freshman* and I was up for a role as an FBI agent who's chasing Brando. I thought the script was incredibly funny and I went in and had a lovely audition. Writer/director Andrew Bergman laughed during my reading, and since he was gifted in the art of comedy, I thought that meant I had a good chance of landing the part. When I got the call saying the job was mine, I was told there was very little money involved. I don't remember how it worked out, but during the negotiation, Bergman personally put some extra money in for me, which was a very sweet gesture.

The film was partially shot in Toronto and I was put up at Sutton Place, which was *the* place to be in town. After checking out the bar, I got into an elevator to go back to my room. When the doors slid open, I saw three people already in there. I faced forward and pressed the button for my floor, and suddenly felt a chill on my back. I thought, *What the hell is that? Who's that short man behind me?* I turned around, and there was Brando. For someone who wanted to be subtle, he was wearing a wide-brimmed hat and looked very Truman Capote-esque. On one side of him was a woman who would read him his lines through an earpiece, and the other person was his makeup man. I started stammering and braying: "Oh my God! Oh my God! I'm going to be working with you!" He was sixty-five at the time and a shy man, and he nervously started to back away from me. I remember thinking that it probably wasn't the best of introductions, but I learned he had an actual physical presence.

When we got on the set, everybody was waiting to see what Brando was going to do. He came out of his trailer wearing some kind of Frankenstein shoes that added about seven or eight inches to his height. He wanted to tower over everyone, and I thought that was a wonderful choice, making the character larger than life. In our scene, I confront him in a restaurant kitchen and he accidentally gets shot. We didn't really rehearse – which made sense since this was Marlon Brando – but I knew the blocking and where I was going to come in, so I was ready. As the cameras started rolling, I burst through the door and delivered my line, at which point Brando grabbed Matthew Broderick and said, "Put the motherfuckin' gun down or I'll fuckin' blow your fuckin' head off." When the moment came for him to be shot, Brando yelled, "BANG!" and fell to the ground.

Andy Bergman yelled, "Cut! Okay, Marlon, that was great. However, this is a PG-rated film. We're not allowed to curse."

Brando said, "I'm sorry, I just went with my impulse. I hope you don't mind." Then he turned to me. "Jon, I hope you don't mind, I just went with the moment."

"No, Marlon, I don't mind," I replied calmly, although I was bursting at the seams inside. Brando had tried to justify his acting choice and asked for my permission to pursue it!

With each successive take he'd do a family-friendly version of his lines, but he kept saying, "BANG!" whenever he got shot. Nobody could understand why, and when somebody finally got the courage to ask, he simply answered, "I always say it. Just fix it in post." He should've had the phrase "fix it in post" tattooed on his forehead. I think the man believed films were based on the moment in the room and everything else could be corrected and improved later.

Brando, who was notorious for being on a shoot for a week or two at most, was pretty much there the entire time. He loved doing the movie as far as we could tell, but I don't think he was very fond of me. Sometimes he'd sit next to me on the set and wouldn't say a word. As the production was winding down, there was still one major sequence of Brando ice skating that needed to be shot. The man was heavy – *very* heavy – but he agreed to do it. In fact, he practiced extensively with a champion skater named Sandra Bezic.

Meanwhile, the film's producer, Mike Lobell, decided he wasn't going to throw a wrap party. His job was to make sure there weren't too many budgetary excesses, and he didn't feel a party was necessary. That quickly changed when Brando became angered at Lobell's

The Freshman *with Matthew Broderick and Richard Gant*

frugality and decided to pay for it himself. I planned on flying my parents to Toronto, but they couldn't make it. Lo and behold, Turk Mueller – the actor who played my bodyguard in *Crime Story* – happened to be in town, so I took him as my "date." It was a cool event even though Brando continued to ignore me, which was disappointing. I still had a great time with everyone else, especially Matthew Broderick, who was a doll.

Although the wrap party was in the books, there was still another week of filming to complete involving Brando's skating scene. Before it could be shot, his daughter attempted suicide in Tahiti. He left to be with her and when he was ready to come back, he supposedly wanted an additional $1 million. He felt he'd fulfilled his original commitment and if he wasn't going to get the extra money, he wasn't going to finish the shoot. Lobell refused and Brando said something to the effect of, "If you don't pay me, I will kill your film." Nobody really believed him, but we woke up one morning to an interview Brando conducted with a Toronto newspaper in which he said, "This is the worst movie I've ever made in my life." That quote went around the world in less than forty-eight hours. It went viral before there was even an internet! *That's* how much cache Brando had.

A negotiation quickly took place. Three days later, Brando revoked his statement and said, "I was totally wrong... I can't wait to do the sequel." Still, his words changed everything and they hurt a lot of people. It's hard to say how much his attack on *The Freshman* affected the movie but it wasn't a success, critically or financially. However, I thought Brando's performance was lovely and I'm proud to have been part of the film.

With *Miller's Crossing* and *The Freshman* in the can, an offer came from Disney for a movie called *The Rocketeer.* Way before its time, it was a comic book come to life with a lot of James Bond-like elements involving Nazis and a jet pack that Howard Hughes designed for the army. I loved the project but my agents weren't happy. "Why do you want to accept this?" one asked. "It's eight days of work, they only want to pay $5,000 and they don't want to give you good billing."

"I don't care, I want to do it," I replied emphatically.

On the set of The Rocketeer *with Billy Campbell*

During the shoot I experienced another one of those odd, psychic Polaroid events that I couldn't understand. The wardrobe department was set up in an old airport office and there were glass partitions you could see through into the other makeshift fitting rooms. While I was being measured for my period costume, one of the extras turned his head and started looking at me. I literally started to tremble. He was a very good-looking man, but this wasn't something sexual. I felt genuinely disturbed when I met his gaze and had no idea why.

At the end of the first week of filming, I thought it would be fun to throw a little bash in my hotel room for some crew members and a few of the background actors. We drank, did lots of coke and shared funny stories about what was happening on the set. As the hour grew late, people started to leave except for one guy – let's call him "Mark" – who was sitting on the bed. It turned out he was the man staring at me during the wardrobe fitting. Once the last guest had left and it was just him and me, Mark asked, "Can I stay with you overnight?"

"Sure, I have two beds," I answered.

"No, I mean sexually."

I'm always leery of anybody who comes on that strong, and to be honest, I thought it was a set-up. I was very fat and he was extremely attractive and well-built, which made me think this was going to lead to something bad. "No," I said, "but if you need someplace to stay, I don't mind if you use the other bed." Mark spent the night and then I sent him off the next morning.

A couple of days later, he called and wanted to get together again. I refused because I was feeling pressured by him, but then I thought maybe the guy was just hoping to catch a break. When we started the next week of shooting, we were doing scenes at the top of a grandstand and needed people to fill the seats. Since I often pick extras and try to get them noticed in some way, I requested that Mark be placed directly behind me. He was wearing a cream-colored suit and looked incredibly stunning. The director agreed to use him, and he can be seen in several shots as I'm saying my dialogue. I got him upgraded to a featured extra and figured that would be the end of it.

Cutting ahead about six years later, I got a call out of the blue from Mark. He said, "I'm right around the corner from you. Can I visit?" I was shocked because I hadn't heard from him in all that time and, somehow, he'd tracked me down. He arrived looking rather thin but still very handsome. When I asked why he was there, he replied, "I came to spend the weekend. I want us to be together sexually." Again, I politely declined but invited him to stay overnight. The next day we did some touristy things and went to dinner, but that evening he was very insistent on having sex with me. We started to fool around but I wasn't feeling right about it, so I stopped. I made up some excuse as to why, and he became noticeably upset. "I really wanted to start something with you," he admitted. Those shivers I had experienced when I first saw Mark in the wardrobe department kept happening to me, and I felt like it was a warning sign.

A year later, I received a phone call from an unknown man whose voice was quivering. He said, "I've been lovers with Mark for eight years. He's dead."

"I'm so sorry," I replied. "I didn't really know him well."

"Well he certainly knew you. On his deathbed, he asked me to get him a cassette recorder and he taped a message for you. He wanted you to be aware of his illness."

"What did he die from?" I asked.

"He's had AIDS for years."

Mark gave me the shivers, but he would've given me a *lot* more if I'd ignored that psychic, Polaroid moment.

* * *

After *The Rocketeer*, I went back to New York and my lovely fifth-floor apartment. I was so heavy it was getting more and more difficult to climb those five flights, and I'd try to limit myself to one or two trips a day as older people do, even though I was only in my forties. Shortly thereafter, I was asked to come back to *Other People's Money* for a three-month run. An offer was made and since I was still holding a grudge about not being a big enough name to open the show in New York, I said, "Absolutely not! I won't do it for less than $2,500 a week." That was a lot of money to me and it was certainly a lot of money in the theater. It was a steep demand because I only made about $1,200 a week during *Death of a Salesman* on Broadway, and I was shocked when they agreed to my terms.

Mercedes Ruehl was gone by then. She hadn't gotten great reviews or been nominated for any awards, so she finished her run and moved on toward her next goal, which was an Oscar. The new leading lady was the wonderful Priscilla Lopez who sang "What I Did for Love" in the original *A Chorus Line*, and she was a joy to work with. The play was quite successful, and I heard that business picked up when I returned, which made the financial backers very happy.

During this time, another script arrived from the Coens called *Barton Fink*. It was about a 1940s playwright who comes to Hollywood and has a haunting experience. The role being offered was a minor character named Lou Breeze, and when I read the script, I thought it was ridiculous because the only part I *should* be playing was that of the studio chief. I wanted to convince the brothers they were absolutely wrong so I invited them to see me in *Money*, figuring that once they saw my performance they wouldn't be able to imagine anyone but me playing the boss. Joel and Ethan came to the Minetta Lane Theatre to watch the play – Ethan was with his wife Tricia, and Joel was with Frances

McDormand – and all of us went to the Minetta Tavern for food and drinks afterward.

It was one of those violently rainy nights in New York, and while we sat in the restaurant, the Coens couldn't have been more complimentary about my performance. "Well, there's no question, then. I'll be playing the studio boss in *Barton Fink!*" I declared triumphantly.

They kind of giggled as they do in their nerdy way and Joel said, "No... Lou Breeze is what we wrote for you."

Upset that I wasn't going to get the prime character I'd hoped for, I respectfully passed on the project. They seemed disappointed, and as the evening came to an end, we all exchanged kisses and hugs. I started to walk up the street with my tiny umbrella barely shielding the rain when I heard someone call my name. I turned around to see Frances running up to me. "You've *got* to do this movie," she said dramatically.

"Well, Franny, I've been doing these lead roles—"

"—You *have* to do this movie!" she interrupted.

"Why?"

"Because they wrote it for you. I didn't want to do my cameo in *Raising Arizona*, but it was one of the best things that ever happened for me. I wanted to play the lead, but the smaller part showed I could do character work and it helped my career. You *have* to do this role. It'll help your career, too."

It's hard to argue with Frances McDormand so I said, "Fine, okay, I'll do it," and I turned and walked away. As I strolled home in the rain, I knew she was right. It *was* a good part, but more importantly it was *different*. A couple of months after I finished *Other People's Money*, we began shooting *Barton Fink*.

Lou Breeze is a man who used to run the Hollywood studio but was kept around so he could be brow-beaten by the new chief played by Michael Lerner. In the first scene I shot, I present Barton Fink – portrayed by John Turturro – to the boss at poolside. Lerner embarrasses me horribly and demands that I kiss Fink's feet. It's a *great* scene; one of those moments that an actor rarely gets to play. I was excited about what was written on the page but had no idea what Lou was

On the set of Barton Fink

going to be like physically. Joel and Ethan came to my hotel room and Ethan decided he wanted Lou to have a comb-over. A beautiful hair-piece was designed, and I'd chosen a pair of antique glasses to use, which the brothers both loved. When we talked about wardrobe, I said that since Johnny Caspar in *Miller's* looked like a bowling ball with a mustache, I wanted Lou to look like a bowling pin: tiny shoulders, wide in the middle and tiny feet. I felt he should look tentative even when he was walking, and I suggested that his voice should be very nasal.

And with that, Lou was officially born.

I assumed Barry Sonnenfeld was going to be the director of pho-tography because that was my history with the Coens, but Barry was moving onward and upward and directing his own films. They brought in a guy named Roger Deakins to be the DP, who I now know is a ge-nius behind the camera. He's one of the all-time greats, but at the time I didn't know him or his work and I had a little attitude toward him. I saw a couple of dailies with these weird and artistic shots of typewrit-ers. They looked good but beautiful shots of typewriters don't make a film, so I still had my doubts. Our location for the poolside scene was the cottage that Joseph Kennedy – the father of JFK – had bought for Gloria Swanson. Roger was doing a lot of shots of Michael Lerner, and I finally got to see what Michael was going to do with his performance. It was wonderfully frightening; he didn't give himself time to breathe. He was a frantic maniac; a really obnoxious prick. He put himself into a bathing suit that was horrendous and was showing a belly even bigger than mine.

John Turturro and I were facing Michael as the cameras rolled, and then they turned and did shots of John. When they got to me, the sun had changed and the reflection in my antique glasses was hurting the shot. Roger was being very polite about it, but he was whispering to Joel and Ethan, "We have a problem. I can't get rid of that reflection." That was because the glasses had regular lenses and we had never had time to change them to the non-reflective kind for filming.

"Don't worry," I told them. "I have an idea." My solution was that when I walk up to the pool with Fink and I'm wearing a wool suit in ninety-degree weather, my pathetic little character gives in to the heat by removing his glasses instead of taking off his jacket. If you look closely, the grooves on the side of my head make it clear that this is a man who *never* removes his glasses. It provided a strong structure for how I was going to play Lou. Sometimes the accidents or conditions imposed by props or wardrobe imbue an actor with character choices *if* he agrees to accept them instead of fighting them. It's an excellent example of being able to take whatever is thrown at you on that day and using it to your advantage.

The rest of the shoot was as smooth as could be, and when we were able to see the final product, I thought it was the darkest, weirdest thing I'd ever seen, reminding me very much of a Roman Polanski movie. *Barton Fink* was shown at the 1991 Cannes Film Festival, and who just happened to be the head of the jury that year? Roman Polanski! Everybody saw the magic on the screen and *Fink* won awards for Best Actor, Best Director and Best Film. *The New York Times*, which had bitched about *Miller's Crossing*, now said the Coens were the greatest thing in the world! People were starting to realize the boys were making art, they weren't going to be limited to making one type of movie, and they were going to attack each genre with venom and panache.

The film wasn't only a winner for the Coens, it was also a winner for me. I was beginning to get a repertoire: the gangster from *Miller's*, the bombastic guy from *The Rocketeer*, the prick from *Other People's Money*, and now the nerd from *Fink*. Character actors gather different personalities and put them in a box from which they can pull them out when needed for an audition. Although the gangster would eventually become my bread-and-butter, *Barton* did what Frances McDormand said it would do: it opened a door to do interesting types of roles. I'm incredibly proud of my work in *Barton Fink*, and at that point in my career, I was easily doing my best acting with the Coens.

* * *

I went back to New York hoping to find a good project to work on when my agent called and said I was being considered for an Aaron Spelling TV show. While Spelling was primarily known for some hugely successful primetime dreck, his name was also attached to incredibly great art projects. "This is a special one he's working on," my agent enthused. "Read the script and let me know what you think."

It was called *Jack's Place*, and the premise was that a rough-and-tumble, motorcycle-riding hunk has a father who runs a casino in Las Vegas. When the father dies, his will requests that his son, Jack, take over the business. It was a well-written script by a guy I'd never heard of named Eric Roth, who would eventually go on to win an Oscar for *Forrest Gump*.

The role I was up for was an old Jewish pit boss overseeing the transition of the business from father to son. The character was nicely conceived, and the pilot was a gritty two-hour epic with a lot of dark, seedy Vegas undercurrents, which was very unusual for an Aaron Spelling show. After the audition, I heard I was definitely in the running but there was someone else they wanted more: Michael Lerner. He'd been

Jack's Place with *Catherine Mary Stewart and David Beecroft*

busy sending Academy members a copy of *Barton Fink* just in case they hadn't seen it and was rewarded for his efforts with an Oscar nomination as Best Supporting Actor. He was now a "name" and had no interest in doing *Jack's Place* at all. Once he passed, the part was officially offered to me. I asked for what I thought was a ridiculous amount of money, almost three times what they were proposing. My agent was convinced we'd never get it and I said, "That's fine if we don't but let's try anyway." Well, they gave it to me and I was treated like gold. I was flown to Los Angeles on MGM Grand Air for wardrobe fittings and then whisked to Las Vegas and put up at Caesars Palace, where filming would take place.

Jack was played by David Beecroft and Catherine Mary Stewart portrayed his indispensable assistant. Once the pilot was in the can, Jeff Sagansky – the head of CBS at the time – said, "We're not going to drop this project but we're not going forward right now. You're on hold for the next five-to-six months and we can pick it up at any time."

Jack's Place may have been in limbo, but I was still getting hired for work, even though my reputation as a drug addict was starting to spread. I was a character guy with a problem and everyone knew it: "Polito's good but he's a chore." It was a rocky road, but I was approaching a period that would be my most fruitful.

It was truly the best of times and the worst of times.

7
Crapping Out in Vegas

While waiting for news on the fate of *Jack's Place*, I settled back in New York and was quickly becoming a mess. My drug use was so out of hand that I began to order in. That's always a bad thing to do when you're in a fifth-floor walk-up because you need to get outside to stroll and exercise. Once you start to close in, once you're stuck on that floor and you make that space your cave, you're in trouble and that's what was happening to me. I was gaining weight like crazy, staying inside and ordering meals from the local diner. You're not supposed to treat food delivery to your home like room service but that was my mindset. Drug addiction is never good, and I believe it's even worse if you can afford it. At that point in my life, I certainly could.

My friend Michael Morin was now living on the fourth floor. Anne DeSalvo – who introduced me to the *Benno Blimpie* project years earlier – had also moved into the building, and across the hall was a young actor who worked with Michael in a play. The situation was like something out of *The Honeymooners* because when we came home, all of us would eventually get together to talk and see how everybody's day went. At this point I started to notice Michael wasn't quite right. He seemed a little more extreme. I was sensing that something about him was "off," but because I was self-centered and on drugs, I brushed away those concerns.

One day, I got a phone call saying that *Jack's Place* was finally being picked up by the network with an initial order of seven episodes and a brand-new title. When my agent, Jinny Raymond, called to say that I'd gotten the part, I was coked out and drunk. She said, "We have to finalize a deal. They're offering $10,000 an episode."

Stoned out of my mind, I told her, "Oh no, Jinny, we have to go much, much higher."

"Well, Jon, the problem is you don't have a very high quote." A "quote" used to mean a lot in the business; it showed that you had done good work in the past and were worthy of making a certain amount of money. If you earned $30,000 per episode for your last show, it meant that negotiations for a new gig started at $30,000. I'd done *Crime Story* for $5,000 an episode and *Ohara* for $10,000, so that's where my negotiations were starting.

I told Jinny, "I want $25,000 per episode." I just made up the number, and since Aaron Spelling was rich, why not try?

The producers rejected my demand so I politely said I wouldn't be participating. Shockingly, they came back and agreed to $22,500. It was more money than I'd ever heard of in my life! I knew other people made more but I felt like I'd just hit the jackpot.

Spelling sure knew how to welcome his stars. I was told I'd be flying to Vegas on MGM Grand Air, the airline of the rich and famous. There were only around thirty seats on each full-size jet, and a round-trip ticket would set you back a tidy sum! I packed about six months' worth of clothes in a huge suitcase my mother had given me because I didn't know what the weather would be like. The morning I was to hop on MGM's luxurious plane – carrying the wealthiest passengers on Earth – I was drunk. I mean fall-down, ridiculously drunk. I'd stayed up all night throwing nearly everything I owned in my bag, and at seven o'clock in the morning, I had to drag a suitcase the size of New Jersey down five flights and cram it and myself into an airport limo. I was wasted when I boarded – which was embarrassing enough – but when I went to put on the seat belt, I couldn't buckle it. I was *that* fat! Naturally, a blindingly attractive flight attendant had to fetch the unbecoming me an extension. I couldn't have picked a more exclusive environment to make a fool of myself.

When I arrived at Caesars, I was offered a small room in the hotel. I said, "No, no, this won't do. I need something better." The greatest part about this show was that Caesars was just beginning its expansion. The casino was in transition and the management wanted us to shoot there to advertise the new additions. They gave us the run of the place, and the room I was eventually given was in the old area that hadn't been remodeled yet. Everything in there was vintage and reeked of 1940s nostalgia, which I loved. We'd shoot in areas of the casino that were blocked off and we'd sign autographs for all the tourists. Nobody knew who we were but it was a really good time.

David Beecroft

The show, however, was changing drastically. It no longer remotely resembled the dark pilot Eric Roth wrote about a man who was going to deal with the seedy undercurrents of the city. In fact, the feeling among the cast – myself included – was that we were now doing *Love Boat* in a casino! David Beecroft and I would often call Eric to complain about the silly stories, but he said that was the direction the show was going. He basically confirmed the network was willing to move forward with the project on the condition it was produced in a manner most viewers associated with the Spelling brand. Eric was barely involved with this new incarnation, and while I was disappointed, David was livid and decided to make his displeasure known.

One afternoon during a break in filming, David was supposed to shoot five brief promo spots for the show, which was now called *Hearts Are Wild*. He was furious with the title because it made no sense, and I had to agree with him. *Hearts Are Wild* has nothing to do with poker; it was just a dreadful play on words. The spots were short and to the point: he was to stand in the middle of the casino surrounded by extras and say, "I'm David Beecroft and I play Jack Thorpe on *Hearts Are Wild*. Watch it on CBS." However, when it came time to do those promos, he refused.

I went to his room and tried to talk him into it. "Please come out and shoot these things," I begged. David thought it was beneath him and no matter how much I pleaded, he was determined to stand his ground. Meanwhile, calls were going furiously back and forth from Vegas to Los Angeles, and people were getting pissed because *a lot* of money was being wasted as everyone waited for the star to come back to work.

After about two hours of sitting in his room and listening to him complain about everything he loathed about the show, David turned to me and asked, "What do you think? Do you think I'm right?"

"No. I don't think you're right," I said matter-of-factly.

He stared at me in utter disbelief. "Then why are you up here with me?"

"David, I'm an old union man from Philly. I believe in standing by each other whether you're right or not, but I think you're making a big mistake here. There's no reason not to do the promos because we *want* people to watch. You think you know more about publicity than Aaron Spelling? I'm sorry but I don't agree with that." I knew we were in trouble from that moment on because if David was going to fight against what everyone else was trying to achieve, the project was doomed.

Hearts Are Wild *with Barbara Rush, David Beecroft, Diana Muldaur,
Ricardo Montalban, Bonnie Franklin and Pat Harrington*

As for me, there were great joys during the shooting of *Hearts Are Wild*. Granted, the episodes weren't good, but one positive thing about having a *Love Boat*-esque format meant I got to work with a bunch of wonderful guest stars every week. These were actors I'd admired for years: Tom Bosley, Bonnie Franklin, Ricardo Montalban, Barbara Rush… They were the supporting people I watched when I was growing up who would eventually become stars later in life.

John Astin made an appearance, which was very exciting. He was famous for his role as Gomez on *The Addams Family*, but when I was eleven years old, I knew him from *West Side Story*, a movie that changed my life. Whenever the guests came into town, I always tried to welcome them the night before we shot and pay my respects: "Hello, how are you? I hope you have a good time, and I can't wait to work with you." When Astin came in, I grabbed him and said, "I have to talk to you about *West Side Story!*" We sat down in front of a bank of slot machines on the casino floor and he told me the story of being cast in the movie to play a tiny part that was only supposed to shoot for two days. He took time off from a Broadway play he was doing, went to California and ended up being there for two weeks because Natalie Wood was so nervous about doing her dance with Richard Beymer. This information was pure gold to me, and I hung on his every word.

And then there was Mickey Rooney… I think that as a young actor, Mickey was a genius. With a resume full of incredible work, I consider his performance as Puck in *A Midsummer Night's Dream* to be brilliant. He was also part of Hollywood history, having been friends with Judy Garland and married to Ava Gardner, so I wanted to spend some time with him. On this particular episode he was playing a guy who wins a jackpot but refuses to publicly acknowledge it or have his photo taken, which causes problems for the casino staff. In real life, this simple story was causing problems for the entire production. One afternoon in the middle of filming, we got word that Mickey wasn't happy and was holding up the shoot. I was supposed to do a scene with him, but the production assistant came to me and said, "Mickey won't work. He's angry and he's yelling at the director."

I walked to the set to see what was going on, and surprisingly, he knew who I was! We started to talk, and he began going off about how he hated the scene and the director. "He won't do it like I want him to," Mickey complained. "He doesn't understand the way I work." Give Rooney an inch and he'd take four miles, riffing on the dialogue and doing improv at every turn. You can get away with that kind of spontaneity in films, but television was a completely different beast and required a more rigid structure.

I excused myself and went to see the director, who confirmed, "He's not doing what we need him to do."

I nodded and went back to where Mickey was sitting. After pulling up a chair beside him, I looked directly into his eyes and said, "You've *got* to tell me about Judy Garland. I want to hear all about her." His whole demeanor immediately changed as he started recounting stories about their adventures together. When he finished, I followed up with, "Your Puck in *A Midsummer Night's Dream* is the greatest thing I've

Hearts Are Wild *with David Beecroft and Mickey Rooney*

ever seen on film." Again, his face lit up and I knew I had him. I wasn't lying because I was genuinely in awe of him, but it was a simple case of me paying him his due. He needed people to treat him like the star he thought he was, and I was happy to do it. I asked him about every movie he was in I could think of, all the while reminding him that he was the best thing in the world. We were getting along famously, and when it came time to rehearse our scene, he began to do it. I got him working. I wasn't performing miracles by any means, but we were dealing with a diva. Being one myself, I knew exactly how to motivate him.

Another fond memory involved my mother and sister coming to visit when the guest star was Gene Barry. I was a sci-fi fan and first saw him in *The War of the Worlds* when I was a kid. I loved him then, and he went on to become a big television star in the '60s and '70s. Gene was playing a stand-up comic and I was going to be sitting at a very large table in front of the stage with David, Catherine Mary Stuart and other people. I immediately suggested, "How about putting my mom and sister at the table?" The director agreed and it was wonderful! When I turned to do a reaction shot with my mother, she wasn't looking at me like an actor does. She was looking at me like I was her little boy, full of pride, joy and love. Seeing the footage at the time was kind of funny, but looking back after all these years, it's also very touching.

Those were moments throughout the shoot of *Hearts* that were important to me, but I also learned a valuable lesson about how to deal with producers. When I did the movie *Fire with Fire*, it was produced by Gary Nardino. Gary was very well-known in the business and everybody loved him. I, however, was not so fond of the man. During the filming, he and I became friendly and as the film was running a little behind schedule, he asked me to give him one more day for free as a favor. I was okay with that, but then he asked for another day's work. And then another. When all was said and done, I ended up working a week that wasn't in my contract, which cost me $5,000. It wasn't much money to him, but it was a hell of a lot to me. This guy took me for a ride and I never forgot it.

When *Hearts* was picked up, I was surprised to learn it was going to be run by none other than Gary himself. Because there was such a long time between the pilot and the series, we could make changes to our contracts before they were finalized. I asked to have a special clause put in that stated if any new footage was needed to add to the pilot, I must be paid $5,000. Whether the scene was large or small, I'd have to be compensated if there was a re-shoot of any kind. My agent didn't understand why I wanted to include such a demand, but the company signed off on it, making it a done deal.

As we were filming the third episode, one of the producers said he needed a quick, four-second insert shot of David and me cheering on a fighter during a boxing match for the pilot. "No problem," I said. "Just remember I get $5,000 to do it."

He looked completely stunned and asked, "What are you talking about?"

"Look at my contract. If you have any questions, go see Gary Nardino."

A week later, on a Friday, one of the business people told me I wasn't going to get the extra money because Gary refused to pay it. I said, "That's perfectly fine but Gary's not getting his re-shoot. If he wants to know why, tell him to call me."

Gary Nardino

Gary phoned me on Saturday from a limousine, pissed as hell and ready to battle. "What's this about you getting $5,000?" he growled. "Why are you doing this to me? We're already tight on the budget!"

"Gary, let me be very clear: during *Fire with Fire* I gave you four days of work that ended up costing me $5,000. I really needed the money and you talked me into doing it for free. You didn't pay me then so I'm getting it back now."

"I would never do that to an actor!" he yelled. "I've never done that in my life!"

"Cut the crap, Gary. You know you did it. You may not remember, but if you go back and look, you'll see you never paid me." He started to bitch some more but we got disconnected.

On Sunday, I got a call around noon and Gary was in a great mood. "Polito, I love you! You were right about this and I'm going to pay you. Come and shoot on Tuesday." It turned out I had learned the vocabulary of producers: just say no or challenge them. In this case it worked, and it was a great ending to a problem I'd had as a young actor.

In the end, *Hearts Are Wild* was a bomb. The two-hour pilot was completely re-cut to get rid of the darker story themes that made it interesting in the first place, and the producers even brightened the lighting in post-production to make everything appear more friendly and inviting. It was now a typical Aaron Spelling show, but unlike *Fantasy Island* or *The Love Boat*, it wasn't catching on with the public. For that I have regret, but from the experience I have wonderful memories.

After wrapping *Hearts*, I went back to Los Angeles and checked into the Roosevelt Hotel. I always made a point of stopping by Les Ferreira's place because he was a great friend. Les was the director who cast me in *Sleuth* way back in '77, and he and his wife were like family to me. He said there was a ground floor apartment available in a building beside his house, and I decided to check it out because I was getting tired of hotel life and wanted something I could call my own. I met the insane little woman who was running the place, and she reminded me of Mr. Burns from *The Simpsons*: hunched over and scary as hell. She was willing to rent it for a price I thought was incredibly high, but in retrospect, it was actually pretty cheap compared to most L.A. properties. The place was a two-bedroom, two-bath with a huge living room, dining room and a wet bar. It was a little house that I desperately wanted to make my home.

I asked my old buddy Michael Morin to keep an eye on my New York apartment because I was officially going to start being bi-coastal. I loved Michael but noticed once again that he wasn't acting like himself. In fact, he wasn't really that friendly anymore. I don't know if he was jealous or envious, but he had no shortage of snarky comments to make about me and my career.

I began to settle into my home on the West Coast, ready to start anew because I'd done a little bit of good, a little bit of crap and a little bit of shtick. I never claimed to be great, but I think I've given one or two great performances in my life – which is all any actor hopes for – thanks to the Coens. My work in both of their films was exceptional and showed I could be a first-rate performer if I had an outstanding script and wonderfully creative directors to guide me. Using them as inspiration, it was time to regroup and find something good that could display my skills.

I got a call from my agent saying that something was happening in Baltimore. It was a new TV series about cops, to which I instantly replied, "Not interested."

"No, Jon, this is different. You've *got* to see this script."

I told him, "I don't want to see it. Don't send it to me. What else do you have?" He gave me two other crappy options and I said, "Okay, send me those but don't bother with the cop thing." The next afternoon, I had a package delivered to my L.A. apartment. Inside were two thick scripts, and tucked underneath were four pieces of paper.

Printed on those sheets were the words: "Scene One, *Homicide: Life on the Street*."

Committing Career *Homicide*

8

There are moments in life that may not seem like a big deal at the time, but with the benefit of hindsight, they're critical in determining the direction of your journey.

This was one of mine.

Even though I had no interest in doing the show, I read the four pages from *Homicide*. The pilot's opening scene is a conversation between two detectives who are looking in an alley for some evidence. One of the cops was Irish and the other was Polish, and I immediately fell in love with the writing. The dialogue between these two men was brilliant, but I made up my mind I wasn't going to audition. I was instantly drawn to the Irishman and the producers were only interested in what I could do as the Polish guy. A few days later, my agent called and urged me to go in for a reading. I reluctantly agreed.

When I met the casting director, I asked if I could include a personal message after the videotaped audition. He didn't think it was the best idea but he didn't stop me, either. I knew Barry Levinson – the director and executive producer – was going to be looking at it, I knew he was from Baltimore, and I knew that Baltimore and Philadelphia have nearly the same accent. After the reading, I turned and faced the camera, and in my best hometown Philly timbre said, "Mr. Levinson, I really think this is a great project and I'd love to be involved, but I don't want to be called back unless it's for the Irishman. The Polish guy is nice but it's not me." With that, I was certain I'd never hear from anybody about this show again.

Amazingly, several days later I *was* asked to read for the Irish character. I pulled onto the 20th Century Fox lot with instructions to park in the visitor's area, but being a bit hungover from partying the night before, I chose a spot right in front of the building where the auditions were being held. I walked into the room and there was only one other person there. I waited and waited and waited. I was getting a little impatient when a young man came running in. "Someone's in Barry Levinson's parking spot!" he said frantically. "Is it anyone in here?" Of course, I knew it was me.

As I left the building and approached my car, I saw Levinson standing there talking to Mel Brooks, which I thought was the coolest thing in the world. Instead of just slinking into my car and sneaking away, I stupidly decided this was an opportunity to introduce myself. I walked up and interrupted their discussion, which is something you *never* do in Hollywood. "Good morning Mr. Levinson," I said. "My apologies, I parked in the wrong spot. Hello Mr. Brooks, I'm Jon Polito. We met years ago in a disco in London when I was doing *Highlander*." Brooks stared at me like I was totally crazy, and Levinson was polite while giving me a look that strongly suggested I should get the hell away from them. I got into my car, drove to the visitor's lot and took the long, slow walk of shame back to the audition, which I now figured was going to be a complete waste of time.

Still, I soldiered on and performed for Levinson and his fellow executive producer, Tom Fontana. I was sweaty as could be and probably reeked of last night's alcohol, but I read well… *really* well. A few days later I was offered the role and was told we'd be shooting in Baltimore in six weeks. I was ecstatic! This was another character I couldn't wait to dig into. Besides being a cop, he was a big-bellied common man with basic problems; not too smart but good-hearted. I thought it was another role of a lifetime.

The only bad thing was that there wasn't any money. After working on *Hearts Are Wild*, my quote was now in the $25,000 per episode range. However, we were told everyone would be paid a flat rate: $15,000 for the "top" actors, $10,000 to others and $5,000 for the rest. I was being offered their top and had no choice but to accept because the project was too good to pass up. I had an apartment in Los Angeles, one in New York and now I was heading to Baltimore, which was only two hours away from my family in Philadelphia. My parents were happy that I was close by, as were my sister, brother and teenage niece, who was impressed that her Uncle Jonny was a movie star.

A couple of months earlier, I had lunch with Marcia Gay Harden at a restaurant in the Village. As I was about to walk in, I was recognized on the street by three black drag queens who seemed very excited to meet me. They were lovely and it was a joy to spend a few moments with some fans. I was taken to an outdoor table where a black man was already sitting. He said, "Hello, my name is Andre." He was a very well-spoken and interesting-looking guy.

Marcia arrived with a few other people and as everyone was getting settled, I told her, "I just had this wonderful experience with some black drag queens before you got here."

Andre was quick to chime in. "Why did you have to say they were black?"

"Because they *were* black," I replied.

"That's the problem with the world today," he said, clearly annoyed. "Our perception of people is defined by their color."

Suddenly I was stuck in a friggin' argument about race with this man named Andre... Andre Braugher. I'd heard of him because he was doing some impressive theater work, but I left that lunch thinking, *I don't care how good of an actor he is, he's kind of a prick.*

Fast-forward to Baltimore... Everyone was put up in a condo building in Fell's Point. I had a lovely apartment, and the production offices were two floors below. I went downstairs to introduce myself to the department heads, and at one point I asked, "Are any of the other actors here?" I was told Kyle Secor had already checked in and Andre Braugher would be showing up later that day. I thought, *Andre Braugher? You've got to be kidding! I'm going to be working with that son of a bitch?* Still, I knew this was the perfect opportunity to re-introduce myself and I couldn't wait to see his reaction. When he was dropped off at the building with bags in hand, I was part of the welcoming committee.

I went up to him and shook his hand. "Andre Braugher, I'm Jon Polito. Do you remember me?"

"Yes, it's so great to see you!" he answered enthusiastically.

He couldn't have been nicer. I wasn't expecting that, so I borrowed a line from *All About Eve* and said, "Andre, a situation pregnant with possibilities and all you can think of is, 'It's so great to see you?' I was hoping for a battle of the ages." He gave me an odd look that set the tone between us: he didn't quite know what to make of me, and I didn't quite know how to feel about him.

Daniel Baldwin, Yaphet Kotto and Clark Johnson – who was going to play my partner – eventually arrived. Clark was a piece of work and I loved him instantly. I knew he was either going to be a blast to act with or a pain in the ass, and he was both. Then there was Richard Belzer, who was beginning the role of *his* lifetime. He was playing John Munch, who went from *Homicide* to *Law & Order: SVU* to many other appearances over the years, becoming one of the longest-running characters in

The cast of Homicide: Life on the Street

the history of television. Before that happened, though, I knew him as a damn good stand-up comic and he knew me from my work with the Coens, so we hit it off right away.

As we were gearing up to start shooting, I was finalizing my character, Steve Crosetti. I wanted to let my belly show and have the jacket be kind of tight with my badge squeezed somewhere on my belt. I felt he should look bloated but capable of doing what was necessary, albeit with a bit of a groan. Since I was paired with Clark, who was quite fit and handsome, I thought being physically opposite would be visually beneficial.

The first night of filming, we did the scene I read at the audition. Clark and I were wandering around talking and you couldn't quite tell where we were or what we were looking for. I was commenting on the mystery of life and how it's not about finding things, it's about looking for them. Clark was complaining about being tired and just wanting to go home, but he couldn't

Homicide *with Clark Johnson*

because we were searching for a shell casing. That became more obvious as we got closer and closer to the body on the street and the flashing lights of the police cars. I even got to deliver the tagline before the title sequence: While standing over the corpse, I looked down and said, "That's the problem with this job. It's got nothing to do with life."

It was a great opening, and it didn't look like anything else on television. Barry Levinson wanted to find a new way of shooting the show, so he chose Wayne Ewing – a documentary guy – as the director of photography. Wayne was circling us like paparazzi, moving around for one take and then moving in a different direction for the next take. The camera was handheld, and he'd come in close or circle around. When it was all put together in editing, it had such rawness to it. There were jump cuts and things looked kind of out of sequence. It shouldn't have worked, but to me it was like hyper-reality. It was magical and I was so proud to be a part of it. On the second or third day, we were filming in a cemetery and that's when we *really* began to work out the music of how to perform. Everyone had to clear the area because you never knew when Wayne would be shooting from an angle that might accidentally show a crew person. Our dialogue felt like we were having a real conversation because there weren't fifty people standing ten feet away from us.

After we finished the first episode, Levinson's plan of action was to hire good film directors to helm subsequent installments, and the next man up was Martin Campbell. He was a talented guy who would go on to do some big action movies and a couple of James Bond films, but I found him difficult. He'd complain from morning till night about everything. I felt like he was trying to prove we couldn't do a quality show on a quick schedule, but the truth is he was used to leisurely days on a movie and was incapable of completing the sixteen pages a day needed for an hour-long TV drama.

In fairness, though, I didn't make Campbell's life easy. I was partying like crazy and the drugs were making me incredibly obnoxious. Because I felt so confident in the role, I figured that gave me the freedom to comment on every aspect of it. I'd also coerced Tom Fontana into giving me access to the dailies, so I'd watch the footage and get excited about what I was seeing, which made me even *more* opinionated.

One of the arcs for Crosetti involved a young police officer played by Lee Tergesen, a terrific actor. Even though nothing was specifically said, it was clearly implied in our interactions that I was his mentor and loved him like a nephew. The third episode was called "Son of a Gun" and revolved around Lee being shot in the head. As he was lying in the hospital on the verge of death, I spent the rest of the episode fighting to lead the investigation because the boy was like family.

In real life, there was a family event going on in a Philadelphia hospital with my father. My sister called and said something was wrong with Dad, but his doctor wasn't very proactive in addressing it. She was worried, and since we were close and I trusted her judgment, we agreed he should get a second opinion. She made an appointment with a new physician, and as I was rehearsing for "Son of a Gun" in Baltimore, the news came back that my father was going to be dead in a month unless he had quadruple bypass surgery.

In this episode, I taught my wounded protégé about jazz, and I was ecstatic because I personally love that music. I'm a huge Miles Davis fan and had the privilege of meeting him when he was a guest star on *Crime Story*. I remember one day he wouldn't come out of his room to shoot a scene, and I was tasked with getting him to the set. I'll never forget the moment of knocking on his door, and when he opened it, I looked at him and saw the most dilated pupils I'd ever seen! That man was flyin' high on something, but even in his altered state he proceeded to play some of the greatest music I'd ever heard.

The "Son of a Gun" script contained a few passages of dialogue in which I mentioned teaching Lee about jazz, so I went to Tom Fontana and begged, "Please let me talk about Miles Davis." For whatever reason, Tom wasn't interested in the idea. In the very last scene of the episode, I was in the hospital room with Lee, who was in a coma. I had a cassette player and put a set of earphones on him and a set on myself, and we listened to music together. I lobbied hard for that music to be Miles' but was told it was out of the question. I wasn't happy and I vented to Richard Belzer, a fellow jazz fan who sympathized with my frustrations.

Before we filmed a major scene where I'm told that Lee was shot, I had to go see my father because I was warned he could die during his operation. One of the crew members drove me to Philadelphia, and I sat with Dad for about an hour saying my goodbyes, just in case. It was a teary time with my mother, sister and brother, and then I was driven back to Baltimore. I managed to get about two hours of sleep before shooting the scene where I burst into the hospital. I can honestly say I didn't do much acting in that episode because my real-life fears and worries were fueling my fictional emotions.

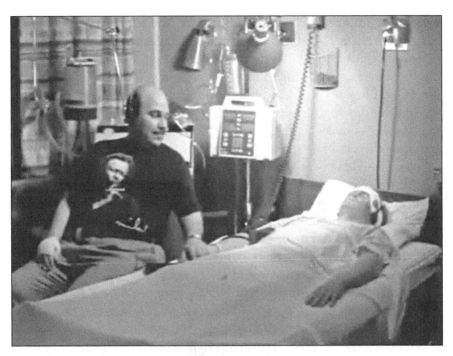

Homicide *with Lee Tergesen*

I was in my trailer preparing to film the last scene when Belzer suddenly showed up. "I bought you a present," he said. It was a black tee shirt with Miles' face on it! I immediately ran to the set and talked to director Nick Gomez and Wayne Ewing. As the scene unfolded, I entered the hospital room and took off my jacket and dress shirt, revealing Belzer's gift. Nick and Wayne – God bless them – made it a point to focus on the shirt, which meant the producers were pretty much obliged to use Davis' music in the scene. I finally got the opportunity to pay my respects to the late, great master.

I loved working on *Homicide*, and there were moments when I thought, *This show could be life-changing.* Everybody was finding their rhythm in working with Wayne's ever-moving camera, and the directors coming in were very interesting and talented. However, we were starting to get a lot of changes from Fontana – Levinson wasn't around that much – and we knew NBC wasn't happy. They began to move the show in a different direction, delving into the home lives of the detectives. I thought it was a mistake to get too personal, feeling that the cases were more important. It wasn't until later that I learned Fontana was having problems with his marriage and my character started to incorporate and reflect the issues he was experiencing. I wasn't fond of playing those scenes and, stoked by the increasing amount of drugs I was ingesting, I had no problem bitching about it to anyone who'd listen.

On Sunday night, January 31, 1993, *Homicide: Life on the Street* was poised to make its debut on NBC. Half the country was already watching the network and its broadcast of Super Bowl XXVII, and we followed it! There isn't a better time slot in all of television to launch a new series. We only filmed six episodes and had no idea if there would be any more after that. Warren Littlefield, the head of NBC, wanted to see what the reaction was before deciding whether to continue with it, so we had a break. The critics loved us, but the show wasn't landing with the public. The camera work made it look almost amateurish, and although it was a style that would later come into vogue, back then it was new and different and probably too jolting for most people.

Despite the ratings, Littlefield decided to continue the first season and produce three more episodes. Once the cast and crew reconvened in Baltimore, the problems picked up right where they'd left off. Yaphet Kotto was always pissed about something, and Ned Beatty – who'd been through almost every film situation imaginable – hated how the show was being shot. Since the camera was handheld, the area the actors worked in was limited ahead of time to make it easier for lighting and things like that, which Ned felt was too confining. There was a lot of complaining from everybody, especially me. I was drugged up, and although other cast members were able to hide their substance abuse, my erratic behavior was on full display.

With the show's fate hanging in the balance, my father was still in recovery after his surgery, so I went to Philly for a visit while waiting for news about *Homicide*'s future. Would I be going back to Baltimore, L.A. or New York? The network had to make a decision by a certain date, and when that date came and went, I started to look around and was offered another job. Shortly thereafter, Fontana called and said, "Jon, we might get picked up. Will you come back for the same money if the show continues? I need to know who I've got."

"Yes, I'll come back but I need to know immediately because there's another project pending."

He phoned the next day and said, "We're doing it. Please make yourself available." I cancelled the other gig and told my agent I was sticking with *Homicide*. Everything was settled.

Three days later, I got another call from Fontana. "Jon, they're picking up the show but they're not picking up you." The executives at NBC apparently thought I was too fat and unattractive, and their idea to lure viewers was to replace me with a pretty girl. After Tom broke the news, he said, "I'll bring you back. I'll figure out a way to bring you back."

I didn't believe him. I'd been through too many events with too many producers who promised me the world and then cut me off. This was yet *another* situation where I originated a role and couldn't continue it. I immediately went into anger mode, which was escalated by drugs. I called a writer named Gail Shister from *The Philadelphia Inquirer*, and the first words out of my mouth were, "Have I got an interview for you!" I proceeded to tell her how pissed I was with the producers of *Homicide* for listening to NBC. By giving in to every little demand from the network, Fontana and Levinson were – in my opinion – slowly starting to sink a great show. In fact, I metaphorically compared the current state of *Homicide* to the voyage of the Titanic.

"Do you feel that Tom Fontana is like the captain of the ship?" Gail asked.

"No. I believe Tom is standing on the iceberg and screaming, 'This way! Come this way!'" It was a horrible comment to make, but it went to print and was featured up and down the East Coast.

Fontana got angry. He released a statement saying, "Jon Polito is a very sad and troubled man," and he put it in *TV Guide* no less! We now had an in-print battle, which wasn't a smart move on my part. As the years went on, I realized it was especially stupid because Fontana is – if

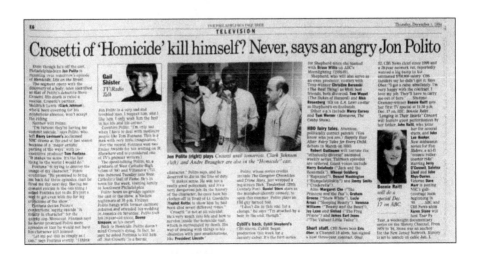

nothing else – faithful to all the actors he likes, and I believe he *did* like me. He elevated the careers of Lee Tergesen and Edie Falco by giving them small roles on *Homicide* and eventually casting them in breakout parts on *Oz*. I think Tom would've done the same with me if I'd simply played it cool and kept my mouth shut.

As the new episodes were being aired, I called him one last time and said, "Tom, whatever you do with Crosetti – you can kill him off if you have to – please don't do something like a suicide because it would go against everything I was trying to create with that character. Please don't have him kill himself. Please, please don't." And of course, that's *exactly* what Fontana did. It turned out to be a beautifully written episode but there was officially no going back. At this point, I didn't know if I'd be going anywhere.

Portraying Steve Crosetti on *Homicide* was one of the greatest artistic endeavors of my career. It was also one of my greatest failures.

9

The Crow and Other Horror Stories

Homicide doesn't quite sum up everything happening during that time in my career. After shooting the first six episodes, I went back to Los Angeles and was immediately offered two roles. One was for a movie called *The Crow*, and the other was for a cameo in the Coens' *The Hudsucker Proxy*. Since both productions were going to be shot at the same time at the same studio in North Carolina, it was a no-brainer to do both.

The Crow is based on a comic book about a man who's viciously murdered and comes back to avenge his and his fiancée's deaths. The part being offered was Gideon, a guy who runs a pawn shop and is selling stolen goods. My wardrobe consisted of an old, loose-fitting gray sweater and a shirt that was coffee-stained and kind of disgusting. I looked like I smelled, and my hair was a mess. Gideon was a disturbing character who was also familiar; a creepy dude audiences would immediately recognize.

When I arrived in North Carolina, there was a darkness that seemed to hover over the production. The first evening on the set, a young man about twenty-four years old was driving a vehicle used as part of the lighting system. As he was moving it across the lot, the vehicle fell into a hole and catapulted him into the air and onto a utility pole, electrocuting him. The early moments of the shoot were clouded by this horrible accident, but whatever negative feelings we all might have felt were gone because of the sweetness and positive attitude of Brandon Lee.

Brandon was more than just the son of Bruce Lee. Although skilled in the martial arts like his father, he was determined not to let that be his defining attribute. He was a promising and eager young actor, and when he walked onto the set you could tell he was excited to be there. Brandon was a happy guy playing an incredibly dark, depressed and angry character. He looked scary in the makeup but as soon as he spoke, his beautiful voice and wonderful demeanor immediately put you at ease.

The Crow *with Brandon Lee*

The first major scene I shot involved Brandon breaking into the pawn shop and confronting me about having his dead fiancée's engagement ring. As we rehearsed, he smashed through the sugar glass, which is a candy-like substitute that looks and breaks like the real thing. On the first take when Brandon burst through the door and started coming toward me, I noticed blood on several parts of his body. As soon as we finished the shot, I yelled, "This boy is bleeding!" People immediately rushed over and started to patch him up, yet he was as perky as could be and acting as if nothing was wrong. A few minutes later, he came up to me and asked, "How do you think that went?"

I said, "Brandon, I don't like that you were hurt. I know you're going to do your own stunts but please don't pull a Vic Morrow." I don't know why that came out of my mouth, but it did. Vic Morrow was a terrific actor who was killed when a helicopter crashed on top of him and two young children during the filming of the *Twilight Zone* movie. I was always mindful of that story because it brought up the issue of how far some producers and directors will go to get the shot, regardless of how dangerous a situation might be. It was the first thing I thought of when I saw Brandon bleeding, and I think subconsciously I needed him to at least be aware of it.

The cast and crew were back on the street set for the second night of the shoot, and as we were waiting around during a camera set-up, people started to notice a lot of smoke. At first we thought it might be from the other movie shooting on the lot – the Coens' *Hudsucker Proxy* – but there were suddenly screams that the prop truck was on fire! Thankfully, nobody was hurt, but oddly enough, the cause of the blaze was never determined. Two nights of shooting and already two accidents. I was sure these were omens.

A couple of weeks into *The Crow*, the Coens were ready for my cameo. They were on the studio's major soundstage, a set filled with beautifully designed offices and an incredible miniature of the building used in the beginning of the film. During the lunch break, Ethan approached and said, "We have a script we're calling *The Barbershop*. We might do something else first, but we'll contact you when it's time because we want you to be involved." Again, the Coens were coming through for me. Here I was working on one of their projects and they were already keeping me in mind for another one!

The Hudsucker Proxy

I finished *Hudsucker* in one night and went back to *The Crow*. We were going to be filming a continuation of my first scene with Brandon, in which my character is blown out of the pawn shop in an explosion. My stunt double was going to fly through the air, slam into a brick wall and then fall to the ground while on fire. The gag went off without a hitch, but when he landed, he turned and started to run. The head of the stunt department said, "It looked good, but I don't know what we're going to do about that last part."

I went to our director, Alex Proyas, and asked, "Do you need something more here?"

He said, "We're going to have a hell of a time cutting it together unless you do the end of the stunt yourself." I have a lot of respect for stuntmen – they always made me look better than I actually was – so if I could do something to help make the illusion convincing, I'd do it.

I volunteered my services to Alex, which didn't make the head of the stunt department happy. He never liked using actors for anything but reluctantly agreed to let me do the shot. My legs were covered with an anti-flame gel and then wrapped in safety material. I wasn't actually going to fly through the air; I was supposed to jump-land into frame and then react when I noticed my legs were on fire. One of the stunt guys came over and said, "Look, your pants are going to be lit just before we start the shot. If it starts to feel hot, yell 'Hot!' and we'll come put you out."

While the lights were being set up I practiced how I'd move, trying to figure out my character's reaction to being on fire. When the cameras started to roll, I nailed my jump, stuck the landing, and then looked down to see the flames dancing on top of my legs. I was absolutely petrified and started to scream "Hot!" while doing a little jig and hopping out of frame, which was nothing like I planned. It wasn't acting, it was real. That's Jon Polito on fire, and not in the best theatrical way! In fact, that one take was all we got because I couldn't go through it again. Although it doesn't look like much on camera, I assure you it *burned*.

A couple of weeks later, things got weird again: there was a hurricane coming. Although I'd seen footage of them on television, I'd never experienced one in real life. Let me tell you, it's as insane as it looks on TV. Cape Fear was getting battered and the water kept rising and rising, eventually reaching our hotel. There were a lot of alarms going off, and out of curiosity, I dashed into the elevator and went down to the lobby to see how bad things were. As soon as the doors opened, I saw water filling the lower part of the building. The employees shut down the elevator, effectively stranding everybody for the rest of the night. Part of the hotel lost electricity, and since the refrigeration system was knocked out, the manager decided to open the restaurant. Staff members moved the tables into an area that wasn't flooding and began making food. Everyone was sitting around eating and drinking as we rode out the storm.

The next day, the water started to recede, and we were able to check out the aftermath. Sure enough, a few of *The Crow*'s sets were heavily damaged. In my mind, all of these seemingly random acts of bad luck were happening too frequently to be dismissed as coincidences.

The Crow *with Tony Todd and Bai Ling*

My last day on the set, I had to complete a scene with Michael Wincott, Bai Ling and Tony Todd. Wincott confronts me, then pulls out a sword and shoves it through my throat. I'm not dying fast enough for him, so he takes a machine gun and shoots me. I thought this was going to be the coolest death I've ever had on screen – and I've had many – but I felt uneasy. We were shooting on the fifth floor of an old, creepy factory and it was as dusty and dirty as could be. It was already uncomfortable for me, but was made worse by the memory of something that happened during *Crime Story*. On that show, there was a scene with an explosion in an elevator shaft that went haywire. It was completely uncontrolled and ended up doing some real damage. I was later told that when dust builds up over many years, the flames become much stronger. With this information in the back of my mind, I was nervous about the muzzle flash that was going to come out of the gun barrel, fearing it might start a fire. I was also concerned because I was going to be wearing squibs, which are the explosives that make it look like you're being shot. They planned on putting eight or nine of them on my chest, but since I was wearing only that stained shirt underneath my sweater, I wasn't able to add any layers of clothing to help protect me from the squibs when they were detonated.

That night's shoot went on and on and on. We were in the sixteenth hour of filming, and during a break I spoke to the gun wranglers, who were old acquaintances of mine. They didn't seem very excited about shooting this late, nor did the special effects people who were preparing the squibs. Everybody was really tired, but the producer was pushing the cast and crew to continue. I asked the wranglers to show me what they were going to use in the machine gun in my death scene, and they brought out what they call one-half blanks. They fired a couple of shots and I was seriously freaked out by how much flame came out of the barrel! It was way too much, so they tried one-quarter blanks, which I also didn't like. I felt weird. Something about the gun just didn't seem right. It scared the hell out of me, so they went to one-eighth blanks, and I still wasn't happy. I approached the producer and said, "I think we should wait until tomorrow to film this. I don't feel safe."

"There's no way," he replied. "You cost too much money to keep for another day."

"I don't care, I'll do it for free. We've been here sixteen hours, everybody's tired and we haven't even started this scene yet." The producer refused, which pissed me off, so I said, "Fine. I don't want any kind of blanks used in the gun." He was furious, but the wranglers backed me up because if an actor says he doesn't feel comfortable, they won't proceed until a resolution is reached that satisfies everyone. We shot the scene without any blanks in the gun and the special effects went off without a hitch, although my chest was burned by the squibs.

Brandon told me how important *The Crow* was to him. He said a movie was being made about his father's life – *Dragon: The Bruce Lee Story* – and he was asked to star in it. He declined because he wanted to distance himself from his dad's legacy and forge his own path, and this was an opportunity for him to do so. From there we segued into a conversation about the famous "curse" on the Lee family. It was one of those stories that was passed down over the years. I certainly had heard about it when I was younger, but now that I was working with the son of Bruce Lee, I felt like that curse was hanging around the edges of the production.

With my scenes completed, I went back to Los Angeles. Less than a week later, I heard the horrible news that Brandon was accidentally shot and killed on the set. I was devastated. He was a wonderful young man who had just begun to show his potential as an actor. I was also convinced the movie would never see the light of day because there were still some important sequences that Brandon never got the chance to complete. Through the magic of Hollywood, however, it was finished, released and became something of a success that many fans still hold in high regard to this day.

Director Alex Proyas and Brandon Lee on the set of The Crow

The Crow combined moments of real fear with real sadness. In fact, that description could well sum up that entire year in my life. It was intense, but it was nothing compared to what was coming next.

* * *

In 1993, the old television show *The Untouchables* made a comeback. Having grown up with the original, I watched one or two episodes of the remake and was underwhelmed. What I *did* like was William Forsythe, a great character actor who I'd first seen in the Coens' film *Raising Arizona*. Watching him work had been a joy, and when I finally got to meet him, he turned out to be one of the sweetest guys in the world. Forsythe played Al Capone in this revamp, but when he was going to be unavailable for a few weeks to do a film, I was offered a new gangster character named Tommy Palumbo who would fill-in for Capone. I was guaranteed two episodes for a good amount of money with the possibility of a third. The show was filmed in Chicago, which is a city I adore, and the actors were housed in the wonderful Ambassador East hotel. I accepted the gig without hesitation.

Upon checking in, I discovered that guest stars were always booked in a regular room. I wanted something nicer, and my drugged stupor and diva attitude made it easy for me to bitch about getting an upgrade. I made quite a fuss with the producers about it, but they refused to budge, so I said, "Put me in a suite. I'll pay for it myself."

I shot my first episode and things went fairly well, even though I delivered nothing more than a basic, over-the-top, Gangster 101 performance. After my last day on set for the week, I asked my old friend Carol Korda – the ex-wife of John Santucci, the son-of-a-bitch crook from the *Crime Story* days – to come over. I'd arranged to have lots of drugs on hand and we began to party heavily. By ten-thirty that night, things were winding down when I got a call from my dealer in California who asked for a big favor. A "friend" (aka client) of hers was empty-handed and wanted to know if it was possible to pay me a visit. About half an hour later, there was a frenzied pounding on my door. When I opened it, I was greeted by a plain-looking, angry man... and Juliette Lewis! I was a *huge* fan of Juliette, so when they walked in, I laid out all the drugs I had and invited them to dive in. That's when she introduced me to her buddy. His name was Tom Sizemore.

As the hours passed, things kept getting crazier and crazier. Juliette was a bundle of energy and Sizemore kept trying to be the center of attention. Dear God, I'd never met a man who was so aggressive, mean-spirited, and full of himself. In the wee hours of the morning, they finally settled down enough to talk about being in town to shoot a film called *Natural Born Killers*. At dawn, all of us took a break to go out for breakfast before resuming the drug-fueled chaos. The day went on... and on... and on. What began as a spontaneous party night had now stretched into the late afternoon.

I was wiped out. When Tom and Juliette finally left at five o'clock, Carol went home, and I began to look at the script for the next episode of *The Untouchables*. I wasn't in a state of mind to read it with any kind of clarity or evaluate it creatively, but I did it anyway and immediately decided it needed a rewrite. In my exhausted, hungover and spaced-out condition, I got on the phone with the writer and started to complain. The producer got wind and called me to a meeting. I pulled myself together as best as I could, but it was obvious to everyone I was a mess. That's when I was told my services would no longer be required for the second episode. The script actually *was* rewritten, but only to replace my character with another new gangster.

Despite my behavior, I was offered a really great opportunity on a film called *Blankman* starring Damon Wayans. Damon had become a star on TV with *In Living Color* and was now branching out into movies. He created a silly character – kind of a sweet but vacant mental defective – who becomes a superhero, and through accidents and quirks of fate, actually ends up doing some good. The director, Mike Binder, was really in my corner when I read for the role and he actually convinced Damon to hire me. My agents negotiated a remarkable salary – the most money I'd ever been paid at that point – to play a character named Michael Minelli, another evil gangster.

The night before filming my first big scene, I was partying my brains out with coke and alcohol. I had a portable Sony CD player which, for some unknown reason, I placed on top of a lamp in my bedroom. I was out of it, I had no idea what I was doing and I completely forgot it was there. At five o'clock in the morning, I woke up, got out of bed, turned on the bedroom light and stumbled into the kitchen to make some coffee. Suddenly, I heard a beeping sound, but it wasn't the coffeemaker. Some other kind of alarm was going off and I couldn't figure out where it was coming from. I walked back to the bedroom and found the CD player on fire! As black, toxic smoke filled the room, I yanked the cord out of the wall and grabbed the device. Liquid plastic poured onto the rug as I ran to the bathroom and threw it into the tub, dousing it with water.

While I began to catch my breath after this chaotic event, I looked at my foot and saw that I'd stepped in the molten plastic. There was a huge hole in my big toe, which was burned down almost to the bone. It was very painful, and as I wrapped it up, I noticed there was another hole in the bottom of my other foot. When I arrived on the set, I was limping around, and people knew something was awry. A nurse came in during a break and advised I go to the hospital, so I went after work and was told I had second-degree burns on both feet. With the wounds taken care of, the only thing left to do was celebrate and stay up all night doing more coke.

On the second day, I arrived at the studio and my heart began to go crazy. I tried to act like everything was fine, but the nurse came into my trailer and said, "The producers sent me to check on you because you don't seem right." She discovered my heart was basically going a mile a minute. Filming had to be stopped because I was being sent to the hospital.

I was humiliated. My agency was informed immediately, which further added to the embarrassment. Here I was in a hospital bed with everyone aware the situation was caused by my excessive drugging and drinking. My agent said, "Look, Jon, we have a real problem here. They're thinking of firing you."

"Please do what you can. I didn't mean for this to happen," I replied, repeating the same old regretful bullshit line that every addict knows by heart. Miraculously, my agent convinced the producers to keep me on as long as I arrived on set the next morning with a clean bill of health. At 5 a.m., I insisted on being examined by a doctor and my vitals were normal. I got dressed, ran home to shower, and went back to the studio, swearing I'd never be a problem again.

Well, at least until the next time.

Blankman *with David Alan Grier*

In the ensuing days, things were going well and my performance was starting to come together. I'd resumed my partying but was doing a good job of not letting it interfere with the work. The week of Thanksgiving, I had to shoot on Monday and Tuesday but was told I had Wednesday off. When I got home on Tuesday afternoon, I started a huge holiday binge. One of the production assistants called and left a message around 9 p.m. saying there was a change in the schedule, and I was needed to shoot on Wednesday. I didn't respond. I was too stoned.

A second call came in and then a third, and I didn't answer those. I just sat in my apartment drugged out of my mind, oblivious to everything in the world. I then got a call from Damon, who left a message saying, "Please, Jon, you're going to ruin this film. We need you." Sometime around midnight, I called and told them I wouldn't be coming in. On Wednesday around ten o'clock in the morning, I was hunkered down in my apartment and my agent came knocking on my door to tell me I was about to sabotage my entire career.

I had officially hit a new low point, both personally and professionally.

In his infinite kindness, Damon didn't fire me. Somehow over that Thanksgiving weekend I pulled myself together, and during the last week of shooting I was doing my best work. I think I finally realized I was in danger of screwing up everything and managed to finish the movie on a positive note. In the end, I think the performance is manic, but it fulfilled the needs of the story in an otherwise unfunny film. To this day, my biggest thanks go to Mike Binder, the director. Mike was in AA, and even though I caused an extraordinary amount of pandemonium, he was very supportive of me not only keeping my job, but also in getting me help and getting me well.

Not that I got help, nor did I get well...

10

Artistic Highs, Realistic Lows

The mid-'90s – and in some ways, the entire decade – are a black hole in my memory. While details of my day-to-day life are something of a blur, there is clarity about the times when I got to act. One of the gifts an artist has (or perhaps it's a curse?) is that moments of life are remembered through the work. On a twelve-hour day in which you only perform for ten minutes, you remember those ten minutes more than anything else.

I also remember that thanks to my recreational excesses, good jobs were becoming more and more difficult to find. There was enough work to keep me going and enough money to spend on coke, but it was obvious to everyone that I was in trouble. I was dropped from Writers & Artists, the agency I'd been with since I was twenty-six, and now had to look for new representation. There were five or six smaller companies out there and I ended up going through all of them. I'd land at one, do a couple of jobs and then move on. In the span of four years, I'd gone from the beginning of a promising career to being a has-been. That was the journey I was on, and I had only myself to blame.

Thankfully, a very good opportunity presented itself. I met the director for a movie called *Bushwhacked* that was going to star Daniel Stern. I'd been a fan of Daniel's for a long time – I loved him in *Diner* – and now he was being cast in leading roles thanks to the huge success of the *Home Alone* movies. I don't want to be unkind, but the director was one of those types who was so eager to please that he didn't really take a strong stand. Although I had a lovely audition with him and eventually got the job, I wasn't quite sure what he wanted for the character. I played an FBI guy who was chasing Daniel, an innocent man framed for a crime who ends up posing as a scout master for a group of kids going on a mountain hike.

Bushwhacked *with Daniel Stern*

It was a great gig but there was a problem with the film that still exists to this day: Daniel Stern. I was shocked to see a man work so hard yet sabotage his own performance. He'd do a scene and it would be wonderful, spontaneous and fun. Rather than moving on to the next shot, he'd say, "Wait a minute, I can do it better," and he tried to home in on what he thought made the bit funny. Over and over again I'd see the spontaneity of the first take slowly evaporate, and by take fourteen there was absolutely nothing left. It was painful to watch natural comedy created in the moment being replaced with over-calculated shtick. After the first week I expected the director would try to rein him in, but it never happened and it was driving me crazy.

My own approach was much simpler, as I felt I'd gotten to the point where I could successfully complete a scene in three takes. I'd nail the first one, repeat it precisely during the second and then do something a bit different for the third. As a little insurance, I went to the producers and told them I suffered from a bad back and any prolonged shooting time would risk aggravating it. Fortunately, the producers and director loved me, not only because they were happy with my work but also because I was saving them a ton of time.

One day, I met one of the producers for lunch to finalize my billing in the credits. Out of the blue he said, "You don't really have a bad back, do you?"

"What makes you say that?"

"I'm looking at you and you seem fine, but you always want to stop after the third take."

"Are you watching dailies?" I asked.

"Yeah, you're really good," he responded. "You're always good on the first and third takes."

"That's right. How many takes are you watching of Daniel?"

He sighed. "Okay, I get the point."

Bushwhacked was an important film for me in many ways. In fact, I've run into adult directors who said they loved it when they were kids. Although not a great success critically or commercially, it was an enjoyable job that helped get my career back on track.

In 1995, I was cast in an episode of the hospital show *Chicago Hope*. Chris Penn played a man whose dying brother needed a heart transplant. When a donor organ comes in and is assigned to someone else, Chris' character holds the doctors and nurses in the operating room hostage, determined to get the transplant for his brother. The big twist at the end was that Chris ends up shooting himself in the head in the OR, which then makes his own heart available to save his brother's life.

Chris was a wonderful actor but he was a mess… even worse than me! He was coked, drunk and completely out of it. He openly kept bottles of liquor in his trailer, whereas I hid my little flask to sneak a drink now and then to take the edge off. Somehow, when that camera came on, he managed to get his dialogue out, but he confided to me that he couldn't remember his lines and asked me to work with him. I wanted to support him, but it was the blind leading the blind since we both had our problems. When we got to the final scene, Chris shot himself in the head, fell to the floor and passed out. He literally passed out! Everybody was waiting for him to stand up, but he didn't. The schedule had gone haywire earlier in the day because of difficulties with him getting through his other scenes, so the decision was made to continue shooting. Everyone remained very quiet as they set up the next part of the shot, and they quickly knocked out three scenes with Chris on the floor, snoring. He was a lovely man, and it was sad to see someone in a situation worse than my own, which unfortunately he didn't survive.

I was next asked to do a spot on a show called *High Society*, a half-hour sitcom with Mary McDonnell and Jean Smart. It was modeled after

Absolutely Fabulous, the glorious British show that everyone was trying to replicate. Although my character wasn't much, the role became important for a personal reason. Jean is a wonderful actress and we had a history, having done *Fire with Fire* together several years earlier. During that shoot there was a night at our hotel in Canada when we had dinner together and ended up back in my room, talking through the night. One of the things that came up during our conversation was my friend Kate Reid's alcoholism, and Jean expressed concern for Kate's health. I knew the signs of being a cocaine addict – I looked at it every day in the mirror – but I never really thought Kate had a drinking problem. In a very sweet and caring way, Jean explained in detail just how bad it was.

Somewhere around four in the morning, Jean, who is diabetic, began to feel ill. I asked if there was anything I could do and she said no. I was lying on the bed at the time and I told her, "Come here and lie next to me." She did, and I held her in my arms. It wasn't in any way sexual; it was human, a lovely moment that was never spoken about afterwards... not the next day, and not for years later.

High Society *with Jean Smart*

Since I was going to be working with her on *High Society*, I hoped we'd be able to spend a little time together to catch up. During our dinner break on the day of the shoot, I wandered through the studio halls and found her sitting in her dressing room. As we were chatting, something was brought up that led me to say, "I remember that night in Canada."

She said, "I remember it, too," and I was ecstatic to have that acknowledgment from her. In life, especially in this business, there are circles where people come up over and over again. *High Society* offered me the chance to close one of those circles with the wonderful Jean Smart.

I was next offered a brief appearance on an HBO series I loved called *Dream On*. Brian Benben was the star, and this was a chance to close another circle because he had played Michael Lasker in *The Gangster Chronicles*, the first television project I'd ever done. The hook of *Dream On* was that the network had access to a ton of old film and TV footage, so whenever Brian's character would encounter odd or stressful situations, he'd have flashbacks to scenes from old movies that were used to hilarious effect. Brian's boss was played by the brilliant Michael McK-

The cast of Dream On

ean, an actor I'd admired from *This is Spinal Tap* and many other things. Denny Dillon – a terrific little powerhouse comedienne – was Brian's secretary, and the great Wendie Malick portrayed his ex-wife. The show was produced by John Landis, who I was apprehensive about because of the horrible accident that happened on the *Twilight Zone* movie. Although I personally felt he was to blame for that tragedy, he was a sweet man and I tried not to let that incident affect my dealings with him.

I was cast as Louie, the criminal cousin of Denny's character. Brian was intimidated when he talked to me, so there would always be a cutaway to some terrific old gangster footage whenever I said anything. It was a small role with a couple of good gags, and the producers were so happy with my work that I was invited back for two more episodes. In the third one, Denny decided she was going to become a performer and take dance lessons. When Brian asked who she was going to train with, she said, "I'm going to train with Louie. He's a professional choreographer." The concept of this gangster knowing *anything* about dance was hysterical, and the fact that I was a big old lump made it even better. We came up with the idea that Louie considered himself the ultimate choreographer simply by trying to mimic everything he'd seen in the movie *All That Jazz*, right down to the pill-popping and scarf around his neck. I was having a ball, and what started out as a minor role turned into a character rife with comedic possibilities.

By this time, I'd gotten to know the show's writers and I stopped by their office one day after filming was completed. "I just want to thank you guys," I told them. "This keeps getting better and better. In fact, I've got an idea for something if you want to hear it."

One of them said, "Well, we've been trying to think of things for you. What do you have in mind?"

I immediately went into pitch mode. "What if Louie is also an author? Since Brian works at a publishing company, what if I tried to sell him a book I wrote about finding love in prison?" They laughed and agreed to give it some thought. A short time later, I was given a script called "All About Louie," which was a riff on *All About Eve*. The story consisted of me taking over Denny's job while she was away, much to Brian's horror. Louie is a gangster who think he's a choreographer; he's never going to be a good secretary. As it turned out, he was a *great* secretary, doing the job better than Denny did.

As the episode went on, Brian loved what I was doing and I eventually made a pass at him. He says, "I'm sorry Louie, but I'm not gay," and I say, "Well I'm not gay, either. I just want to make love to you and bring you fresh croissants every morning." It was a great experience made even better because it was wonderfully directed by Michael McKean. The role was a gift and showed I could take a staple of my repertoire – the gangster – and by moving it here and a little bit there, I could play the drama of Johnny Caspar in *Miller's Crossing* and the comedy of Louie in *Dream On*.

During this time I was still making occasional trips to New York, but as much as I loved the city, it was becoming less and less appealing. Anne DeSalvo had moved out, which left Michael Morin, the man who housed me when I first arrived in the Big Apple. My visits with him were becoming more and more difficult. He was different… angrier. I loved Michael unconditionally – we'd been friends since our college days at Villanova – and I treated him like family, but he didn't seem to feel the same way about me.

One night when I was back in town, Michael came over for dinner, had a large glass of vodka, went into convulsions and started foaming at the mouth. Panicked, my first reaction was to rush him to the ER, but he came out of his stupor and said, "Don't take me to the hospital. I don't have insurance." He passed out again a few minutes later and I was frozen in terror, torn between acting on my instincts and honoring his request. I stayed with Michael that night and held him. He was never one to show any kind of physical affection like hugging, but when he passed out, I held on to him and stayed awake to make sure he kept breathing.

Somewhere around seven the next morning, he came to and seemed almost completely sober. He immediately went into my kitchen and asked, "What do you have to drink?"

"Michael, you've got to stop."

He began to shake and looked at me with the saddest eyes I've ever seen in a human being. "I can't," he said softly. Michael opened my freezer, found a bottle of Stolichnaya, swilled down half a glass and walked out of my apartment. Exhausted, I fell asleep and woke up around two in the afternoon, at which point I decided to go out and get something to eat. As I passed by Michael's apartment, I noticed the door was ajar, which is something you *don't* do in New York. When I called his name and got no response, I walked in and found him unconscious on the living room floor.

I realized my friend had a real problem, and with nowhere else to turn, I called my mother. I gave her all the details and asked for her advice. "You have to call his family and let them know," she said. "You have to get him help."

"I can't interfere with his life," I explained.

"This is something you have to do right now! Contact his family and tell them what's going on. If he dies, you're going to feel terrible and you'll have to live with it."

I knew Michael loved his sister very much, so I tracked down her number and called. She said, "Keep him there. I'll come up and get him."

I went downstairs to find his door locked. I knocked and was genuinely surprised when he answered. He seemed to be perfectly fine. I walked into his apartment and said, "Michael, I'm concerned about what happened last night." He started making all kinds of excuses and I told him, "I've done something you're probably never going to forgive me for. Your sister's coming to pick you up and take you back to New Jersey." He instantly became upset and began rambling on and on until his rambling turned into tears. I went to hug him but he turned away, walked into his bedroom, pulled out a suitcase and began packing his clothes. I had come back to New York for work and ended up putting my dear old friend into rehab. The problem was that I honestly didn't know if I was saving his life or ruining it.

When I went back to Los Angeles to see if there were any new jobs around, *Roseanne* was heading into its final season. I was a longtime viewer, and despite the tabloid stories of her diva-like behavior and behind-the-scenes fights with the producers, I remained a fan.

Roseanne with Roseanne Barr and John Goodman

Roseanne was going to change her character's life – and the direction of the entire series – by winning the lottery. I was hired to play a small role as a lottery official, but it was a bittersweet situation. As an actor, I was thrilled to get the part and the exposure that would come with it. As a fan, however, I was disappointed because an audience of millions who clearly identified with the struggles of this lower-middle class family was now going to be alienated after the Conners became instantly rich. During rehearsal, I never actually got to work with Roseanne. She apparently didn't rehearse with the other actors because she was too busy supervising every other aspect of the production. Goodman was there – he's an old pro with whom I'd worked on *Barton Fink*, and he was as kind as could be – but I had to hand the lottery check to a stand-in. It was kind of difficult to do because everything we had carefully planned and staged was being done without the person with whom I was actually going to be doing it.

Little did I know that Roseanne was watching me on the set, and for reasons unknown, she agreed to do the final rehearsal before the actual taping. She was fine to work with but was using cue cards, and I felt like she was phoning it in. After I did my bit in front of the audience, someone grabbed me and said, "Roseanne wants you in another scene." This doesn't normally happen in television, especially on a shoot date, but she wanted more of me. There was a scene at the end of the episode of the family's celebration party, and they put me in and gave me a couple of lines. I got to meet Laurie Metcalf – an actress I've admired for years who's only gotten better with age – as well as the young actors playing the kids, who were all lovely. Although my role was a minor one, I was going to be seen by a huge number of people in one of the most successful sitcoms in television history.

My work on *Roseanne* should've been a high point in my career, but it was tempered with a sad dose of reality. Michael had gotten out of rehab and sent me a letter. He wrote about what a bad influence I'd been in his life and pretty much blamed me for his addictions. Reading his words was terribly depressing, and I was caught off guard that he was putting all his problems on me. He claimed I made things worse by enabling him, and in retrospect, he was probably right. We used to get stoned together and I'd say, "Don't go to work tomorrow. Stay with me and I'll give you money." I wanted him to party with me and felt responsible to make sure he wasn't losing out financially, especially since he was already having trouble keeping jobs because of his drinking. After getting his letter, I tried calling him a couple of times, but he never answered.

The third time I called Michael, I received important news. An old friend of ours from Villanova named Tony Torrice – a young, gay actor who I put into a couple of movie projects and theater roles – called to say he was dying of AIDS and wanted to see me. I went to visit Tony, and he passed away two weeks later. I decided to get tested for HIV, which was kind of late considering how long I'd known about the disease. Fortunately, the results were negative. I phoned Michael to share the bad news about Tony and he didn't really have a response, which I thought was strange. I then told him about my own testing and tried to stress the importance of getting himself checked out. He gave me a bunch of excuses and quickly ended the call, making it crystal clear he didn't want to talk to me anymore. In modern terms, it was our official "bromance" breakup. It hurt me badly, but I'd heard from other people that he had bad-mouthed me quite a bit over the years and wasn't the friend I always considered him to be.

I loved him, and as difficult as it was, I accepted his rejection. Maybe I really was, in part, to blame for his problems.

11

With Friends like *Seinfeld* and *Lebowski...*

There were times when I'd fall head-over-heels in love with certain projects. I'd jump in with both feet and shoot it, but due to the long post-production process, it would be several months before I could see the finished product. During that waiting period, everything that excited me about it – what I believed would be absolute gold – might disappear. Such was the case with a script called *Whiskey Down*.

The movie takes place in a diner (the title is lingo for "rye toast") and the premise is that an old man learns he has a winning lottery ticket worth $6 million and then immediately dies. A group of people in the diner begin scheming to get their hands on the ticket, and mayhem ensues. The script was well-written and the cast was impressive: Virginia Madsen, who I'd worked with on *Fire with Fire*; Carroll Baker, who was nominated for an Oscar for *Baby Doll*; Bill Erwin, a wonderful character guy; and two young actors named Jon Favreau and Vince Vaughn, who'd made a movie called *Swingers* that had yet to be released. There was also Flea from the Red Hot Chili Peppers, Ernie Hudson from *Ghostbusters*, and Mike Starr, whom I knew from *Miller's Crossing*.

Months later, a screening was held for the cast and crew, and although we were hoping for the best, we knew it just didn't work. What had looked so promising on the page somehow got lost in translation. It was released overseas on VHS and made its American debut in 1996 under the title *Just Your Luck*. The movie didn't amount to anything for anyone involved, and for that I'm sorry. It was a performance I'm proud of.

My acting career at this point was kind of like a boring roller coaster ride: flat with no thrills and very few hills. The top show on television was *Seinfeld*, which was coming to a close. I wasn't that big of a fan,

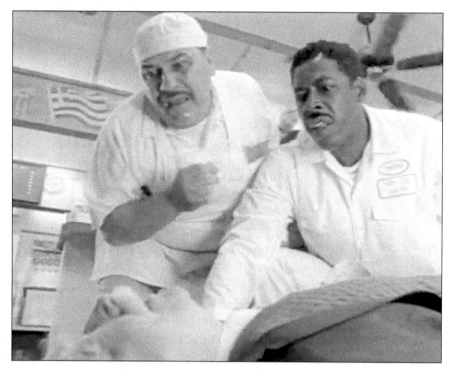

Just Your Luck *with Bill Erwin and Ernie Hudson*

but like many series that have since become classics, I watched the re-runs and only later came to realize its importance. My agent called on a Friday afternoon saying I had an audition the next morning to play Silvio, Jerry's landlord. My upstairs neighbor had an old fax machine, and when I explained they were going to fax me the script, he kindly brought it down to my apartment and set it up for me. It was a primitive device, and the quality of the print came out horribly, but I received the pages at six o'clock that evening.

One of the first scenes was a hallway confrontation with Michael Richards' character, Kramer. He was reversing the peephole in his door and my line was, "Kramer! What are doing?" That's what was printed on the paper: "What are" – scribble, scribble – "doing?" It didn't make much sense to me, but since other scenes included conflicts with Jerry and Newman, I knew Silvio was an angry man. I went to my room with the crinkled papers and began to prepare for the audition. I couldn't figure out what my voice would be or how I would carry myself. When I read the line, "What are doing?" out loud with a very generic mid-Eastern European accent, I thought, *That's it! I've got it!* The dialogue was easy to learn once I knew how I'd say it, but there was still something missing. I pulled out all the hairpieces I'd saved over the years and lined them up. That's when I saw the comb-over piece originally designed for *Barton Fink.* I put it on, greased the few hair strands on it and started talking with the accent. Confident this was the way the character should be, I studied the lines over and over because I *really* wanted this role.

On Saturday at 10 a.m., I arrived at the CBS Studio Center lot and walked up to a line of small cabins that served as office space for the shows currently shooting. I went inside the *Seinfeld* building and sat down, hoping in my heart of hearts that maybe I was the only one who was being seen. Within minutes, in walked six of the finest character people I knew, all of whom I would've cast in anything because they were excellent. As everyone was chatting, Jerry Seinfeld entered and greeted us on his way to the back room. It was 10:20 a.m. and the audition was about to begin. I was number one, the *worst* position to be in. I looked at my competition and said, "Guys, give me a hint. What accent are you using?"

They all gave me a puzzled look. "What do mean? What accent?" one of them asked.

"The character's first line is, 'What are doing?' I took that to mean he was a foreigner."

He looked at me and said, "The first line is, 'What are *you* doing?'" I gazed at his beautifully printed script pages and immediately started to freak out, realizing I had prepared a character based on a typo!

Before I could even begin to think of a plan B, my name was called. I entered the room – Jerry was sitting at a table with the writer and several other people – and I immediately approached him. "Seinfeld, I'm screwed here!" I blurted out. "I thought the line was, 'What are doing?' so I came up with this accent." I just started rambling on and on about what I did, how it happened and why I chose the hairpiece.

Jerry looked at me and said, "Whoa, whoa, whoa... Where's the hairpiece?" I pointed to the strands running across my head and he nodded. "Oh, okay. Let's hear the accent." I began to calm down immediately. He was a good man who put me right at ease. When it was over, I went home convinced there wasn't a chance in hell I'd get the part. I'd made a lot of mistakes in my preparation, but as fate would have it, *none* of the things I did were mistakes. They were, in fact, the very things that made me stand out from everyone else, and the role was mine.

Seinfeld *with Michael Richards and Jerry Seinfeld*

On Monday morning, we were shooting an exterior scene in which Kramer explains that Jerry is a bit of a "dandy," and I launched into this very silly, overly expressive mocking of him. Everybody thought it was funny, especially Seinfeld. In fact, the reaction was so good that some rewrites took place. When I got home that night, I received a revised scene that introduced my character (it's always a good sign when they add material for you instead of cutting it down!). The plan was to have a run-through Tuesday morning and tape in front of an audience that evening, and while the cast seemed to thrive on the tension of limited rehearsal before going out and performing, I was extremely nervous. As intense as it was, everything went well and I had a ball. I'm told "The Reverse Peephole" is considered a classic by the *Seinfeld* faithful, and to this day it remains a nice little feather in my cap. What started out as an honest mistake turned into the creation of a character unlike any I'd ever done.

During the mid-'90s, major changes were brewing, both personally and professionally. My niece and I were very close, and after graduating from high school, she decided she wanted to come out to L.A. and live with me. Her mother – my sister – was adamantly opposed to the idea, but I loved my niece and decided to make whatever adjustments were necessary to accommodate her in my home. It was also around this time

I concluded that after years of being bi-coastal, I was ready to let go of my New York apartment and settle permanently in Los Angeles.

In 1996, Marcia Gay Harden was getting married in Texas at a resort she'd gone to as a child. My niece had met Marcia once and was very starstruck, so I paid for both of us to go. On the plane was a woman with a newborn baby. At one point when she stood up to go to the bathroom, she saw me and introduced herself. "Marcia said we have to meet. I don't know why." The woman was Maryellen Mulcahy, Marcia's manager who worked at Framework Entertainment. After finally arriving in Texas, I was in the process of renting a car when Maryellen came up to me with her baby and said, "I'll go with you." I was okay with that, so my niece got in the passenger seat and Maryellen sat in the back. It was a helluva long drive made even worse because the baby cried non-stop, I could see Maryellen's boobs flying furiously in the rearview mirror, and she was backseat driving like crazy!

When we finally arrived at the wedding location, we discovered it wasn't a resort at all. The place was a religious retreat for children and there was no alcohol on the premises. Maryellen and a few others were panicked about not having any booze there, so I'd sneak away and bring back liquor, becoming the unofficial barkeep for the weekend.

On the way back to the airport, Maryellen made a lunch date with me. Years after being dropped by Writers & Artists due to my excesses, the agency had been sold and I was asked to come back. None of the people I had dealt with were there anymore, so it would be a fresh start. After our lunch, Maryellen agreed to take me on as a client. I'd never had a manager before, I didn't really understand what her job was, and I wasn't sure why another percentage of my income would be going to her, but I believed she would be beneficial to my career. During our meal, one of the first things Maryellen said was, "You have to lose weight." She was right. I was up to 295 pounds and I needed to do something because it was starting to affect my health. My niece was now living with me and I realized it was time to stop being "crazy Uncle Jonny" and start taking care of myself. Anthony Denison, my buddy from the *Crime Story* days, was married to a woman who sold a weight loss product that actually worked. I diligently followed the diet she suggested and the pounds began to melt away. I dropped from 295 to 240 within a few months.

Life was pretty good at that point, but the cherry on top came from the Coens. They wanted me to do a cameo in their new movie, but I couldn't make heads or tails out of the script, something called *The Big*

Lebowski. My part was so small that it was referred to as "Figure in a Volkswagen." There was no definition about who he was until he announced himself as Da Fino, a private dick who'd been hired to keep tabs on a guy called "the Dude."

The Big Lebowski *with Jeff Bridges*

I arrived at the location on a Wednesday night having no idea what I was going to do with this character. While waiting for Joel and Ethan to get to my scene, I spent the entire time trying to figure out how in the hell to play it, but I kept coming up empty. When Jeff Bridges – a fun and lovely guy – came on the set, it was time to shoot. My time had run out. He was taller than me, so when I got out of the car, my hands suddenly shot out and my body was contorted in a weird position. I was trying to look threatening in an apathetic way, leaning forward on my tippy-toes trying to be taller and intimidating as I delivered my dialogue. These were physical things I was making up as I went along, and Da Fino was being born on the spot. It was the usual Coen magic at work. Of all my many performances, my best have been with them because I was always in great hands.

Truth be told, I had no idea what the movie might turn out to be, but less than a year later I was invited to the premiere, and I thought it was one of the funniest, strangest and most beautiful pieces of art that would never make a nickel. The after-party was held at the bowling alley where some of the film was shot, and I spotted John Goodman, whom I hadn't seen since working on *Roseanne*. I went up behind him and hugged his waist. He immediately turned around and there was happiness in his voice when he said, "Polito!"

"Mr. Goodman, I think you're the best," I gushed. "You're one of my favorites."

He said, "Well, you didn't make it easy for me in New York." I gave him a puzzled look and he proceeded to explain that he was doing theater there the same time I was. I watched a lot of actors around that time, but he was one who flew under my radar. He knew of me, though, because I was starting to get a lot of press. Early in the 1979-1980 season when I was up for the play *Emigrés*, John said he was in contention for the role to the very end before it was given to me. "You don't know how much I wanted *Emigrés* and a lot of the other parts that you got."

I told him, "Well, you certainly got the best of me now, don't ya?" We had a good laugh about that, and it was the last face-to-face experience I've had with John. I look at him and his work with such admiration. He's done things as an actor that I could never do. He should've been nominated for *Lebowski* (as well as several other performances) but I believe that one day he'll finally get the Oscar recognition he rightly deserves.

In 1997, another circle of life came around when I got a call from Bobby Costanzo asking me to be in a movie. I had first met him during my audition for *Ohara* – he said how much he needed the part that I eventually got – and over the years we continued to battle each other for roles. Bobby was starring in a low-budget film called *With Friends Like These...*, and it had a fun premise: a group of buddies, all of whom are character actors, learn about a top-secret audition for a new Martin Scorsese project, and they turn against each other while trying to land a coveted role. Bobby's character had a backstory about an actor he hated competing against named Rudy Ptak, and Bobby said, "Jon, you *have* to play Rudy because this is you. This is us!"

There wasn't any money involved but Maryellen agreed I should do the movie because the cast was incredible: Adam Arkin, David

With Friends Like These... *with Robert Costanzo*

Strathairn, Jon Tenney, Beverly D'Angelo, Michael McKean, Amy Madigan, Bill Murray and Scorsese himself. I had a mustache at the time which I had worn proudly ever since *Miller's Crossing*, and they asked me to shave it off. I wasn't happy about it but knew it was essential to the punchline of a scene where Bobby and I have a confrontation on a golf course, which showed just how much we do look alike. In fact, Bobby told me stories about fans mistaking him for me and him signing my autograph for them. Unfortunately, despite a stellar group of actors and a clever script, *With Friends Like These...* didn't generate much interest. It is, however, a wonderful film that perfectly encapsulates the professional – but very friendly – rivalry between me and the great Bobby Costanzo.

I next got an offer for a show called *Millennium*. It was a companion piece to *The X-Files* starring Lance Henriksen as an ex-FBI guy who investigates serial killers and supernatural events. I'm a huge fan of Lance. My last job as an extra in New York was in the Al Pacino movie *Dog Day Afternoon*, playing one of the cops in the background. When I saw the film – you *always* went to see whatever you were in and hoped for something good – I remember being impressed with Lance and began following his career. It was a dream come true to finally get an opportunity to work with him, but I also wanted to learn. I'd made a fairly good living being bombastic and over the top, while Lance is an actor who's subtle yet powerful, and I decided to imitate him. During our scenes together, I was quiet and simply said the words, just like he did. It's not a great performance to anyone else, but to me it's one of my most important and I'm grateful to have had the experience.

Millennium *with Lance Henriksen*

In May of 1999, I promised my mom I'd come back to Philadelphia to attend an event for her, but I ended up getting booked on a show. In this business, it's inevitable that you get a job as soon as you make plans for a trip or vacation. In this case, though, I was kind of excited about the gig because it was a TV series shot in San Francisco called *Nash Bridges*. It wasn't very good, but it starred Don Johnson, whom I liked and had worked with on a couple of *Miami Vice* episodes.

I arrived at the set on a Monday and was supposed to be done by Thursday, meaning I could still leave for Philly on Friday. However, Monday's shoot never happened, and Tuesday's filming was also cancelled. I knew one of the assistant directors and asked him what in the world was going on. "Don doesn't like the episode and he wants it rewritten," he explained. "Until that happens, he's not showing up." It was a display of the old-school diva behavior that peaked in the '80s. That kind of mentality was winding down in the '90s, and it certainly wouldn't be tolerated at all today. I told the AD about my planned trip and asked how long this stalemate was going to last. "You'd better cancel," he answered. "Even if we start tomorrow, you won't be done in time."

I called my mother and gave her the bad news. She was incredibly disappointed, but I left the door open a bit and said, "Let me see what I can do." Wednesday came and there was no shoot. Everyone thought we'd surely be going to work on Thursday, but noooooo... In fact, it looked like Don wasn't going to show up on Friday, either. When a rumor began to spread that we probably wouldn't start filming until Monday, I went to the airport and made an all-night flight from California to Philly. I arrived in time for my mother's event on Saturday and then flew back to San Francisco, landing around midnight on Sunday. There were lots of messages waiting in my hotel room because word had gotten out that I'd left. It was a bad situation – Maryellen wasn't happy with me at all – but it ultimately didn't matter because Don didn't come to the set on Monday. Later that evening, we were told he was finally happy with the script and shooting would commence the next morning.

Nash Bridges *with Don Johnson*

Of course, Don couldn't be bothered to rehearse the scene! I laughed at the star treatment as I worked with his stand-in while the director went through an extensive series of shots he was going to do, moving from one set to another. We finished our run-through and waited for Don, who arrived just before lunch. He looked at the scene, the director explained how he was going to film everything, and without any hesitation, Don declared, "No. Absolutely not."

"What do you mean?" the director asked, stunned.

Don turned to me and said, "Polito, how ya doing?" – he remembered me! – and then addressed the director. "We can do this in a oner," meaning a single shot. And I'll be damned if he wasn't right! We did the entire scene in one walking, handheld shot and it was beautiful. It worked much better because there was no interrupting our flow. I thought his choices were great and it reminded me of a famous story about Orson Welles when he was making *Touch of Evil*. Welles would spend an incredible amount of time rehearsing and the producers were concerned he was falling behind schedule. When he finally turned the camera on, he got the shot in a single take. It's a great story about how his process not only ended up being economical, it made for a much more effective movie. *Nash Bridges* isn't *Touch of Evil*, but Don took something that was convoluted and stripped it down to the essentials, which ultimately improved it.

Meanwhile, I began to realize I was in trouble. On the domestic front, my niece was living with me and I was still doing drugs, which often led to screaming matches between us. My life was an intense series of highs and lows, and it proved too much for her to stomach. She began listening to her mother's hateful comments about how horrible I was, which led to her getting her own apartment for a short time before finally going home to Philadelphia. The coke, booze and gambling were taking their toll, and like any other addict, I was spending more than I was making. My bank accounts were dwindling, and by the end of the '90s I was $265,000 in debt. Anything I earned went toward keeping the apartment and fending off creditors, who were hot on my heels. A decade that started with great artistic and financial promise was coming to a bleak and uncertain close. I needed any work I could get.

Maryellen called about a young director named Morgan Daniel who wanted me to appear in a film he was making called *Flies on Cupid*. She wasn't a fan of clients doing low-budget projects, but I told her I'd at least like to hear what he had to say before passing on it. Morgan was quite the charmer. By the end of his pitch I was mildly interested, even though the title was unappealing and the role was just another Johnny Caspar rip-off. The biggest problem was his offer of $1,000 for one day's work. It was all he could afford, so I asked Maryellen how to respond. She advised asking for $2,000, and if he agreed, I should take it. Morgan said yes, and since it would help make that month's rent, I officially signed on to *Flies on Cupid*.

It was a movie that changed my life forever.

12
Love, Loss and Closure

The end of 1999 wasn't looking good. Years of financial irresponsibility and indulgences had caught up with me. I was $265,000 in debt and whatever money I was making barely dented my bills. It was a constant worry and I was finally starting to acknowledge the cost of my addictions. I also began questioning how my behavior affected personal relationships. In early September of 1999, I felt a need to compare notes with everyone from current pals to my oldest and best friends. I didn't know where it would lead or if it would solve anything, but I made some calls.

Two of them were to Carol Korda and Michael Morin, both of which went unanswered. I wasn't surprised about Michael since we were estranged after I helped put him in rehab. Deep down, I knew he'd probably never speak to me again. On the other hand, Carol's silence was more curious. We talked at least twice a month, so it was unusual for her to not respond to my messages. After trying a couple more times that week and not hearing anything, I worried that something was wrong. I started having that weird psychic feeling, and that's when the proverbial shit hit the fan.

I got two calls in one day, the first from a woman I didn't know. She said, "I'm a friend of Michael Morin's. He died last week." As I tried to process this news, I got word less than an hour later from Carol's sister-in-law that Carol had just passed away. I was crushed. I loved Carol. I visited her every time I was in Chicago and we'd chat on the phone for hours at a time. I was so happy she was finally doing well for herself, and now she was gone.

With Carol's death there was at least some clarity about how it happened. Her family had a history of heart problems and her father had dropped dead in his forties. Carol had just turned fifty and her heart simply stopped. Michael's situation, however, was quite different. I learned he'd been diagnosed with AIDS in the early '90s and he never said a word about it. I remembered his strange reaction when I told him I was HIV-negative and how he started drinking heavily and became so bitter and vicious toward me. All those memories came rushing back and began to fill in the story about my friend's life that, in the end, I really knew so little about. When Michael found out he was HIV-positive, he was actually on a campaign to kill himself. I didn't know it, of course; I just thought his drinking was excessive and he needed help, so that's why I put him in rehab. He wanted to take himself out and I ended up extending his life… and as it turned out, his suffering.

A strange bit of irony about Michael involved the World Trade Center. It was one of his favorite places to visit and he'd find any excuse to go. It was truly one of the few things in life that made him happy. Michael died in 1999 on September 11th, and when the attack happened two years later, I was glad he wasn't alive to see it.

Within a week I'd lost two of the most important people in my life. It was a slam to my heart, but as an actor, the only thing I knew how to do was to keep plugging away, and that's what I did. Having accepted the small role and salary for *Flies on Cupid*, I asked to be driven to and from the set, and they agreed. In fact, they said yes to everything I requested. The movie had been shooting for at least a month and this was the last day of filming. On a Sunday morning, I got in the limo and arrived on location at dawn. It was very disorganized, as is often the case on low-budget independent productions, but I was excited to be working and determined to treat it as seriously as I did everything else. I thought, *Who knows what this might bring?*

Of all the cast and crew members, one who caught my eye was the first assistant director, a very handsome man in his mid-thirties who bore a strong resemblance to actor Sean Astin. I've always had a thing for the Sean Astin-type: short, strong, cute and Germanic. Everyone on the set was making quite a fuss over me, but this AD had no idea who I was and seemed singularly indifferent about my presence. After asking around a bit, I learned his name was Darryl Armbruster and he was very efficient and professional. Morgan Daniel, the writer/director/leading man, was fawning over me so I knew Darryl was going to be the person I needed to rely on to get some objective feedback.

I pulled Darryl aside during lunch and asked him to go over the scene with me. He said, "I don't really know who you are but everyone else is impressed by you. Should I call you *Mister* Polito?" It was a semi-sarcastic, smart-ass comment that I found to be adorable, and since he was pretty damn cute, I was a little flirty with him. Although I'd lost

some weight, I was still a big boy at this point – around 250 pounds – but in my mind I was a slender, gorgeous thing, so I shamelessly flirted with whoever I could. As a single man, all I could do was throw it out there and hope somebody would take the bait. Unfortunately, Darryl wasn't biting, but he got me through the day's filming without a hitch, keeping the set moving and helping everyone stay focused.

At the end of the shoot, Morgan invited me to the wrap party being held a few days later. It was the kind of event usually reserved for people who worked on a movie from beginning to end, and since I was only there for the last day, I wasn't sure if I should attend. However, I said politely that I'd love to be there. On that Wednesday afternoon, I got a phone call from Ken Marino – a wonderful comedian and actor I worked with on *Nash Bridges* and *Carlo's Wake* – asking me to come out for drinks with him. I agreed immediately, thinking it would be a good excuse to leave the wrap party early.

When I arrived at the *Flies on Cupid* gathering, Morgan and his wife, Rhonda, cornered me. She said, "One of the reasons we wanted you here is because we think you'd be a great match for Darryl Armbruster."

"The assistant director?" I responded, somewhat stunned by this revelation. "Oh... Okay." It was like something out of high school the way they seemed to be plotting this, but God bless them, they had my heart in mind. When Darryl came in with his best friend, Jenny Moss – one of the stars of the movie – I went over and spent some time drinking with them. I was trying to court him, and he seemed to be responding. This was new for me because it had been *many* years since any of my advances had actually worked!

Right around this time I was regretting my promise to meet with Ken Marino. I anxiously told Darryl and Jenny, "Don't leave. I have to go do something, but I'll be back." I ran out, jumped in my car, and drove through Los Angeles traffic to a bar where Ken was waiting. As we sat at the table, my knees were shaking and I was bouncing all over the place. It was like a scene out of a Hitchcock film: the clock was ticking and I had to get out of there quick! Ken wanted to go to a different place for another drink, so I said I'd follow him there. After staying behind for one block, I sped away and rushed back to the party. Just as I arrived, Darryl and Jenny were leaving. I ran up to him and said, "I need your number. I've got to call you." He pulled out a business card and handed it to me. I had no idea what, if anything, would come from this encounter but I was anxious to find out.

During the next two days, I tried phoning Darryl and didn't get a response. I figured I misinterpreted the signals between us but as it turned out, he was just playing hard to get. He called back on Saturday and we had a long, lovely conversation. We were laughing and having a great old time and made a date for the following week. Two days before our get-together, he said he'd watched *Miller's Crossing* because he had no idea who I was. I *think* he liked it but I could tell he wasn't that impressed. Me playing a gangster didn't really mean that much to him, especially since I'd just reproduced the same performance for *Flies on Cupid*. The next night, he called and excitedly said he got a much better idea of my acting abilities because he'd just seen *Barton Fink*.

He was learning what I did for a living, but aside from his assistant directing gig on *Cupid*, I really didn't know much about his work. I got a call one day from Morgan and Rhonda saying they were going to see Darryl sing. I thought, *Darryl sings???* We met at a club called The Mint in L.A. and I finally got to see Darryl in his element as a member of the Dan Band. Actress Kathy Najimy was married to a man named Dan Finnerty, who would go to karaoke events in L.A. and sing women's disco songs as a joke. He developed something of a following, which led to Dan organizing a show. Word spread that this weekly karaoke thing was the place to be.

Dan was a grungy-looking guy with a backwards ball cap, bad boy attitude and dirty mouth, and he was backed up by two singers, one of whom was Darryl. It was a comedic rock 'n roll band and the show was brilliant. It was funky, it was fast, and it was funny. I thought I was witnessing something that was hot but had no idea at the time how hot it would be. The Dan Band became quite a big deal, and in the midst of it, Darryl and I were becoming a couple. For the first time in many years, I had a boyfriend.

In November, I got a call from my manager. "Well, you're not going to believe this," she said. "Despite all of the problems you've had, they're asking if you'll appear in the *Homicide* movie shooting in Baltimore next month." After executive producer Tom Fontana had my character commit suicide off-camera just to spite me, I stopped following the show. The plot of the TV movie was that Yaphet Kotto's Lt. Giardello gets shot and is facing death, at which point he wanders through the white light and has an encounter with all of the cops in his charge who'd died over the years.

"Is there any money involved?" I asked.

"Very little," she responded. Even though this wasn't going to be a financial windfall, it was an opportunity to put my finishing touch on

Homicide: The Movie

Crosetti. Of all the characters I created that were taken away from me, that one hurt the most. As much as I needed the cash, I needed closure even more, so I immediately agreed to do it.

I took off for Baltimore and was put up at the same condo in Fell's Point I stayed in all those years before. It brought back some wonderful memories, but the nostalgia turned out to be the highlight of my trip. It was made clear to me that I was just being used for one group scene, they weren't going to pay to keep me there long, and I was given very little time to prepare. I got the feeling that my being asked back didn't mean this was a reconciliation or an apology. It was more like a mild handshake between the producers and me, with both parties putting aside our differences for the sake of the show. When I sat down at the table to read the script, it was as if I'd never left. Richard Belzer was terrific, and Clark Johnson was wonderful. Yaphet was his old grumpy self, still making life uneasy on the set. I don't think he was a happy camper from the beginning of the series to the end, and he was never more than casually polite to me. The filming of my scene went well, and when all was said and done, I was finally able to close the door on *Homicide* and walk away with my head held high.

* * *

When the year 2000 rolled around, life was pretty damn good. I was finding steady work, but most importantly I came home to Darryl, who was now staying at my place three or four nights a week. Although our relationship was going well, my financial issues had yet to be resolved. Conversely, Darryl was doing a little better for himself. The Dan Band became the house band for a show called *Pajama Party* on the new Oxygen TV network which Oprah Winfrey co-founded in 1998. My boyfriend was on television every week, he was making a tidy sum and we were starting a nice life together. Things were going so well that I wanted to share my joy with friends who were in relationships of their own. I'd been the fifth wheel for so many years and here was a chance to show that I was now happily part of a couple. Ironically, by the time Darryl and I got together, a lot of my friends were splitting up. It was bizarre timing, but instead of using all those breakups as examples of why not to stay together, we decided to give it a try and forge ahead hand-in-hand. Darryl wasn't officially living with me, but he was pretty much "living with me." It was fun!

Darryl and Jon

Fun... That was something I hadn't experienced in a long, long time. I'd forgotten how much I missed it.

Darryl and I were invited to a Sunday brunch at the home of David Burke – the story editor on *Crime Story* – and his wonderful wife, Wendy. During the meal she revealed she'd been diagnosed with terminal cancer. It was quite a shock, and after everyone had finished eating, David pulled me aside and we went downstairs to his office. He said he had to find some artistic outlet to help deal with Wendy's illness, and he started pitching an idea. A director of photography I'd worked with years earlier named Francis Kenny was doing technical research on a new Sony digital camera that would replicate the look of film. This was back when digital photography was an emerging technology, so it was a big deal to see if you could capture the same kind of aesthetic on a digital device. Francis had to do a project in order to prove the worth of this new camera, so he went to David and said, "I'd like you to write and direct this thing but it has to be done with Jon Polito."

I don't know why Francis insisted on having me involved but David explained those were the conditions. He said, "I'm going to write something about cancer, you're going to star in it and Francis is going to shoot it." I sat there dumbfounded, not knowing what to make of any of it, but I was eager to help David out and I agreed without hesitation. I thought it was going to be like a screen test just to show the camera's ability; something where I just walked on, said a few words and was done.

Two weeks later, I was in Laughlin, Nevada to shoot scenes for a movie called *View from the Top* with Gwyneth Paltrow. She was playing a trailer trash girl who follows her dream of becoming a flight attendant, and I portrayed the head of the airline. It was supposed to be a comedy, and although the film ultimately didn't work, she was certainly giving it her all. I must be honest here: when Gwyneth Paltrow came on the set the first time in high heels with blue eye shadow and pumped-up blonde hair – the same kind of look ladies sported when I was growing up in the '60s – she was one of the most beautiful women I'd ever seen. I was literally stuttering around her! She was sweet as could be, very polite and lovely to work with. As gay as I am, my stomach would start to flutter when I was around her.

After the first day's shoot, I went back to the hotel and got a phone call from David. "I faxed you the script for this camera test," he said. "We'll do it on Sunday and finish it in one day." Thinking there might

Jon and David J. Burke

be one or two pages of dialogue at most, I went to the front desk and was handed a stack of seventeen pages! Entitled *Frank's Last Dance*, it was like a one-act play with me doing a non-stop monologue from beginning to end. It was a beautiful piece of writing, but what scared the hell out of me was trying to learn this material in only two days. I got the script on a Thursday night; I had a full day's work on Friday and then I flew back to L.A., getting home around midnight. On Saturday, I went into overdrive trying to memorize the script, in which I played the owner of a failing Greek restaurant who was dying from cancer. I went to the set not knowing what to expect and hoping for the best. David had rented a restaurant for the day and was totally winging it, using his creative instincts to guide every spontaneous set-up. Unlike movies in which it's very time consuming to properly light a scene, Francis Kenny was able to use this new digital camera to quickly prepare each shot and make it look as if it were put together by a professional crew. It was an incredible experience.

Frank's Last Dance

As we knocked out each scene, I had a great feeling about the project. Even though it was just a test for a piece of equipment, Francis and David were pouring their hearts into it, as was I. This little movie would never be seen by audiences, and for that I felt sad because we were three men working at the peak of our abilities. Instead of being yet another bombastic gangster or oddly eccentric Coen creation, I got to deliver a *really* good performance as a nice, normal, regular guy who was ill and had only a short time to live.

I had no idea how prophetic the role would turn out to be.

13
Wake-Up Calls and Warning Signs

The 2000s had started with a bang. I had a terrific boyfriend and a steady stream of work, but while cash was coming in, even more was going out. Thanks to credit cards, gambling and drugs, I was still over a quarter of a million dollars in debt, and although I was paying the piper it wasn't enough. I even had to borrow rent money from Darryl once, which put him in the uncomfortable situation of having a new beau who couldn't cover his bills. He bailed me out – God bless him! – and aside from that embarrassing moment it was a wonderful and exciting time in our lives.

However, things were a little askew in my hometown. My niece and I were estranged – she had run back to Philly after giving up her hopes and dreams, much to the excitement of my sister – and my parents weren't doing well. Thanks to my mother's love of gambling they were deep in debt, too. I arranged for a bankruptcy on their behalf and got their finances stabilized. It made their lives a little easier, which was good because Mom had other issues to deal with. She'd recently been hit by a motorcycle in Atlantic City and was thrown into the air, which left her pretty banged up and on a long, painful road to recovery. She wasn't someone who got ill or played sick, so it was difficult seeing her in such a helpless condition. At the same time, my father's health was becoming an issue. They were growing older – he was in his early eighties, she in her late seventies – and everyday life was getting tough for them.

Darryl and I, on the other hand, were doing well, but like any couple we'd occasionally have fights. As a German, Darryl would get angry and quiet; as an Italian, I'd scream bloody murder and then want to make up ten minutes later. It was an interesting dynamic, but we were

Jon with parents Dee and John

making pretty good progress in setting up our lives together. I'd met Darryl when he was thirty-six and I was forty-nine, and one year later we were in love. I said those three little words first and spent a frightening amount of time waiting to see if he would answer back. When he did, it was official: we were in a relationship. But something had to change about me, namely my addictions. Drugs were still part of my lifestyle – I always had marijuana and an eight-ball sitting around – and while Darryl wasn't against getting high from time to time, he didn't abuse it.

There was one morning… actually, it was a horrible morning *after*. Anyone who's done drugs or drinks knows what I'm talking about. I blacked out at some point during the evening, and when I woke up, I had a feeling I'd done or said something terrible but couldn't remember what it was. Darryl and I usually slept in separate bedrooms because it was more comfortable, since we were both used to living alone. I walked past his room and told him, "Good morning," but his response was very cold. I knew that look, and I knew that feeling. Something was wrong.

Around 10 a.m. while I was on the patio having coffee, he came outside with a warning: "If you keep doing coke I don't think I can be with you anymore." He then listed all the horrifying things I had done and said the night before. I've been told I can be quite the asshole when I'm annihilated, usually giving an intolerable "Don't you know who I am? I'm Jon Polito!" speech, as if I were more important than anyone else in the room. It was a wake-up call, and because of his confrontation I gave up cocaine after thirty years of daily use. There was no rehab, no meetings; I just quit. I don't know how I did it, but I think the fear of losing Darryl's love was stronger than any hold the drug had on me.

By this time, I was making more money from television than films. I was getting prominent, singular billing in the credits ("and JON POLITO") and "top of show" compensation, meaning I was paid the highest rate offered for guest stars. Things were looking better, but it still wasn't solving my debt problems. I was also hoping a part would come along that would really display my range. *Dear God*, I thought, *if only the Coens had something...*

As if on cue, the phone rang a few days later. Ethan said, "It's time to do that damn barbershop film." I was finally going back to work with my favorite filmmaking brothers! I had *Miller's Crossing, Barton Fink, The Hudsucker Proxy* and *The Big Lebowski* under my belt but I was hoping this next one was going to be the role of a lifetime. In fact, Ethan used that exact phrase to describe it, but I knew he said that to everyone about everything. When I read the script I didn't think it was the game-changer he made it out to be, but it certainly *was* interesting.

Ethan first mentioned *The Man Who Wasn't There* while I was doing my cameo in *Hudsucker* several years earlier, and although he said Brad Pitt was going to be starring, by the time the project was ready to go Billy Bob Thornton was the leading man. Billy Bob had come on to the scene with a movie called *Sling Blade*, which was brilliant. Anyone who's seen that film knows what an amazing performance he delivered, and I was excited beyond belief to be working with him. *Man*'s story takes place in the late '40s, focusing on Ed Crane, a barber who's having marital problems. Looking to create a better life for himself, Ed decides to blackmail his wife's lover so he can get money to invest in a dry-cleaning business that my character, Creighton Tolliver, was pitching.

Creighton was a closeted homosexual. In fact, the script refers to him as the "pansy salesman." The hairpiece was crazy, curly and much too excessive, but it *was* something this pansy would've chosen to wear. The outfit was beautiful, created by the Coens' terrific and Oscar-nominated wardrobe person, Mary Zophres. I started work in the middle of the shoot and on my first day in the makeup trailer, I asked how things were going because that was *the* place to get the best news and gossip.

I was told the person causing the biggest stir was a young actress named Scarlett Johansson. I didn't know who she was, but everyone was utterly mesmerized by her beauty and talent. Unfortunately, I never got to work with her, but she was wonderful in the film.

The Man Who Wasn't There

In one of my scenes with Billy Bob, Ed Crane tells Creighton he thinks he can get the money to invest in my dry-cleaning business. That news perks me up, I put the hairpiece on and I'm ready to talk business. We have a drink, and the script says that Creighton looks at Ed and there's a silence. Ed's next line is, "Was that a pass?" I say, "Maybe," and he responds, "Well, you're out of line." There was no stage direction as to what the pass was going to be, and during rehearsal Joel and Ethan asked me what I could do with my face to flirt suggestively with him. Aside from arching my eyebrows, my only other gift is being able to wink with my left eye without squinting. It's kind of creepy but the Coens thought it was hysterical, so we went with it.

When I met Billy Bob, he was rail thin and on the verge of being unhealthy. While we rehearsed, I kept looking at him and thought, *How could this be the same guy from* Sling Blade*? How in the hell could he physically transform himself like that?* I even said to him, "Billy Bob, this is a joy and an honor for me. You gave the best performance of the year in that movie and I still can't figure out how you did it." It may have come across as me being a little starstruck, but the feeling was genuine. During a coffee break before filming the flirtation scene, I noticed him whispering something to Joel and Ethan and then to our DP, Roger Deakins. When it was time to shoot, Billy Bob sat down not as Ed Crane but as his character from *Sling Blade*. He had hitched up his pants, jutted out his jaw and started talking in that unique voice. I swear to God, that man instantly gained twenty pounds and was a completely different person! It was sheer genius, and for a character guy like me, truly inspiring.

During the production, I was invited to a screening at the Writer's Guild for *Intolerable Cruelty*, a film Joel and Ethan directed starring George Clooney. It wasn't quite a red-carpet event, but it was still exciting because there were a lot of movie stars there. Billy Bob and Angelina Jolie were a couple at the time, and he introduced her to Darryl and me. She couldn't have been sweeter, and when Darryl made a comment about finding a true partner in me, she responded by saying she'd known Billy Bob since their days in ancient Egypt. It was a funky, "We've been kindred spirits since the beginning of time" kind of thing, but she said it with such charm that I immediately fell in love with her. At the end of the evening I went to get our car, and while I was gone Billy Bob pulled Darryl aside and told him, "Before you leave, I have to talk to you. I want you to know who you're with. If I never act again, it would be okay because of the joy I've had working with Jon. He's one of my favorite actors of all time." Whether or not that was his true feeling, it was a classy and generous thing to say. When Darryl got into the car, he looked at me and beamed with pride.

My first appearance in the film was the last sequence to be shot. Movies are filmed out of order, and this sequence was critical as it introduced the character and helped set the plot in motion. A few days earlier, my cousin and her family had come to town for an extended stay. In the midst of entertaining my guests, I lost track of the shooting schedule and wasn't fully prepared for my last day of work, which happened to feature the largest amount of dialogue. I went in that morning hoping I had the lines down but as we filmed, I felt I was taking too long. I could say the words, but it took a lot of work and a lot of time to get the rhythm and the meaning the Coens intended.

Honestly, I was pissed at myself because I really wanted to impress them with how wonderfully I was doing without drugs, hoping my newfound clarity would keep me employed with them for the rest of my days. Doing that scene was tough, and because I struggled so badly, we went over schedule. Feeling terrible, I pulled Joel aside near the end of the day and said, "I'm so sorry. I'll give you a free day if you need it."

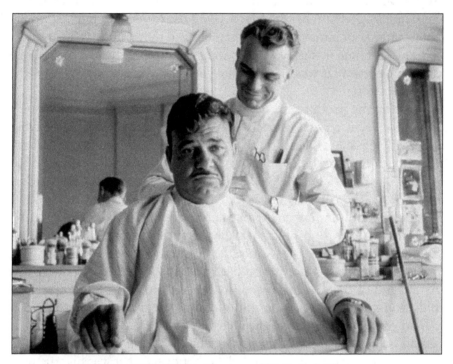

The Man Who Wasn't There *with Billy Bob Thornton*

"Don't be silly," he replied. "We got it. It's in the can." Despite his reassurance, I was concerned it was a performance that wouldn't work. To calm my fears they invited me to come and watch the dailies. Now, viewing dailies with the Coens is a very special time. It's like being in church: you let them sit up front, you don't say a word, and you don't make a sound. Since my cousin's family was visiting, I asked if they could come on the set as my guests. It was an act of kindness I instantly regretted because they laughed, made comments, and had to repeatedly be reminded to stay quiet. It was a situation that I don't think reflected well on me.

I'm trying to find excuses as to why this is the last movie I've done with the Coens, but the fact is there isn't one. I've looked at who's been in their films since then and they're all stars. It's a new, A-list repertoire they're working with now. Ethan has said they're planning a film in which they'll use me, and I pray that's true. I feel proud to have been a member of their company, and until the day comes – if it ever does – that I'm asked back, *The Man Who Wasn't There* served as my finale with the Coen brothers.

It had truly been a decade of magic.

As my time with Joel and Ethan was coming to an end, Darryl and the Dan Band were on the rise, playing at bigger venues and high-profile events. In fact, they shared top billing with Olivia Newton-John at a benefit concert hosted by Drew Carey. I was a real fan of Drew and loved his stand-up, and he went nuts when he saw me. It was a mutual lovefest, and he said, "I'm getting you on the show." He had a hit sitcom with a very talented cast, but I took his comment with a grain of salt. Whenever someone says they're going to get you a job, it very rarely happens. True to his word, two weeks later I got a gig on *The Drew Carey Show* as the voice of a baby! I had a ball doing it and my work led to two more episodes in which I appeared on camera. I still run into Drew occasionally and he's one of the sweetest, kindest men I've ever met.

In 2001, a gift came along when I got a call to read for a TV pilot called *The Chronicle,* a show about a trashy tabloid newspaper. It published stories about flying saucers and monsters and other nonsense, but the gimmick was that the stories were *true.* The show had a good creative pedigree: Bob Greenblatt and David Janollari, who'd done *Six Feet Under*, were producing a script by Silvio Horta, who went on to develop *Ugly Betty.* The character I was auditioning for was the editor of the paper, and I loved the part. There were some great people up for it and only five of us were brought back to go in front of the brass at NBC. There's nothing more nerve-wracking than five actors sitting in a room together, each one wondering what the others are going to do differently to try and make the best impression. I had a lot riding on this reading because my agent secured a very lucrative contract if the show was picked up. It was the best television deal of my life, almost $30,000 per episode. That's not big for TV, but for me it was huge. There were only two problems: I didn't know if it would be green-lit, and I had no idea if I would even be cast.

I went home to Darryl, and about an hour later, the call came that I had gotten the role. I was going to be in a major pilot for NBC! We flew to Vancouver to shoot the episode; there were beautiful sets and wonderful special effects. It was an expensive production and the finished product turned out to be damn good. Days turned into weeks as we were all waiting on pins and needles to see what would happen, and word finally came down that the network had passed. It was a crushing blow. I made some money from the pilot, but it wasn't going to be the financial salvation I was hoping for. Two days later, I learned the Sci-Fi Channel – now known as Syfy – was looking for a new series and agreed to buy *The Chronicle*. This meant my NBC deal was out the window. One of the new producers called to say I was wanted on the show, but he couldn't match my salary quote. So, do I refuse to be paid less than I deserve and walk away? Unfortunately, I wasn't in a position to do that. I desperately needed the money, so I quickly accepted his counteroffer.

The producers promised that if the series continued beyond seven episodes (Sci-Fi initially ordered seven to see how the audience reacted) they'd try to increase my salary for any additional installments, and that's exactly what they did. Every week's check went toward paying a credit card bill, and slowly but surely, I was starting to make some progress with my finances. *The Chronicle* was good but not great. While it got decent ratings and some positive reviews, the biggest joy came from finally paying off over a quarter million dollars of debt. I was starting a new chapter … broke but with a clean financial slate. Darryl had gone through some bad times when he was younger and had to declare bankruptcy, so the two of us made a pact that we'd never allow ourselves to get into such dire straits ever again, and to this day we haven't.

After *The Chronicle*, I went back to my bread-and-butter work. David Burke, for whom I portrayed the cancer patient in *Frank's Last Dance*, had written a play and was trying to get it produced. Several people came together to help him get a reading at a theater, but when things didn't work out he decided to rewrite it as a script for Showtime called *Women vs. Men*, about two married guys who go to a strip joint. It was directed by Chazz Palminteri, and Darryl and I were both cast. While I was getting ready to film my small contribution, David pulled me aside and asked that I look at some dailies from *Dance*. As I was watching the final scene in which I reveal that I have cancer, I had another psychic moment. It wasn't like any of the others in the past; it was a different feeling, like I'd better get checked out by a doctor.

In 2002, I went to a wonderful local physician who said, "Jon, you have something in your system called a monoclonal protein. It doesn't mean much now but it has to be monitored." He referred me to an

The Chronicle *with Reno Wilson, Chad Willett and Rena Sofer*

oncologist who explained that a monoclonal protein only develops in the body to fight off a particular type of blood cancer called multiple myeloma, which can be a death sentence. I had to have my monoclonal protein numbers checked every three months to see if they were within normal range. Sometimes the numbers would be a little high, sometimes they'd be a little lower.

I asked the doctor if I should I start taking some kind of cancer drugs. "No, you *don't* have cancer," he responded. "You have a mono-clonal protein but that doesn't necessarily mean you're going to get multiple myeloma. It's just a warning sign, and we have to keep an eye on it."

While I now had a new focus on my health, my acting career was taking an interesting turn. I was invited to two auditions in one day. That's the way it goes sometimes: you don't get anything for three months and then you get two spectacular ones on the same day! The first was for a film remake of the British TV mini-series *The Singing Detective*, which was going to be produced by Mel Gibson and star the newly-released-from-prison Robert Downey Jr. At the end of the reading I was asked to wait until all of the other actors had been seen, but I politely said I had an important errand to run and would be back as soon as possible. I fought my way across town in bumper-to-bumper traffic to make my second appointment, which was for a gig on an ABC show called *Push, Nevada* being produced by Ben Affleck and Matt Damon. When I walked into the office to meet the director it turned out to be John McNaughton, the wonderfully grumpy man I'd worked with on *Homicide*. "Polito, I don't need you to audition," he said, gruffly. "I just needed you to come here, tell me you'll do it, and then leave." Not missing a beat, I told him I was in, and then rushed out the door, hoping I could make it back in time to meet with the *Detective* decision makers.

It was a crazy day. And as it turned out, the beginning of an even crazier part of my life.

14

Family Turmoil

Having a job as an actor is wonderful. Having two is absolutely amazing! This was the enviable position I was in after being cast in *Push, Nevada* and *The Singing Detective*. The best part was that both roles were very interesting and very different. In *Push*, I was playing a scuzzy casino owner being investigated by an IRS agent. There was one very strong scene I was looking forward to, in which the agent confronts my character and vows to take me down. It was a lengthy monologue from the leading man – played by Derek Cecil – where I sat quietly, looked at him, and came back with a big zinger. That's the kind of scene I really like, where you don't have to memorize too many lines.

Push, Nevada *with Derek Cecil*

When I met Derek, I instantly loved the guy. We bantered back-and-forth, and I found him to be both funny and challenging. During our rehearsal, he confided that he felt his character's speech was far too long and needed to be cut down. I immediately said, "No, my friend. This has to be done as written, and you'll do an amazing job with it." And in fact, he did. Our scene together was incredible, and although my character was killed at the end of the episode, I was convinced I was so brilliant they would bring me back from the dead. Alas, they didn't. *Push, Nevada* was a terrific experience because I could finally perform calmly. I was getting to the point where I didn't have to be bombastic; I could simply rest and just look at someone with great power in my eyes, and this show gave me an opportunity to do that.

The Singing Detective was something completely different. It was written by Dennis Potter and had previously been staged as a TV miniseries in England. The film version was being produced by Mel Gibson, who was also playing a psychiatrist, and the leading man was Robert Downey Jr., who had been through hell in his life with drug addiction and a prison sentence. From what I understand, once he was released he couldn't get insured to work on movies, but Gibson told him, "You're coming back to work, I'm going to pay for your insurance myself and we're going to restart your career." The rest of the cast was filled with other amazing people: Robin Wright, Jeremy Northam, Katie Holmes, and a young fellow named Adrien Brody.

The plot is about a man who has a horrible skin disease that causes his mental condition to deteriorate. He's in a hospital wrapped in bandages from head to toe and starts to have hallucinations that are very film noir-esque. That's where I came in, playing a character identified as "Second Hood," with Adrien as my counterpart, "First Hood." We were a cross between *The Maltese Falcon* heavies and a *Guys and Dolls* duo, which was appropriate since *Detective* was a musical. As our shoot began, Adrien was getting a lot of buzz for his role in *The Pianist*, a movie that was causing quite a stir and winning all kinds of awards. He was preoccupied with all of the accolades and attention and would come to the set asking people what he should wear to the ceremonies. It was difficult working with an actor who was more concerned about getting nominated for an Oscar than he was with rehearsing and learning the lyrics to the song we had to sing. The whole situation was very frustrating, and we got along begrudgingly, at best.

The Singing Detective *with Robert Downey Jr. and Adrien Brody*

Conversely, Robert Downey Jr. was an absolute delight. He was fresh out of rehab and doing wonderful work, with a sponsor around at all times to keep a close eye on him. On the set, Robert was very accessible, but during his off time it was difficult to see him because people were trying to protect him from negative outside influences. I desperately wanted to talk to him because I'd stolen something of his and needed to confess. He had done a movie with Sally Field called *Soapdish*, a wonderful screwball comedy about the behind-the-scenes chaos of a TV soap opera. Robert portrayed a flunky producer who's obsessed with an actress played by Cathy Moriarty. During a live broadcast, Moriarty's character is revealed to be a man who had had a sex change operation. The head of the network looks at Robert in disbelief and says, "She's a boy," at which point Downey stands up and calmly says, "We knew that." He appears unfazed by the revelation, but his hand was twisting in such a nervous, hysterical way that I burst out laughing. Don't ask me why, but I thought that little bit of movement was so brilliant that I did the same thing in *Barton Fink*, and I was determined to thank him for it.

One afternoon, I cornered his sponsor and asked for a few minutes alone with Robert. Permission was granted, and when I walked into his trailer, his son was there, closely guarding his dad. When the boy finally left, I sat with Robert and told him about me stealing his bit. He got a kick out of the story and complimented my work, saying that he was a fan of *Barton Fink*. When big stars tell you things like that you never know if it's true or not, but it was nice of him to say. *The Singing Detective* wasn't a success, but it was to me, especially coming on the heels of *Push, Nevada*. To be able to do two performances back-to-back in which the looks, the voices and the characters are completely different is rare. *That's* the fun part, and that's when you really feel you're displaying your range as an actor.

While things were going well for me, the same couldn't be said about my father. After almost losing him several years earlier, his health continued to deteriorate. Darryl and I would periodically visit my parents, but we had to play it cool because my father and I had never had an open talk about my homosexuality. The rest of the family knew but they all warned me not to tell Dad. Whenever we made the trek to my parents' house, Darryl and I slept in separate rooms and avoided talking about anything too personal so as not to tip him off.

Darryl was lovely interacting with my father. Dad had been a contractor – he was an artist when it came to construction – and Darryl was fascinated by the craft, asking one question after another. My father was charmed by his enthusiasm and the two began to bond, with Dad eventually nicknaming him "the boy." During one of our trips, Darryl and I were sitting with my parents in the kitchen having a meal and exchanging small talk. Dad was at the head of the table, and out of the blue announced, "I have something I want to say." The room immediately became silent. We all stared at him, waiting to hear what was on his mind. He looked at me and said, "I just want you to know I'm glad you found the boy." He then turned to Darryl. "And I'm glad you found my son," he concluded. We sat there quietly stunned, words failing all of us. Darryl smiled at me and I smiled at him. It truly was a wonderful moment.

At the end of our visit, I went into the bedroom and kissed my father goodbye. He said, "Send the boy up." When Darryl went upstairs, Dad told him, "I want you to take care of my son." During that trip, a part of my life with my father that had always hung in the balance – something that was never previously spoken of or acknowledged in any way – had finally come to a close.

* * *

Nearly everything was going my way for the first few years of the twenty-first century. Not only was my apartment becoming more of a home, Darryl and I officially started living together. His career with the Dan Band was thriving and ABC was considering a pilot built around the band. It had a great cast but Dan Finnerty, the head of the group, couldn't act, so the show never got past the development phase. Meanwhile, I was getting a steady stream of work. I appeared on a revival of *Dragnet* starring the wonderful Ed O'Neill, I did a show called *The Lyon's Den* with Rob Lowe, a low-budget film titled *The Box*, and a couple of gigs on the series *Gilmore Girls*, which was created by my friend Amy Sherman-Palladino, whom I first met on the set of *Roseanne*. These weren't big roles in high-profile projects, but they were enough to keep me going.

While my West Coast life was pretty wonderful, things on the East Coast weren't so great. Dad was dying and Mom was coming to the realization that she'd have to get their affairs in order. Sadly, my sister continued her negative and destructive influence. On Christmas Day, we convened in Philadelphia for a family gathering. During dinner, Darryl went upstairs to change my father's diaper, and when he came back down, my sister – who refused to spend any time with Dad – started spewing venom. "I can't believe you just did that," she uttered in disgust. "I certainly *won't* be doing it."

In front of everyone, Darryl turned to her and said, "What's wrong with you? You'd do it for a baby, wouldn't you? Why can't you do it for your father?" The room instantly went quiet and I loved my man all the more for speaking his mind. Still, the pride I felt was tempered by the undeniable fact that my family was in turmoil and there wasn't a damn thing I could do about it.

Darryl and I went to Maine for New Year's and then back to Los Angeles to face 2004. Three weeks later, I got a call saying I needed to come to Philly immediately. This was it for my father... I went by myself and spent as much time as I could with him, but on the fifth day of the visit, he passed. It was the end of a major stage of my life, and as sad as it was, I was at peace with it.

I returned to Los Angeles and discovered that Darryl was having problems with the Dan Band. The group was bringing in much more money – playing venues for a thousand people instead of a hundred – and was making appearances in big Hollywood movies. They were hot, and Dan Finnerty hired a manager who did nothing but look out for his best interests instead of the whole group. Darryl and Dan finally had a confrontation in which Dan admitted, "This is *not* about you and this is *not* a band. This is about *me* and my career!"

Old School *with Darryl (far left) and the Dan Band*

At that point, Darryl quit. It was a big decision, both professionally and financially, but I told him, "I have enough money coming in. Why don't you pursue your acting career?" He was involved in the Elephant Theatre and his performances were being nominated for awards. He joined an agency and did a couple of national TV spots, but I don't think he could stomach the steady stream of rejection that comes with those cattle calls. I know what it's like to go on ten movie auditions and lose out on seven or eight of them. Commercials are even more difficult; you're lucky to land one gig out of a hundred. Rejection is part of the business, and while you have to get used to it, it can still be frustrating and depressing.

While Darryl kept himself busy in the theater, I was offered a part in a remake of *The Honeymooners*. As a fan of that classic show, I'll be the first to admit it didn't need to be remade as a movie, but somebody got the idea to do a version with Cedric the Entertainer as Ralph Kramden and Mike Epps as Ed Norton. It also featured Gabrielle Union, Regina Hall, Eric Stoltz and John Leguizamo. What was really strange was that they were going to shoot it in Dublin, Ireland! I have no idea why Dublin was doublin' for New York, but I know the film's producer was fond of working in Ireland and, in the old days, financial assistance was offered to production companies as an incentive to shoot there.

I was in a scene packed with extras, and as we were setting up the shot, they brought over a beautiful Irish girl named Laura Way. She was fun and well-spoken, and I was immediately enchanted by her. In the past I sometimes coupled myself with a bit player whose presence would enhance my character, and I told the director I wanted to upgrade Laura and give her a chance to speak. He said, "I don't want to change the shot but if she has something good to say we'll let her do it." I went to Laura and told her to start thinking of a line.

The shot was complex, designed to start with Cedric, Mike and Leguizamo entering a dog track and talking to each other. The camera then dollies past them and comes to a stop on me and Laura, who was to say her dialogue and then walk away. We rehearsed it over and over, but the problem was that she hadn't come up with a good line yet. When we did the first take, the camera moved over to us and Laura blurted out, "I don't know anything about dogs, but I sure do know about pussy."

"Cut, cut, cut!" the director yelled immediately. "*What* did she say? Did she say she knows about pussy? This is a PG movie!" He was pissed off, but I stepped in and took the blame. I told him I thought the line was funny and encouraged her to use it, even though I had no idea what was going to come out of her mouth. He calmed down after that, but it was decided Laura would no longer speak. However, he allowed her to still have some interaction with me, which meant she got to keep her upgrade.

The Honeymooners *with Laura Way*

I was so in love with this woman I wanted her around me all the time, on-screen and off. She listened intently as I told stories about my life and shared some personal things with her, like how my family called me "Jonny Boy" and that I had the monoclonal protein in my system. Darryl came to visit during the shoot, and we went to Laura's home in Wexford, where we got to spend a wonderful weekend with her family. *The Honeymooners* was, unfortunately, another one of my duds. At this point I'd been doing movies for twenty-five years, and although there were a couple of artistic hits, I didn't have any big moneymakers. There ain't no *Star Wars* on my resume!

Back in Los Angeles, I got a call from John McNaughton. He said, "Polito, I'm doing this piece of shit up in goddamn Vancouver called *Masters of Horror*."

"Is that like *Tales from the Crypt*?" I asked.

"I don't know, I don't watch this shit. It's got something to do with horror stories by famous writers, and the one I got is by Clive Barker."

"Haeckel's Tale" is a strange account of a man following in Frankenstein's footsteps, wanting to create life. I loved the script and John offered me the role of a necromancer in the mid-1800s. This was a

Boris Karloff part if ever there was one! However, John had a dilemma. When filming in Canada the rule is that you must use a lot of Canadians in the production, and if you're bringing in Americans, they have to be approved based on their success level. John wanted Derek Cecil – the actor I worked with on *Push, Nevada* – to co-star, but Derek didn't have enough credits to be accepted. After brainstorming with John, I ended up writing a letter on Derek's behalf, bringing up a lot of his performances and saying how important it would be for me to work again with this on-the-rise actor. We were pulling things out of our ass to try to convince them to let Derek join the show, and after about a week, he was finally approved.

On the set of Masters of Horror: Haeckel's Tale *with Derek Cecil and John McNaughton*

Once that problem was solved, I focused on creating the character, starting with the wardrobe. I was dressed in layer upon layer of uncomfortable burlap, and they wanted me to have long hair and a very sloppy mustache. The costume and wig changed me vocally. I enunciated everything and had to do a speech in a kind of fake Pig Latin. In my mind, I *was* a necromancer and I *could* bring animals and people back from the dead. The story may have been inspired by *Frankenstein*, but this wasn't like any old Karloff movie I ever saw. It was a scary, gory, tasteless piece of horror that was a total blast to make. I also did an on-camera, in costume interview about the project which was included as an extra on the DVD. In fact, that sit-down conversation got some better reviews than the episode itself!

In November 2004, I had a bomb dropped on me. Paul Bettis was not only one of my mentors, he was one-third of what I called "The Trilogy of Great Influences." The first was Dominic Garvey, the Christian Brother who was responsible for getting me a scholarship to Villanova. My acting teacher was a woman named Irene Baird, who insisted her students get to the gut of a character through movements, exercises and indulgences. Simply put, she was a professor of the process. Into this mix came Bettis, whose first words to me were, "I have no interest in process. I just want results." I loved the combination of these three teachers, and their lessons have been extremely beneficial.

Paul and I had become lifelong friends, and every Sunday would bring a phone call dedicated to our catching up with each other. During one of our weekly chats, he made a comment that he was unhappy about the way he looked. A friend of his had just died of cancer and he suspected he might have it, too. A few months later, Paul gave me the news: "Jonny, I have lung cancer." I wasn't sure what to say but I was convinced that with all the medical advancements being made, this was something that could be fixed. As the weeks progressed, however, I wasn't hearing anything positive about his treatments.

I bought him a round-trip ticket to visit me in Los Angeles, and it was obvious when he arrived that he was terribly ill. I had a feeling the cancer wasn't being dealt with medically and I wasn't sure why. We didn't really talk about his condition but it was the elephant in the room. The most difficult thing was watching him struggle to eat. When we'd go to restaurants, he'd order large meals and only be able to finish one or two bites. He was a shell of the man I knew and admired, and it was tough to see him that way. One afternoon, he was lying in my bed – I had given him my room to sleep in – while I sat next to him. A breeze was coming through the window as we were talking about this and that, and I put my hand on his chest, almost as if I was attempting to feel where the cancerous lung was and send him good vibes. We didn't have a tactile relationship – Paul was very

British in that way – but when I touched his chest he said, "Ahhh, Jonny." I said, "Ahhh, Paul." I knew in my mind that this was his way of saying goodbye.

Paul died on August 4th, 2005. In September, a tribute in his honor was held in Canada. I couldn't make the trip, but I wrote a speech that was read to the crowd, and I was told people were moved by it. I then received a call from Paul's best friend, thanking me for the memorial. She said, "Several schools want to devote a section of their libraries to Paul so we're putting together his history. Do you think we should include that he had AIDS?"

I was floored. "AIDS?"

It was a tremendously awkward moment, and she had to pull back and say, "Oh, God… I thought you knew."

Just as I was never told about Michael Morin's HIV status, this information came to me like a slap in the face. Paul's lung cancer was connected to AIDS, which is why they weren't making aggressive attempts to try and heal him. I later learned that he'd been diagnosed many years earlier and had chosen not to tell me because I'd finally found happiness in my life with Darryl and he didn't want me to worry.

Paul was a father figure, a wicked uncle and a talented mentor. Any way you looked at it, I'd lost another member of my family.

15

Swimming Pools, Movie Stars

Shortly after the passing of Paul Bettis, I received a call from our land-lady's son. He said, "This is your notice that you have two months to vacate the apartment."

"Don't be silly," I replied. "You can't evict me." Having lived in New York for all those years, I knew that the rules stated you were se-cure in your living space unless you stopped paying rent or voluntarily gave it up. California, however, used a totally different rulebook.

"Sir, I'm a judge and my mother's not doing well. We're going to move her into your apartment, so you have two months to get out."

As I sat there in shock, Darryl came home from an audition. He walked into the room, looked at me and asked, "What's wrong? Did someone else die?"

"No, but we're being evicted. What the hell are we gonna do?"

"Well, I met an actor today who said he also worked in real estate. Maybe he can help us find a new place."

That man's name was Eddie Bowz and he came over the next day, pitching us on the merits of home ownership. As a journeyman actor always on the move, I considered renting as the most prudent thing to do but was slowly becoming convinced – partially because Eddie *was* a good salesman – that we should at least look at places that were for sale. This was during the time when banks were giving money to any-one; hell, a goat could get a loan for a house! Eddie said we could buy a place for zero down, which was important because I only had about $26,000 left in my savings account. After thirty years in the business and paying off all my debts, that was all I had to show for it.

There was a condo building about a mile away with a unit for sale. We went to look at the place, a former hippie den with black walls that was pretty much falling apart. With only one month to go until our eviction, Eddie found someone who would approve a loan with no money upfront and no guaranteed income. By the time our offer was accepted, we only had fourteen days left to move. Those two weeks were complete pandemonium, but at the end of it, we were officially property owners. We then began renovations, trying to make it as refreshed and inviting as we could. It not only became a place for us to live, it became a home for us to grow old together. Most importantly, it had a pool! We could finally enjoy the California weather in the comfort of our own swimming area.

Meanwhile, my mother was in transition. After my father died, we made sure to keep her as occupied as possible, which meant a lot of traveling to see us. She came out to L.A. for Christmas in 2005, but her visit was interrupted because I was offered two movie roles. The first was called *Stiffs*, which was a script I'd read a year earlier. I told the director, Frank Ciota, that I was interested and encouraged him to continue pursuing it. Frank was a successful businessman but he and his brother, Joe, wanted to be filmmakers and had gotten one of their projects financed through a wonderful man named Roger Marino. Marino was listed in Forbes as a billionaire who co-founded a company in the early '80s that made computer memory boards, and he later bought the Pittsburgh Penguins hockey team. He was a terrific guy and *Stiffs* was going to be his second movie with the Ciota brothers. The premise concerns a funeral parlor in an Italian neighborhood in Boston that's fallen on hard times. Less and less business is coming in and the employees are starting to worry about their livelihood, so one of them – my character – comes up with the idea of murdering people. It was a funny script with mobsters and wiseguys, and Danny Aiello was going to be playing one of the main roles. I was officially booked for the picture, which was going to start filming in Boston in January.

On December 23ʳᵈ, I was offered a part in a movie called *Big Nothing*. Filming would take place across Europe and the money was good, but there was a catch. They needed an immediate decision and I'd have to leave the day after Christmas! The whole situation sounded chaotic so I read the script to see if it would be worth it. My role was an FBI guy nicknamed "The Eye" because he could always see the right person who did the wrong thing. It was a fun and clever concept and I immediately agreed to do it, which meant having to rearrange holiday plans with my mother. I also had to figure out the logistics of shooting *Big Nothing* in Europe while *Stiffs* was slated to start in Boston in January. When you're lucky enough to land two jobs that overlap, agents usually make you choose one, otherwise they have to jump through hoops to create a schedule so you can do both. I pushed my team hard to make it work, mainly because the characters were completely different. I thought I'd finally be able to do two diverse performances in films that would come out around the same time, thus setting my career on fire.

On December 26th, I was whisked to the Isle of Man and met Jean-Baptiste Andrea, the wonderful director of *Big Nothing*. The plan was for me to stay for a day and film one scene, at which point I would then turn around and fly back to America. I found that extremely strange, but I later learned the movie was being financed by European producers who had worked out a deal whereby they would get tax breaks by shooting one day in several different countries. That helped the budget because the cast wasn't cheap: David Schwimmer, Alice Eve, Natascha McElhone, Mimi Rogers and Simon Pegg. This was a *good* group!

Jean-Baptiste and I began to work on the character, which was a joy because it was an attempt to recreate and reinvent one I hadn't done for many years: Lou Breeze from *Barton Fink*. Almost the same physical elements were included – I was a pear-shaped, bespectacled nerd – but the glasses I was given turned out to be a disadvantage. They had magnifying lenses that made my eyes appear much bigger and made the character quite scary looking, which was what Jean-Baptiste wanted. Unfortunately, those lenses were a prescription meant for somebody else and I could barely see. In fact, when I put them on I became im-

Big Nothing

balanced and was having a hard time delivering my lines. I may have also been a bit jet lagged since I'd just arrived, but whatever the reason, I wasn't in top form on my first day. The scene ultimately turned out rather well, but I felt it had to be pieced together and wasn't as flowing as I wanted it to be. I was also a little nervous about what David and Simon must have been thinking as I tried to work through a difficult situation. I wanted to be sure that when it was time for the next shoot, I'd be in much better shape.

I was preparing to spend New Year's back in Los Angeles with Darryl when I was given the rest of the schedule for *Big Nothing*. I had to do a quick turnaround and get back on a plane and fly to Wales. Since there was very little notice, I was allowed to bring Darryl along. We arrived to film the next section of the movie, the glasses had been modified, everything went well, and Darryl and I spent New Year's at a wonderful spa. However, I was getting reports from L.A. that there was a problem brewing with my other gig.

I was supposed to go from Wales straight to Boston and start production on *Stiffs*, but the *Big Nothing* producers needed me to fly to Vancouver for a one-day shoot to finish my introductory scene. The people in Boston didn't like the fact that I'd only be working a couple of days on their movie before leaving to complete the other one, and they were refusing to adjust the schedule to make it happen. After I arrived on the *Stiffs* set, a producer threatened to sue me if I left. It turned out this so-called "producer" was actually an employee of Roger Marino who was trying to impress him by playing hardball. I called her bluff and let her know there was nothing she could say or do that was going to stop me from leaving. It certainly wasn't the best way to begin the production.

I made it to Vancouver to complete work on *Big Nothing*, and it was a very strange situation. They were filming multiple scenes with Simon, Alice and David, and it was quickly approaching three in the morning. I had to be on a plane in several hours back to Boston when I got word that my mother, who had just returned home after her visit with us, had been rushed to the hospital. The medical staff wasn't sure what was wrong and feared she was going to die. So there I was with an emergency in Philadelphia and people yelling at me in Boston while I was waiting in Canada to complete my part. As if on cue, that's when it started to storm. The rain was threatening to delay the shoot and there was talk about postponing my scene. They asked if I could stay another day – which I couldn't – and there was panic in the air. After several moments, Jean-Baptiste asked, "Jon, what do you think about doing your scene in one take in the rain?"

Big Nothing *with Simon Pegg*

"Why not?" I replied, my eyes lighting up. "Let's do it!" Proving that adverse conditions can often spur creativity, Simon and I did a wonderful walk-and-talk that introduced my character in *Big Nothing*. It was an experience that I remember fondly.

I returned to Boston and despite all the animosity about my schedule, Danny Aiello was terrific and we worked well together. He has a bit of a reputation for being particular about his comfort while making a film, so I made sure that my contract was connected completely with his. Whatever he got, I got; that was part of the deal. I knew he was making more money, but I figured I'd at least make sure our accommodations would be the same. Danny didn't like the small trailer provided to him, and every day he insisted on getting a larger one. After bringing in a medium-sized trailer and a double – both of which he didn't care for – he asked for the largest trailer I'd ever seen in my life, and he got it. This thing was the size of New York! As they were rolling it in, I went up to the producer and said, "I'm sure you remember that whatever Danny gets, I get."

She immediately became pissed. "You don't *really* want the same trailer, do you?"

"I'm sorry, but if I don't put my foot down here, it's going to affect me later on," I explained. "If Danny's insisting on this, I'm going to need one, too." We moved from location to location with an entourage of trucks and two of the largest trailers on Earth. Boston welcomed us with open arms, especially the Italian section of the city. Every restaurant in the area wanted Danny there and I would tag along, enjoying first-class service and amazing food.

Stiffs *with Danny Aiello*

Although shooting *Big Nothing* and *Stiffs* back-to-back was a challenge, I was able to mount two very different performances with the hope they would be released in succession to show my versatility. Unfortunately, it didn't work out that way. *Stiffs* wasn't released until a few years later, and only then on DVD. *Big Nothing* opened nicely in London and looked like it was poised for a successful run, but the reviews were very bitchy about Simon using an American accent. Critics loved him and I guess they felt he was going Hollywood, so they were extremely negative toward the film. I was disappointed by the reaction because I was proud of my work. In the end, both movies amounted to nothing but happy memories.

Soon after, I was offered a guest-starring role on a series called *Medium* with Patricia Arquette, whom I loved. Doing the show required more effort than usual because I was still as heavy as could be. The set-up for the character was that he'd just been murdered and was now a ghost who hadn't gone over to the other side. However, he had died in his underwear, so let me be frank here... It ain't easy for a big old fat guy to pick wardrobe when he must be seen in his underwear. You don't want to wear tighty-whities and show your private parts, and you don't want to wear boxers that are too big because you'll look like a real slob. I chose something that was boxer-like, and instead of flaunting my man boobs, I chose a horribly loose old tee shirt that looked like it was covered in chicken fat.

Even more difficult was the actual filming on the streets of downtown L.A. I was 240 pounds, in my underwear and running barefoot through glass, metal, rat poop and God knows what else on those roads. I was also afraid because at this age – my mid-fifties – I was having a hard time doing the physical stuff. We started shooting at one in the morning, and I said to myself, *Okay, Jon, just jump in and do it*. I started running, and I don't know where the strength came from, but I ran from 1 a.m. to 4:30 a.m. as if I was being chased by a herd of elephants! It was a hell of a rough time and I was able to catch my breath in-between shots, but I noticed a couple of pangs in my chest that I hadn't felt before. It didn't seem quite right, but I pushed ahead and did what was necessary for the performance.

I was next offered a part in a movie called *Cougar Club*. I loved the director, a crazy guy making a silly little film about a bunch of college nerds who couldn't get laid. Because some older ladies like being with younger men, the guys turned it into a business. The boys were having sex, the women were having sex, and everybody was happy. My character is a cocaine-addicted businessman, which was easy to play since that's what I used to be. It was a great shoot with wonderful people, but what I was looking forward to most was getting to see Faye Dunaway again, who had a small but important role.

Faye and I had a history together. Back in 1981, it was announced she would be performing on Broadway in a play called *The Curse of an Aching Heart*. There was some controversy over her casting because she was coming off *Mommie Dearest* and people were afraid the movie could ruin her career. I'd auditioned and won a role in *Heart*, and she was wonderful to work with. Instead of demanding any kind of star treatment, she tried very hard to be just another member of the company.

Rehearsals, however, weren't going well. Whatever magic the producers and director were hoping for wasn't happening, and when the play opened it wasn't well-received. In those days you went to Sardi's on opening night and waited for the *Times* review to come out at midnight. Faye was there with her husband, but her table was empty. When the critique finally came in, it was a killer. A negative *Times* review could close a play in one night, and I was shocked no one came to offer her support. She sat at her table alone and I remember feeling bad and eventually going to sit beside her. One of the producers came over and said, "Well, that's it, Faye."

"How long do we have?" she asked.

"We'll try to keep it going for a month, but that's it."

"Okay," she responded, "but only a month."

Ironically, as soon as the production was announced as a limited engagement, sales went through the roof! Shows were selling out left and right, and with money pouring in the producers asked Faye to extend the run, which she declined to do.

One night during a curtain call I noticed a man at the back of the theater who was clapping a little too eagerly. As the cast took their bows, I watched as he started walking down the aisle towards the stage. I didn't know what was going on but I didn't like it. The curtain came down and when it went back up, this guy was standing directly in front of the stage applauding like a maniac. In less than a minute Faye was going to be up there all by herself, so I ran to the stage manager and screamed for him to get security, who quickly arrived and escorted the man out of the theater. The next night I went to Faye's dressing room after the performance. She was so beautiful as she sat in front of the mirror taking her makeup off, and I got down on my haunches next to her. "Faye, I think there's a problem."

"What do you mean?" she asked, still looking in the mirror.

"That guy last night got too close to the stage. We need to increase security."

"Well, they're just fans," she casually replied.

"I don't think you understand. It wasn't safe."

"This is New York, what could happen?"

I stared at her and said, "John Lennon."

She looked down at me and her eyes widened as the weight of my answer began to sink in. "We'll have more security from now on," she conceded. I remember really loving that moment between us, not as actors, but as human beings. I've always loved her and even though I'd heard things about her bad behavior over the years, I was still looking forward to seeing her on the *Cougar Club* set and reconnecting.

When I arrived at the location, I walked up to her and tried to introduce myself, but she was as blank as blank could be. She had no idea who I was and seemed to be quite annoyed I was even there. I was really hoping we could reminisce about our experiences doing *Heart*, but it quickly became apparent that wasn't going to happen.

When we finished the movie I had to do looping, which is re-recording some lines of dialogue that didn't come out clearly for one reason or another. They had one line to do with Faye around 9 a.m. so I was told to come in at eleven, which would give them more than enough time to complete her work. As I entered the lot, there was an idiot in front of me who kept stopping unexpectedly and signaling the wrong way, which prevented me from passing. I was stuck behind this clown and quickly approaching road rage.

I started beeping the horn, as did the people behind me, and this person finally turned into the parking area. I pulled into a spot on a different side of the lot and as I got out of the car, I thought, *I want to see who this asshole is.* As I approached the vehicle, out came Faye Dunaway! Not only was she a terrible driver, she was two hours late for her looping session. At that point I knew it was going to be a long day. As she neared the building, I went to greet her and was completely ignored. I made my way up to a room that overlooked two booths; Faye was standing in one to do the recording, and the director, producer and sound people were sitting in the other. I had a terrific seat to see everybody at work and watch chaos unfold.

Faye Dunaway in Cougar Club

Dunaway only had one line to do and it was a disaster. She would read her line, exit the booth, and look at me very angrily as she entered the other booth. It was like a scene out of a screwball comedy, and it kept going on and on. Eventually I started smiling and waving every time she made her back-and-forth trip, and she looked at me like I was crazy! Finally, on one of her passes through, she stopped and gruffly asked, "Do you have to be here?"

"Yes, I do, Faye," I answered. "I was scheduled for this time and you're running well over it."

After about an hour-and-a-half when it looked like she was finally happy with her one line, she ran into the sound booth and started pointing at me as she was talking to the producer and director. I could tell she was pissed, but as the discussion went on there was finally a moment when she looked at me with some recognition. She walked out of the room and said, "By the way, I adored you in the Coen brothers' films."

"Faye, I'm Jon Polito. We worked together on *The Curse of an Aching Heart.*"

"Oh, of course. I remember you well."

It was clear she didn't know me from Adam, but in all fairness, I was much younger and thinner in those days. Still, I was disappointed. As she frantically gathered her things, she turned at the last moment and said, "I'm making a movie that I'm writing and directing. May I have your email address? I'd love for you to be a part of it." It was a nice gesture, and I gave her my contact information.

In many ways, the *Mommie Dearest* character seemed to rub off on her. Not the cruelty, of course, but certainly the eccentricities. Nevertheless, I still love Faye, even though that was the last I ever heard from her.

16

Between a *Rock* and a Heart Place

I kept my career afloat by making appearances on hit TV series, tacky cable movies and providing voiceovers for animated shows. I wanted to do a little bit of everything because you never know what's going to pay off, and while there were some good times, most of the jobs weren't very exciting. That's when a gig came along that turned out to be a total blast! An amazing man named Declan O'Brien was an up-and-coming filmmaker doing scripts for some cheaply made Syfy movies. One of his projects was called *Rock Monster*, which started the fad of intentionally absurd movies like *Sharknado*. I was offered the part of a retired colonel who, much like Robert Shaw in *Jaws*, stands up and gives a speech to the townspeople, convincing them he can kill the Rock Monster. It was an interesting role, the money was nice, and it was a rather short shoot in Sofia, Bulgaria. The flight there was long, about fourteen hours plus a three-hour stopover. My body started to feel odd midway through the trip, but I didn't give it much thought.

I met Declan and was immediately taken with this enthusiastic Irishman who was going to direct a campy production with every cliché imaginable. Not only was overacting allowed, it was encouraged! Declan was determined to make the experience fun, and it was. The first day, I began to create my physical character. I wore a military uniform that was too tight because he was older and not in as good a shape as he was in his active duty days. I also incorporated a frightening, generic Middle Eastern European accent that wasn't too far from what I'd used on *Seinfeld*.

None of us knew what the Rock Monster was going to look like, and that was one of my greatest joys. When I became an actor, I'd always wanted to be in something where I got to turn, look up and say,

On the set of Rock Monster *with Declan O'Brien*

"It's coming… IT'S COMING!" Whether it was a dinosaur, a flying saucer or some other kind of fantastical threat, I *wanted* to have that moment. I was imagining the creature would be something Ray Harryhausen would've created, and I was playing it with that sense of believability. We were on a short schedule and as we prepared to shoot my big scene, I made a point of letting the camera crew know where I'd be stopping and focusing. I then talked to the lighting people to see where everything was going to be set. I was pretty much doing the "I'm an old pro" thing and setting up my own shot, and Declan was appreciative because it saved some time.

One cast member – Alicia Lagano, a sweet New York fireball – was intensely watching and shooting me looks like, *Who does this guy think he is?*, but I felt she was enjoying it. Since the estrangement from my niece, I hadn't thought of letting anyone else into my life, but I immediately liked Alicia. I wanted to keep her in "my family" and we bonded on and off the set. We'd work all day and enjoy a drink at night, have dinner on our days off and visit tacky casinos. We turned our stay into a wonderful European experience.

Although Declan had good intentions, the special effects turned out to be *horrible*! In fact, the movie was delayed a couple of years because

Alicia Lagano and Jon

the effects were so bad and that's when he did something brilliant. He wrote to all of the major critics across the country and said something to the effect of, "I was raised on Saturday matinees and *Rock Monster* is a tribute to them. If you can, give it a chance. It ain't *The Godfather* but you might enjoy it." Surprisingly, it got some nice notices, and my reviews were *wonderful*. I not only chewed the scenery, I ate the furniture and was praised for it! The critics, for the most part, kept an open mind and didn't apologize for enjoying how bad it was. *Rock Monster* was the birth of the Saturday night Syfy craze, which has worked out well for the network.

Following *Rock Monster*, I was offered a part in a movie called *American Gangster* that was going to be filmed in New York and directed by Ridley Scott. The shock of all shocks was that I got the job after he watched the beginning of my demo reel. As actors, we all have these videos that highlight our various performances, but the irony is that you very rarely ever get cast because of them. Ridley saw the start of my drama reel – the opening scene from *Miller's Crossing* – and that was enough to convince him to hire me for a small role in a big studio film with a massive cast: Denzel Washington, Josh Brolin, Russell Crowe, John Hawkes, Ruby Dee, Carla Gugino; the list went on and on. I was there to film one scene in August and then I was told they were going to do a "drop/pickup," which means after your first appearance they'd carry you on for a period of time. It was more money since my original offer was very low, but I took the job because I wanted to work with Ridley. This new deal meant I'd do my scene in August, come back in September, and stay until mid-October. It was going to be a good six-to-eight-week gig, which certainly helped my finances.

I was cast as a mob flunky, and the day before my first scene I arrived on the set and met Ridley. "Jon, I'm going to ask you to wear a hairpiece," he said. "It's going to be strands of hair that will look like a pompadour you used to have."

"Yes, sir," I responded. Ridley is a very serious man, so you listen to him as if God was talking to you.

"I went to a Coney Island restaurant looking for locations and saw three goombahs talking at a table," he continued. "They were in their seventies and all of them had remnants of their hairstyles from the 1960s. That's what I want for you if you don't mind."

I told him I loved the idea, and after our discussion I went to the hair person and had my piece fitted. My big scene was shot the next day

American Gangster

in Harlem with Denzel Washington who played Frank Lucas, a real-life guy who imported heroin in the late '60s and early '70s. Denzel was quite a guy: a wonderful actor, a true gentleman and a serious pro. My big scene took place in a darkened café where I pass him money in a strange little way. It didn't mean much for the story, but it played well. I finished by giving Denzel a look that was distrusting, and Ridley said, "Nice bit at the end but I don't think I'm going to use it." It was another of my brilliant acting choices that ended up on the cutting room floor.

Part of my deal included a plane ticket for Darryl to visit for a week, and I dragged him all over the city taking pictures and showing him the places that had the most impact on me when I lived there. October 16th, 1999 is the day Darryl and I first met, and I wanted to do something special for our anniversary, so we went for a carriage ride in Central Park. When I got the photos back, there was one the driver took of us in the back of the carriage where I looked frightened. Was this the psychic thing coming back into play? I didn't know but when I saw the picture, I told Darryl I could see the mask of death on my face. I've tried to explain my Polaroid moments to him – many of which were proven true – and he finally conceded that it's possible I have a paranormal ability. Looking at that photo, I felt I had something going wrong inside me. I was still being monitored for that monoclonal protein, but I didn't think that was the problem.

I was certain it was my heart.

The *American Gangster* shoot ended in late October, and when I got back to L.A. I learned that my niece was getting married. Although things weren't good between us, I was invited to the wedding which was taking place on December 2nd, 2006 in Philadelphia. Darryl didn't want to go but being a supportive partner, he planned on making the trip until he was cast in a movie called *Boiler Maker*. It was a role too good to pass up, so I made the journey to Philly on my own. I was scared and nervous, about to face my family drama head on. Not only was my niece and I in a bad way, my mother suffered from failing health and was now wheelchair-bound. To top it off, my sister had distanced herself from Mom and refused to make any arrangements to have her transported to the wedding, leaving that responsibility to fall on me. I arrived on Thursday and got a room at a Holiday Inn close to where the ceremony was going to take place. We had a rehearsal dinner that evening, and on Friday I spent some time with my mother during the afternoon and joined the wedding party at night for drinks. It was kind of fun, but I wasn't really feeling that great.

Saturday was the big day, and at 6 a.m. I woke to a heart attack. I've read that sometimes people have cardiac events and don't even realize it, but this was *not* the case! The chest pain was massive. I felt like I was being stabbed! If anybody had seen me, they would've thought it was the worst case of overacting ever, but it was real. At six-fifteen I called downstairs and asked the whereabouts of the closest hospital. The desk clerk asked if I needed an ambulance and I stupidly said, "No, no, no... It's not a problem." I sat on the bed, took three aspirins, and passed out.

I was awakened by a phone call and when I answered, Darryl asked, "Are you okay?" Why he called me at that time I have no idea. It was three hours earlier in California, but he was thinking about me and wanted to check in.

"I don't know if I'm okay," I told him. "I might have had a heart attack."

He started screaming, "WHAT?! Call 911!"

"No, no, I think I'm all right now."

"Call 911, Jon!"

"No. Let me wait and see what happens."

After several minutes of this back and forth, he reluctantly hung up and I called my mother. I said, "Mom, I might have had a little heart attack."

"Call 911!"

"No. I'm feeling much better now so maybe it was something else." I was lying to myself. There was no doubt it was a massive heart attack. I got in the shower, put on my tuxedo and drove a rental car to pick up my mother, who was looking lovely in her wheelchair.

A friend of hers came up to me and said, "I heard you had a heart attack. Take these with you," and she handed me three nitroglycerin pills. I popped one under my tongue, got my mom in the car and we drove to the church. I was weak and it was a struggle just to push her chair up a slight ramp. I thought, *If I die here, I've at least got my mother in my arms and I'll ruin my niece's wedding, so let's do this!*

I made it through the ceremony and headed to the reception where I had a beer, a shot of whiskey, and pushed Mom around so she could visit with everyone. Although my sister and niece were cordial enough, their civility felt fake. Mom and I were clearly the outsiders. We made it through the meal, and although I was still feeling a little iffy, things were going okay. Everyone was telling me how wonderful I looked; I took lots of pictures with people and I didn't say a word about what happened that morning. My cousin, Frankie, was the only one who

Jon and his mom at the wedding after his heart attack

thought something was wrong. He asked several times throughout the evening if I was okay, and I kept assuring him that I was.

Around ten-fifteen that evening, I took my mother back to her apartment. "You know, I still feel a pain in my chest," I confided to her.

"You're not going back to the hotel," she insisted. "I want you to stay here with me."

I agreed and went to my car to get sweatpants and a tee shirt. I changed clothes and sat at the kitchen table while she was in the bathroom. I was used to these open-door conversations, and as we were talking, I began to feel another pang. "I might be having another heart attack now," I told her.

From her seat on the toilet she shouted, "Call 911! If you don't, I will. Get them on the phone!"

"Mom, I don't think—"

"—Call 911 now!" She was angry as hell, so I picked up the phone and dialed. The operator asked what the emergency was, and I said I might be having a heart attack. As she began to ask for my address, I hung up the phone because like all stupid men I felt like I could deal with the situation. Mom immediately started yelling, "What did you do?! Call them back! You've got to get to a hospital!" And at that point, less than three minutes after I'd hung up the phone, the doorbell rang.

I opened the door and saw a huge man standing there; about six-foot-three with big shoulders and a massive mid-section. In the sweetest voice ever he said, "Sir, we got a call."

"Well, I think I may have had a heart attack," I admitted.

"Oh, my goodness! You're Jon Polito!" The paramedic recognized me, and I didn't know quite how to react. I mean, it's always nice to meet a fan but this was a strange circumstance. He started talking about my movies as he gently led me to the couch, took off my tee shirt and placed some probes on my chest. I'm not sure if he was genuinely star-struck or if the chatter was his way of keeping me distracted, but I noticed his attention was focused squarely on a monitor. After a couple of minutes he said, "Mr. Polito, we're taking you to the hospital right now."

"I'm not going like this," I declared, and I ran into the bathroom and put on my tuxedo. I walked out dressed like a million bucks, got on the gurney, and was wheeled to the ambulance waiting outside.

Fortunately, I was being transported to Crozer Medical, a place ten minutes away and the center for heart instruction and studies in the Philadelphia area. We went in through the emergency entrance and the paramedic – I think his name was Michael but in my mind I nicknamed him "Bubba" because he was a big boy – was pushing me through the hallway, proudly announcing, "This is Jon Polito! Remember *The Big Lebowski* and *The Crow*?" I felt like I was making a grand entrance to my room as a *star*, and in a tux, no less! I tried to get off the gurney and into bed but I was too weak, so Bubba and a couple of nurses had to lift me. I was hooked up to machines and monitors and finally had a moment to rest. For the first time, my whole system relaxed, and my chest didn't feel normal at all. I fell asleep for a bit but was awakened when a female doctor came in and explained my condition. She said I had one heart attack for sure and possibly another, and she started to point to the monitors and describe the damage that resulted. Fumbling for any excuse to leave I said, "You know, I can't really stay here. I'm supposed to fly home tomorrow. I was just in town for a wedding."

She nodded but didn't really care about the story I was telling her. "You have to stay," she said.

"Isn't there something you can do to get me home tonight?"

At that moment, Bubba walked in holding a sheet of paper he had printed from the internet with a list of my credits and some movie quotes. After asking for an autograph, he turned to the doctor and proudly told her, "This is a famous actor."

"Well, this famous actor doesn't want to stay," she replied. "Can you explain it to him?"

Bubba looked at me with genuine concern. "Mr. Polito, you can't go anywhere. You really need to stay here."

As he was speaking, I began to feel odd. "Wait a minute," I said. "Something's going on." I looked at the doctor and began to see a spiral of light, like the one Saul Bass created for *Vertigo*. It filled my vision completely and then everything went white.

I died.

My life literally began to flash before my eyes as rapid bursts of memories started playing chronologically. They weren't particularly notable or important moments in my history, just random snippets, each one representing a year. As I was going through those memories, a warm and wonderful feeling was washing over me. There was no pain, no anguish; it was just memories and relief, and I felt completely at peace as my brain and body were shutting down during one minute and fifty-five seconds of V-tach (ventricular tachycardia).

And then WHAM! I was vacuumed backwards and came into consciousness.

The wonderful Bubba had jumped on top of me with the defibrillator paddles and, as I came to, he was standing over me, sweating profusely. "Oh, Mr. Polito, we lost you," he panted. "We lost you but you're back." At some point I had peed myself and my shirt had been ripped open, but they were kind enough to pull off my tuxedo pants instead of cutting them off. I'd died and fallen into the abyss when Bubba became my unicycle.

My first impulse was to ask for a pencil and paper. When things calmed down and I was comfortably settled in bed, they gave them to me and I began to write down everything I could remember that needed to be taken care of: the rental car, my hotel room, and my luggage. I wanted to see if my brain was still working properly after being in V-tach. The staff was very kind in contacting my mother and telling her I was okay and in good care. When they called Darryl and explained the situation, he told them he'd be there as soon as he could. He still had one more day to film and I didn't want him to give up his last day's shoot. After all, we're actors and the show must go on!

I was initially housed in a room with two other people, which I didn't mind. Within an hour, a nurse came back and said, "We made a mistake. We're moving you." It turned out that my insurance was pretty damn good, and they were putting me in the biggest room on the floor, kind of like a corner suite. Unfortunately, the window view was of a cemetery. I thought, *Well, what are you gonna do?* I laid there looking at it, thinking I could have just as easily ended up there instead of the room I was in now.

A surgeon came in and said I had a damaged vein that needed a stent. He asked which kind I'd prefer and since I knew nothing about them, I wanted to see what they looked like. They were weird little mesh tubes made of either plastic or metal, but the metal kind required you to take blood thinners for the rest of your life. I wasn't fond of blood thinners because near the end of his life, my father would bleed every time I'd touch him, so I chose the plastic kind. Darryl arrived at six on Monday morning, just in time for me to have my first stent put in. By Tuesday, I was told everything was looking good and my recovery was going to be fine, so we made plans to fly home on Friday.

I was now a man who'd suffered two massive heart attacks and was dead for almost two minutes, yet I couldn't wait to jump right back into the craziness that was my life.

After all, what else could possibly happen?

17
The Not-So Bionic Man

Once I was home with Darryl, I was eager to start my recovery and get back to work. I did a guest appearance on the TV show *Las Vegas*, which I really enjoyed. My character was known as "The Cleaner," a guy who specialized in covering up people's indiscretions. I looked pretty damn good after losing some weight from the heart attacks and was now sporting a goatee instead of just my trademark mustache. As we get older, all character men grow facial hair, and the goatee became my freak flag.

I landed a strange little job on a short film by two men – James Baker and Joe Haidar – who worked as animators for Disney. They were upset at that time because Disney was moving away from old-fashioned cel animation in favor of computer animation, and they had been laid off. In protest, they wrote a short called *Animated American* about a studio exec who is confronted by a bunch of out-of-work cartoon characters. I was offered the voiceover role of the ringleader, Max Rabbit. It was a very dark, well-made film that got some nice reviews on the festival circuit.

Shortly thereafter I made an appearance on *Two and a Half Men*, which was making headlines at the time due to Charlie Sheen's backstage escapades. I had a lovely scene with Jon Cryer, who was a dream to work with, in which I was getting massaged and began to experience some ill-timed flatulence. The episode was directed by a wonderful man I'd admired for years named Jeff Melman, and it was a great gig in front of a live audience. Mr. Sheen didn't bother to appear until it was time to shoot, which lent some credibility to the rumors about his erratic behavior. I have to admit, though, that once he was on the set, he was *very* good. He was a man who, like me in my drug days, could pull it together no matter where he had been the night before.

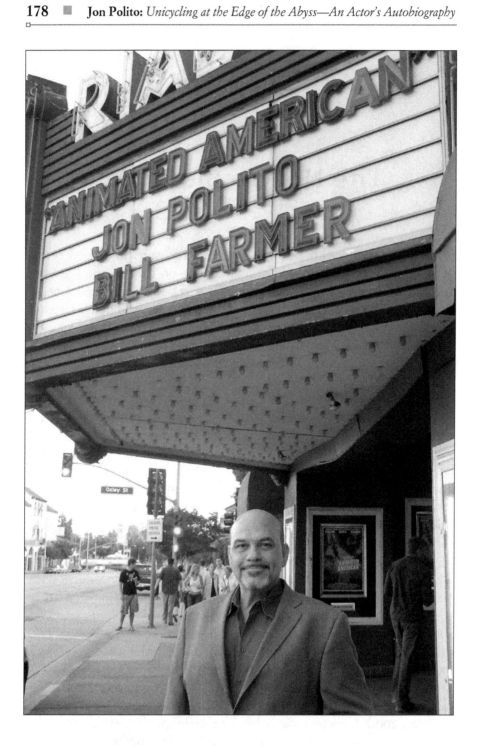

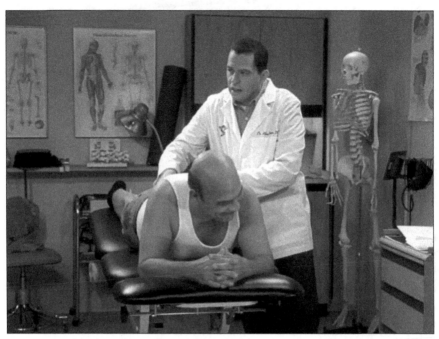

Two and a Half Men *with Jon Cryer*

I was asked to read for a television series that had been green-lit for a six-episode run called *Do Not Disturb*, created by a talented guy named Abraham Higginbotham. When I walked into the casting session on the 20th Century Fox lot, there were only two other people there for the audition, neither of whom looked anything like me. We were all comparing notes and trying to figure out what was going on when we learned the real story. The pilot was completed and had been picked up, and the role we were reading for had been played by Robert Wagner. This was *the* Robert Wagner, husband of Natalie Wood, and a terrific guy who's been around forever. Apparently, the network suits didn't think he was funny enough and would only agree to do the show if his part were recast. So, they paid Wagner some money to go away, and these two other guys and I were going to read to see who would replace him. When I went in, I felt more welcomed than usual. The people were polite and sweet and anxious to see me, particularly Abraham, who was jumping out of his seat. Of course, I figured this was the kiss of death. Too much eagerness on the part of casting people usually means, "You're fabulous but we'll use you some other time."

In this case, however, I was booked within two days of the audition as the new regular on *Do Not Disturb*. The show was about a hotel being run by a crazy bunch of guys and gals, and it starred Niecy Nash, who I loved on *Reno 911!* The cast included Jerry O'Connell, Dave Franco (younger brother of James) and an interesting young actor named Jesse Tyler Ferguson. Jason Bateman, the star of *Arrested Development*, had directed the pilot and came back to film my scenes. I adored Jason but I was kind of intimidated that he was going to direct me. They were going to shoot my scenes for the pilot *and* the second episode at the same time, so I had twice as much work to do. It wasn't an ideal situation, but I thought I could get through it.

However, there was a bigger problem. Jason is a brilliant actor. He does a kind of comedy that is dry and sarcastic but accessible; he's smarmy and sweet. I don't know how you define it, and I don't know how he does it, but I certainly knew *I* couldn't do it and that was the rub. I felt his direction was trying to lead me toward a performance that *he* would do. I don't think it was deliberate on his part, but it was very difficult for my overacting self to do something as subtle and witty as a Jason Bateman performance. It was tough and I tried my damnedest, but in the end, I didn't think it was great, although everyone else seemed happy with it.

Abraham later admitted that he'd always wanted me for the part, and in fact had written it with me in mind. He championed me all the way through development at the studio, but the executives weren't interested. They wanted a "name" actor – like Robert Wagner – but since that choice didn't work out, they were giving me a try. It was a tough shoot because television shows now had sixteen producers, associate producers, executive producers, assistant producers, and consulting producers. I've been on a lot of half-hour shows but I'd never been on a set like that one. After a scene was done, everybody would huddle and have a conference. All those producers wanted to keep their jobs so every one of them had opinions about the way I delivered a line or how my tie looked. It was hell! God bless the cast who were as positive as they could be, and God bless Abraham Higginbotham for being in my corner. Although we were scheduled for a six-episode run, *Do Not Disturb* wasn't getting ratings and was cancelled after three.

But the jobs kept coming! Steven Bochco, the genius creator of landmark TV series such as *Hill Street Blues*, *L.A. Law* and *NYPD Blue*, was doing a lawyer show called *Raising the Bar* for the TNT cable channel. He was no longer the cat's meow at the broadcast networks, but he was still producing some quality material, and this series starred Mark-Paul Gosselaar and a terrific actor named Currie Graham. Even though it was just a small role as a judge, I went in to read for *Raising the Bar* because I wanted to work with Steven. After getting the part, I made a fairly good deal for one day's worth of shooting. When they asked me to continue the role for several more episodes, I made an even *better* deal, which significantly helped my finances.

Around this time, I also started accepting invitations to attend film festivals that were hosting retrospectives and anniversary screenings of my older movies. Not only were these great opportunities to see some old friends and collaborators, I realized making appearances at these events could be a viable financial option in case acting gigs slowed down or disappeared. *The Big Lebowski* was becoming quite a religion, and I was a guest at Lebowski Fest, which is an annual gathering of wonderful, crazy fans devoted to the Dude. It was a good time when I could simply be me and coast on my past successes.

It was during one of these festivals that I happened to see a short film called *Tackle Box*, which I thought was terrific. It had a great set-up about a woman who dies, and her ashes are put into a tackle box because she loved to fish. Her remains are mistaken for drugs and people start snorting them because it makes everyone happy. It was the weirdest little movie, but I really enjoyed it. The director's name was Matthew Mebane and I said to him, "I like your work. Anything you've got coming down the pike, let me know." Matthew eventually landed a job directing one part of a horror anthology called *Locker 13*. His story was "Down and Out," which tells the tale of a fighter – played by Ricky Schroder – who's at the end of his career. He's given a pair of haunted boxing gloves and suddenly starts winning, but everyone he faces ends up being killed in the ring. My role was initially a simple cameo which I was doing as a favor for Matthew. I was supposed to film my part on a Thursday, and I got an anxious call from him on Tuesday night. Keith David was hired to play the boxing coach but backed out of the project the day before production was scheduled to start. In desperation, Matthew called and asked, "Is there any way you can play this part?"

"When do we shoot?"

"Tomorrow morning," he said. "We start at six o'clock."

I'd read the script and thought the coach was a great challenge. Even though I only had a few hours to learn the role, I told Matthew, "Absolutely. Let me know what scenes we're doing and I'll get the rest of the performance together as we go along." I memorized some won-

Locker 13 *with Ricky Schroder*

derful dialogue overnight with no sleep, and I went in at 6 a.m. to begin filming. It was an absolute dream! Everything went smoothly and I looked great, not only because of my weight loss but because of the director of photography, Russell Carpenter. The film was shot digitally; I didn't know how he managed to make me look so gorgeous, but the footage was spectacular. I figured it out later when I realized Russell had shot *Titanic* and won a Best Cinematography Oscar for his efforts! Although the final movie took ages to be completed, making the "Down and Out" segment of *Locker 13* was a fun experience.

My career was in a pretty healthy place, so it was time to get an update on my medical issues. I was going to a cardiologist named Dr. Schreck, whom I liked very much. I'd been keeping on top of things with regular visits and check-ups, and 2009 was going to end with a simple stress test to make sure the ol' ticker was gonna keep on ticking. I had a weird feeling about this stress test, though. I don't know if it was a psychic moment or not, but I really wanted Darryl to come along. Schreck said he wasn't going to be there that day because he had jury duty but would look at the results when he got back. Darryl and I sat in the waiting room and when my name was called, I went into a back room and got on the treadmill. As I started to walk, I noticed the guy running the test seemed very disengaged, and the room was kind of crowded and in disarray. Those thoughts were running through my mind when Dr. Schreck walked through the door. "Hello, Jon," he said cheerfully.

"What are you doing here?" I asked. "I thought you had jury duty."

"They let us out early and I thought I'd come over. There are a few other things I'd like to check out, so you can get off the treadmill."

I stepped off the machine and immediately felt disoriented. "Something's happening…"

I collapsed. My heart went into V-fib (ventricular fibrillation), meaning it flutters instead of beats. It wasn't pumping blood and I was going to die. Schreck immediately got me up on a table, threw two wet rags on my chest and zapped me with a defibrillator. Poor Darryl was in the waiting room hearing chaos and panic, and even though he tried to come in, he was held back. Schreck got my heart into a somewhat normal rhythm, Darryl was finally allowed in, tears streaming from his eyes, and I was whisked to St. Joseph's Hospital about a block away. They couldn't put me under anesthesia but had to immediately go inside to see what was happening. Dr. Schreck performed the procedure himself while I lay in bed looking at the monitors as he put holes in my groin and dye in my system. Instead of being scared to death like a normal person, I was totally fascinated by all of it and wouldn't shut up! Schreck was a nervous wreck and said, "Please be quiet!" but I was excited to see them sticking needles and cameras inside me. I watched as they put in three more stents, and two days later, I was released from the hospital. At the end of 2009 I now had four stents and was feeling kind of bionic, ready to face 2010 and whatever it held in store.

I did a guest appearance on the TV show *The Mentalist* playing a rather officious prick who ran a cooking competition. One of the chefs is poisoned, and much like an episode of *Murder, She Wrote*, it's left to stars Simon Baker and Robin Tunney to figure out whodunit. The most interesting thing about the episode, though, was how I got the role. Six months earlier, there was a casting person who told my agent he didn't want to bring me in to audition anymore because he thought I was "too gay." This guy obviously had a problem and wasn't afraid to say why. My agent and manager got involved and said if he didn't cast me in something by the end of the year, we would bring him up on discrimination charges. He ended up sending me in for the effeminate role on *The Mentalist*, and since I got the part, he and his homophobic attitude

The Mentalist *with Simon Baker*

were officially off the hook. He never brought me in for anything after that, but I was happy to be on the show.

One of the other guest stars in this episode was Robin Weigert, who was famous for playing Calamity Jane on *Deadwood*. I didn't know her, but I got a first-hand look at how serious a Method actress she was. Her character was revealed to be the killer, and during rehearsals she cried as part of her performance. When filming started, she cried during all of the coverage takes instead of saving her performance for her close-up. I remember Simon Baker sweetly saying to her, "You're wonderful, my darling, but you don't really have to give it your all right now."

She turned to him and barked, "I work a *different* way!" which simultaneously shut him down and made the rest of us raise our eyebrows at her intensity. Of course, when it was time to film her close-up, she had dried up completely and had no more tears to give, having wasted them. They shot it three times before giving up and moving on to the next scene. It was an example that reinforced my belief that Method actors perform for the sake of performing. It's not a process I'm fond of but Robin was very good on the show, so God bless her – however you get there, you get there.

Out of nowhere, I was hired to work on a strange project called *The Last Godfather*. A comedian in Korea named Hyung-rae Shim became popular in the '80s by doing Chaplinesque slapstick with a character he created named Young-gu. Over the years there apparently was still a demand for more of the sweet buffoon, so Shim wrote and directed the film, which is about a Mafia boss, played by Harvey Keitel, grooming his son, Young-gu, to take over the family business. It was a silly script but I liked it. I was also *very* excited to be working with Keitel, who I thought was a brilliant actor.

I portrayed the head of a rival family and my right-hand man was played by Jason Mewes, who I knew from Kevin Smith's films. Jason was having a problem with drugs and I recognized it right away. It was hard for him to make it through rehearsals, he had a difficult time getting through a scene and sometimes he was so out of it he'd just fall over. He was in bad shape, but I loved the guy, and I was determined to do what I could to get him through it.

Dealing with Jason wasn't easy, but it was nothing compared to the fact that Mr. Shim, our director and star, didn't speak English. It was, "Me Tarzan, you Jane" time. He'd give direction and it would be filtered through interpreters; likewise, if you had a question, you'd have to go through them to get an answer. Mr. Shim directed the film from a visual standpoint because he didn't know what any of his actors were

The Last Godfather *with Jason Mewes*

saying. I put all of this together and was kind of enjoying the process, making sure my performance was clear enough visually that he would be able to understand it even though it was in a different language.

Acting-wise, I was able to hold my own with Mr. Keitel. It wasn't an easy situation for him, and I don't think he was very happy to be there. He was doing what he could, but I think he was frustrated with everything. In the end, *The Last Godfather* was barely released in America, and Mr. Shim lost so much money that his Korean investors took him to court. Even though few people saw it, the movie was an enjoyable gig and a full-blown starring role that put some money in my bank account.

The first decade of the 21ˢᵗ century had been filled with a lot of work, a lot of love, and a lot of loss. My heart condition had taken center stage but there was something else lurking behind the curtain: the monoclonal protein that was discovered in 2002. It wasn't something that was dangerous in and of itself; it was simply a warning sign about the *possibility* of developing multiple myeloma, an incurable cancer. In all the years since that diagnosis, I have stayed on top of the situation, checking in regularly with my oncologist so he could monitor my numbers. In June of 2010, I went in for a scheduled visit. The doctor told me, "It's been eight years and I'm pretty sure nothing's going to come of it. I'll call you in a week with your results."

Instead, he called me three days later. "Jon, you need to get in here immediately. You have multiple myeloma."

18

Sunny Days and Stem Cells

On June 10th, 2010, I was facing the abyss.

Dr. Olsen had been my oncologist for eight years, and truth be told, I loved him. He looked like a doctor straight out of a Norman Rockwell painting, so I always felt secure around him even though my visits were to monitor a potentially life-threatening condition. With Darryl by my side, Dr. Olsen said that I'd developed multiple myeloma. He spoke for a while but all I heard were soundbites: "Cancer." "Incurable." "Six months to live." According to Darryl, however, Dr. Olsen also talked about treatment, which I don't remember hearing at all. I was just thinking about how I was going to tell my mother that my numbers had spiked so much within two months that I went from having a cautious warning sign to full-blown cancer.

I decided it was time to do some investigation. I found an article online about Geraldine Ferraro, the vice-presidential candidate from the '80s, and discovered she was a multiple myeloma survivor. She talked about her treatment using drugs that were incredibly expensive and not easily accessible to most people because of their price. The piece, which had been written several years earlier, led to more recent stories in which she made speeches at symposiums to raise awareness of the disease. She was proving multiple myeloma wasn't the quick death sentence it used to be, and I was starting to feel a little bit of hope. Three of the top hospitals in America that dealt with this form of cancer were in New York, Chicago, and Los Angeles. The L.A. hospital, coincidentally enough, was called City of Hope and was just twenty-five minutes away from our condo. A doctor named Amrita Krishnan who worked there was listed as a leading specialist in the field.

After a weekend of crying many tears – alone and with Darryl – I spoke to my mother and brother and gave them the news. It was a time of reflection and fear that sparked *the* fight for my life. We met with Dr.

187

Olsen and he explained that the most aggressive treatment would be a stem cell transplant. My age, however, made the procedure questionable because it was usually done for people 55 and younger, and I was approaching 59. After delivering that bit of depressing news, he smiled and said I'd been accepted by Dr. Krishnan, and an appointment would be scheduled to begin the process.

Around this time, I was hired to appear in a movie version of the book *Atlas Shrugged*. Darryl and I had become friends with a man named Paul Johansson, whom I liked very much. Paul was an actor – handsome and hunky – who was looking to branch out into directing. When the original director of *Atlas* had a fight with the producers and quit the project, Paul was offered the job. It was a small production with little money, and when he asked me as a favor to be involved, I couldn't say no.

My scenes were scheduled the day before my first meeting with Dr. Krishnan. I had only a few, one of which was with my old *Barton Fink* cohort, Michael Lerner. I hadn't seen him since then, and when I got to the set, he wasn't the same man I used to know. He looked great, having lost over 100 pounds since the *Fink* shoot. When he asked me to come to his trailer, I thought it would be a good opportunity to discuss our scene because I hadn't read the book and the dialogue was all political jibber-jabber. To my surprise, it turned out Michael wasn't at all concerned about his lines, saying he didn't really put much effort into low-paying jobs like this. He then proceeded to talk about his personal life and how well things were going for him. I was kind of shocked he was speaking about such things, because it's not like we were good friends or close in any way.

My first scene involved a great actor named Matthew Marsden, and we knocked it out quickly and smoothly. I portrayed a simple business guy and didn't do much to make it a "character" performance. I thought it was something I should play as naturally as possible while looking as good as I could. My body was changing, my weight was going down, and while I used to think it was because I was making healthy choices, I now realized it was due to being in the grip of cancer.

When we got to the part that involved Michael, it was an absolute nightmare. He didn't know his lines and had no idea what he wanted to do with the character, so he would try something, stop mid-way through, and start over. It was a simple scene that should've been shot in an hour or two, but it kept going on and on. Paul pulled me aside

Atlas Shrugged *with Patrick Fischler, Michael Lerner and Matthew Marsden*

and said, "Can you help me out with your friend? He's not listening to me. He insists on doing his own thing and it's screwing everything up."

"I'm not really friends with him," I admitted. "Besides, I don't know what his problem is. I don't think there's anything I could say that would help."

This dilemma was made even more dramatic because I had to be at City of Hope in the morning, and it was now eleven o'clock at night. We still had to finish the scene with Michael and do his close-up, plus I had another scene to shoot after that. I spoke with Darryl on the phone during the breaks and gave him updates on the chaos. He was already upset that I had gone to work the day before my medical appointment, and hearing of Michael's behavior made him absolutely furious. It was a tough situation that felt like something in a Hitchcock film; a ticking time bomb that could explode at any minute.

We finally wrapped Michael's stuff at one in the morning, and after working all day and all night, everyone was exhausted. As much as I wanted to go home, I knew I couldn't leave without finishing the job. I pulled Paul aside and said, "Let me be honest with you. I'm going into the hospital this morning for a very important medical issue and I don't know if I'll be able to come back. Please, can we shoot my last bit now? I'll do anything to get it done as quickly as possible."

He called for the assistant director and we all had a meeting. The scene consisted of me at a bar talking on the phone, and at one point I look up at a staircase to see another character enter. I told Paul I felt we could do the whole performance in one take, and if he used multiple cameras, he could get enough coverage to intercut the different angles. Instead of a full-blown rehearsal, I did a quick walk-through and explained, "I'll move here, I'll touch this ashtray, I'll pick up the phone here and then I'll turn this way." We started at two in the morning and we were done forty-five minutes later. With my scenes for *Atlas Shrugged* in the can, I got an hour's sleep before meeting with Dr. Krishnan.

Multiple myeloma is a bone marrow blood disorder where a monoclonal protein recreates itself and takes over your immune system until it's destroyed. This cancer was on the rise, and like any medical condition that's starting to flourish, there was research funding for it. Money was being spent on tests and studies, and although the disease was incurable, work was being done in the hope of extending life. I guess if you're going to have a cancer, it's good to have one that's popular! My treatment consisted of taking a series of pills and drips for about three months which were slowly going to break down my system and bring my blood to a level with less and less multiple myeloma. There were two types of medication available in my medical plan (thank God I had insurance through the Screen Actors Guild!) that Dr. Krishnan was going to use. One was a chemo drug called Velcade, and the other was a companion called Revlimid. The amazing thing is that Revlimid is a thalidomide derivative. Thalidomide was introduced in Germany in 1957 for pregnant women who suffered from morning sickness and anxiety. It worked as advertised but had tragic, unintended side effects. Babies were born horribly deformed with fins instead of legs and stumps instead of arms. These images were plastered all over the world in newspapers and magazines. Thalidomide was a nightmare I grew up reading about, but it did end up having some benefits, one of which – many, many years later – was found to be useful in treating multiple myeloma.

I began chemo at the end of June when my mother came out for her summer visit, scared as hell that I was going to die. She and Darryl were both there when I took my first pill, but instead of feeling bad, I felt kind of energized because I had to take it with steroids. It was like I was back in the coke days, revved and ready to go after a sniff or two... or twelve. The drugs were lowering my numbers so that my blood and stem cells would be pure enough for removal. The plan was that I'd return to the hospital in December and have the stem cells injected back into my system, in the hope that the transplant would help rebuild everything so that I'd have more time to live. I must admit, the cosmetic side effects of chemo were fabulous! As the months passed, I lost almost twenty pounds and was starting to see good lines and angles in my

Darryl, Jon's mom and Jon

face that I hadn't seen in a long time. My energy was up enough to keep auditioning and people were complimenting me on my appearance.

I'd been a fan of a comedy series on the FX network called *It's Always Sunny in Philadelphia*. The show was on the verge of being cancelled after the first season, so Danny DeVito was brought in to give it a boost, delivering one of the most offensive and hilarious performances I've ever seen. Although we'd never met, I had a bit of history with De-Vito. During my time in *Other People's Money*, I told people he should play my character if there was ever a movie version. I heard a rumor that he initially turned down the film role, but when I returned to do the second run in New York and he watched the production, he agreed to do the adaptation. I didn't know if the story was true but that was the word on the street. Another connection I had to Danny was an internet troll. Every time my name was mentioned on certain websites – for reasons good, bad, or otherwise – there would be one guy who would always comment that I was "the fake ass Danny DeVito." I'm not sure if he hated me or was just unfavorably comparing me to DeVito. Hell, it might have been Danny himself trolling me! All of this played into my desire to be on *It's Always Sunny*. I was still able to work while doing chemo and didn't say a word to my agents about the illness. I wanted to do as much acting as I could because I thought the clock might be ticking not only on my career but my life, as well.

As fate would have it, a part *did* become available on the show. It was only a one-day guest spot, but I was excited as hell to do it. However, I became sick. As soon as I learned the job was mine, I developed pneumonia and was rushed to City of Hope, forcing me to give up the gig.

September rolled around and it was time to have my stem cells removed. Back in the old days when you'd see a laboratory in a movie or TV show, there would be bubbling vials with tubes running everywhere, and a scientific device that looked suspiciously like a reel-to-reel tape recorder. Those sets were primitive and fun, like something you'd make in your basement. Well, my procedure took place in a room just like those old Hollywood labs. A needle was inserted into my arm, I was told to sit back and relax, and I watched as my blood made its way through a tube and toward a tape recorder-like device. At the bottom of this machine was a plastic bag containing a clear liquid that was very slowly becoming pink. My stem cells were being collected in there, and I was hoping for as many of the damn things as possible. When I went to see Dr. Krishnan two days later, she reported over eleven million cells had been gathered and I was to come back on December 12th.

Life went on in those three months. I was weak in some ways and used a cane from time to time, but I was still looking fabulous. However, as the weeks passed, I began to appear a little drawn. My skin was starting to hang a little too loosely, and instead of having good angles I had melted wax. I didn't like the look and I didn't like the way I was feeling.

The battle in my body had begun.

I returned to City of Hope with Darryl on December 12th. We met another patient – a podiatrist named David Sterling – who also had multiple myeloma and was there to start the same treatment as me. David and I chatted while Darryl talked with David's wife, and we felt some camaraderie. One of the most important things I learned about cancer came from Wendy Burke, David Burke's wife who had inspired him to write and direct the cancer-centric short film I starred in, *Frank's Last Dance*. Being a survivor of the disease, she was one of the first people I called after my diagnosis to ask for advice. She said, "Whatever you do, don't get into support groups. Don't make friends with people because you'll compare notes with them, and if they die that's just one more thing you'll worry about. Keep yourself around healthy people." I thought that was a *brilliant* recommendation, and while we were social with the Sterlings, we kept our relationship very businesslike as we approached our mutual goal of getting better.

The first step in the transplant was to bring my immune system down to zero. Everyone coming in and out of my sterile room had to wear a mask because any germ could kill me. The whole process took seven days, and as my immunity was being lowered and I was becoming more and more vulnerable, Dr. Krishnan started the next part of the procedure, which was to put the stem cells back. It was a simultaneous treatment, and by the time my system reached zero, she wanted to see if any stem cells would begin rebuilding my blood. It was a hell of a week. No one could talk to me except through masks, and the food options were extremely limited. As the days went on, I tried to keep myself busy by reading, watching bad TV shows and playing with my new laptop, finally making the technological leap into the twentieth century even though we were well into the twenty-first. I also refused to wear the open-back hospital gown, insisting instead on wearing sweatpants and a shirt. I didn't want to look like a patient, I wanted to look healthy. When the week ended, I was told my system was starting to rebuild rather quickly, and within twenty-four hours my numbers had already begun to rise.

It was encouraging news that couldn't have come at a better time. With the holidays quickly approaching, I really wanted to be home for Christmas, but it didn't look promising. Over the next two weeks, I was being monitored daily and my numbers kept going up and up. It didn't mean I was out of the woods; I would have to be retested a month later, but things were looking good. Back in Philly, my mother was going through a tremendous amount of anxiety. We spoke on the phone five or six times a day, with me always being as positive as possible, but this was going to be the first year she wouldn't be able to spend Christmas with us since my father died. I was released on December 24th, but I couldn't really go anywhere because of the threat of germs, so Darryl and I stayed home and celebrated the holiday together. I had skirted the abyss yet again and my unicycle this time was Dr. Krishnan, who saved me from falling in. I was about to face 2011 with cancer, a whole bunch of new stem cells and cautious optimism.

In January, life became *Sunny* again. Charlie Day, one of the stars and producers, told my agents he had an even better role to offer. Char-

It's Always Sunny in Philadelphia *with Danny DeVito*

lie was under the impression I had turned down the first one because it wasn't big enough. He was a fan of mine and was now proposing I play Danny's older brother who comes for a visit. This was like manna from Heaven! The script was terrific and featured flashbacks of our lives together that involved wigs, disco, drugs, guns and fucking! DeVito's character had sex scenes in other episodes of the show, and he had the most unusual way of screwing. The writers figured it would be funny if it were revealed that I taught him how to do it, so I had to recreate Danny's unique method. At sixty years old, I was going to have my first on-camera sex scene. I knew at that moment the gig was going to be a blast!

My first appearance with Danny was one in which I walk in and say his name; he turns and looks at me, and instead of hugging we get into a fist fight. During rehearsal we walked through the sequence, saving our energy until the cameras were rolling. As we began to shoot, I realized just how weak I actually was. I couldn't catch my breath and almost collapsed. The producers came running up and a nurse was called in. This was drama. I didn't want them to know I had just gotten out of the hospital – and I certainly didn't want them to reconsider my casting – so I started stumbling and stammering for some kind of excuse. God bless him, Danny saved the day by saying, "I know how we can do this." In addition to being a wonderful actor, he's also a great director, and he re-blocked the fight so it would be less strenuous.

During some downtime on the set, he and I were discussing a few things when I mentioned how much I enjoyed his performance in the movie version of *Other People's Money*. I told him that during the first week's rehearsal of the play, I predicted he would star in the film if there ever was one. "I wouldn't have played it if I hadn't seen you do the character first," he replied. Danny confirmed the rumors of turning down the role and then changing his mind after watching me, and I have to say that made me feel pretty damn good.

It's Always Sunny in Philadelphia *with Danny DeVito*

I'd like to say, "Thank you, thank you, thank you!" to those wonderful people on *It's Always Sunny in Philadelphia*. It was the first burst of light and laughter I'd felt after an extremely difficult six months of dealing with multiple myeloma, and it's a gift that I cherish to this day.

19

Facing Mortality

With *It's Always Sunny in Philadelphia* in the can, I wanted to keep working as much as I could while recovering from the stem cell transplant. There was a post-*Sunny* party I went to hosted by John Goodner, the show's video assist man. He approached me and said, "I've got a project I'm working on and I'd like you to be in it." Even though I had no clue what he had in mind, I wasn't turning down anything at this point and told him to let me know when he was ready to shoot.

I needed to do a lot of things I'd been putting off. When you're faced with the end and you make a list of everything you *haven't* done, the urgency intensifies to *get* them done, which is part of the reason why you're reading this book. One of the ideas brewing in my mind involved the movie *Whiskey Down*, which had been released as *Just Your Luck*. Even though it had a wonderful cast, it bombed. The reason it didn't work was because it never should've ventured outside the diner where most of the action took place. I always thought the story was more suitable as a play, and I had talked to Darryl about it off and on over the years. One day he said, "You want to turn *Whiskey Down* into a play? It's time to get to it."

I went to writers Gary Auerbach and Todd Alcott and asked for permission to adapt their screenplay for the stage. They thought I was crazy but gave me their blessing. I still had the original script, and Darryl and I spent six weeks going through it page by page and reworking it as a play. We called it *86'd* – a restaurant term used when something was off the menu, as well as slang for the people being killed in our story – and we felt it turned out pretty well. Darryl was involved with the Elephant Theatre, a prominent and well-respected establishment in Los Angeles, and they agreed to stage a reading. We gathered some of their finest actors and presented it to the company, but the head of the theater, David Fofi, didn't feel it was right for him.

On the set of Jonny Boy *with Laura Way*

The project was put aside but at least it was completed, and I checked it off my bucket list.

I'd done some voiceover work for *Thundercats* and *Batman: Year One* when I received a phone call from Ireland. Laura Way, the wonderful girl I befriended on the set of *The Honeymooners*, had kept in touch over the years and said, "I had an idea, you're the reason it happened and I got approval to do it!" I had no clue what she was talking about, but it turned out she'd been inspired by all of the stories I told her while we were making the movie. Laura was getting some cachet as a director after doing a short film called *Sugar Stick*, and she went to the Irish Film Board and proposed another short called *Jonny Boy*. She asked me to star in it, and without knowing anything about the script, I agreed immediately.

The set-up involved a man whose wife is dying in the hospital. It's revealed that we married so she could keep her family intact, and although we had a great life together, I sacrificed my own happiness to help her. She then confesses she's been hiding letters written to me over the years by the true love of my life. After she dies, I find the correspondence and fly to Ireland. I walk toward a house in the middle of the countryside and come upon a beautiful woman who's hanging her laundry outside. As the sheets are blowing in the wind, she looks at me and says, "My God, is it you?" We embrace and then she says, "Are you here to see Bernie?" I turn and see her brother, the man I'd been in love with all those years ago. It was a wonderful payoff to a beautiful film. *Jonny Boy* played festivals and earned some good reviews, and I'll be forever grateful to Laura for including me in a project of which I'm extremely proud.

When I got back to Los Angeles, it was hard to figure out what was going to happen because my body was giving way to other health issues. I was like an old Ford in dire need of an overhaul, so I had both hips replaced. I also needed a new knee but decided to wait because I wanted to do some more work before undergoing another operation. The problem was that I began using a cane to get around and word was starting to spread about it. That was nothing, though, compared to what happened when people found out about my cancer.

City of Hope asked if I'd do a promotional piece about stem cell transplants for a local news channel. It was a simple bit in which I talked to a lovely woman named Lisa Sigell about my experiences during the transplant procedure. My episode of *The Mentalist* had aired recently, so the spot was advertised by the station as, "Actor from *The Mentalist* fighting cancer!" Instead of airing it in the lower-profile five o'clock afternoon slot, they put it on during the nightly news at eleven. My health was now out there for everyone to know, and people interpreted it in different ways. The TV piece made it clear I had incurable cancer, but thanks to the transplant I was now in remission. Remission, though, doesn't mean you're healed or cured, so some people heard that I *had* cancer while others heard that I'd *beaten* cancer. I was noticing during auditions that people would hesitantly ask, "Well, doesn't he have cancer?" It was a scary time. What was going to happen to my career?

That's when John Goodner called and said, "I've got the financing together for my movie." The short film was titled *Anti-Muse* and my character was the devil on a depressed man's shoulder who'd tell him, "Don't follow your dreams, it's not worth it. Just kill yourself." There was no angel on his other shoulder to keep his spirits up; I was the lone negative voice in this guy's head. He eventually fights back, defeats his demon, and survives. John wrote a terrific script and I knew I needed to play against a *really* good actor. Unfortunately, the people being called to audition were extremely amateurish.

There was a man who worked with Darryl at the Elephant Theatre named James Pippi. James' demo reel was cool to watch because he played a lot of different characters, and he edited it to make it appear as if they were all interacting with each other. It was like Lon Chaney working with Lon Chaney working with Lon Chaney. Not only was it impressive from a technical standpoint, it showed that James had a lot of range and talent. John asked if I knew anyone who'd be right for the role; I suggested James and, after viewing the reel, John immediately cast him. As the shoot began, I thought it was going to be a pleasant and creative experience, but truth be told, John wouldn't let me do *anything* that he hadn't already planned. I had no creative input into the character and had to do everything precisely as instructed. Surprisingly, I won a Best Actor award from the Hollywood Reel Independent Film Festival, and during my acceptance speech I thanked John by saying, "This is no joke: I owe my entire performance to him." Although I wish *Anti-Muse* had been a more collaborative effort, I was happy for the recognition and thankful for the experience.

Aside from the cancer, life was pretty manageable at this point. My finances were okay because I'd claimed my Screen Actors Guild pension early. I didn't know how long I'd live, so I decided to take the money from that and my Social Security, which created a decent cushion in case jobs became scarce. The East Coast was a different story. My mother was becoming very frail and it was difficult for her to visit, so Darryl and I would go to Philadelphia to see her. One day, she lost her balance, fell,

At the Hollywood Reel Independent Film Festival

and had to be rushed to the hospital. While my sister was convinced Mom was faking it for attention, tests revealed that her heart was so bad, oxygen wasn't getting to her brain whenever she stood up. She had an honest-to-God medical condition my sister refused to acknowledge, and that's when I decided to eliminate her from my life. It was a difficult choice to make because I was all about family, but her unpleasantness and hateful attitude toward our mother made it necessary.

Besides the heart issue, Mom was also going blind. She never said anything, but I noticed she wasn't seeing things clearly and was simply pretending that she did. In order to get her some fresh air and away from the hospital bed, I'd take her to a little alleyway behind the building where the nurses smoked. It was nothing but brick and concrete, but she thought she was in a lush backyard with gorgeous scenery and kept saying how beautiful it was. That's when I knew things were bad. Back in her room, I'd play old music for her, including Nat King Cole's "Smile," which was the very first record she ever bought. We'd talk and I'd make her a little drink because she loved her martinis and Manhattans. One day, the nurse practitioner who ran the place came over to talk to us. My mother asked, "How bad am I?" Being the direct person that she was, the nurse practitioner laid it all out there: her heart was weak, other organs were starting to fail, and they didn't believe she'd survive much longer. I'll never forget that moment when Mom looked at me with those incredibly clear blue eyes that could barely see and said, "Jonny, I'm dying."

"Well, aren't we all?" I replied. It was meant as a joke but deep down I knew she was scared. I tried to encourage her by saying, "I died once, and it wasn't that bad!" As much as I tried to make light of the situation, I knew we were sharing a moment when she was facing her own mortality.

She wasn't the only one. My mentor, Dominic Garvey – the man who got me into acting when I was sixteen years old – told me he was suffering from a variety of ailments, including heart conditions, stomach issues and blood disorders. He wasn't doing well so I made a point of calling him twice a week to check in.

Back in L.A., things were a little better. I went in for an interview with a young director named Ruben Fleischer, who had made the terrific *Zombieland* with Woody Harrelson and Jesse Eisenberg. He was going to be doing a movie called *Gangster Squad*, and I thought the script was quite campy, featuring square-jawed detectives fighting an evil mob guy. The part I was reading for was very tiny – it was pretty much a cameo

Jon and his mom

– but I wanted to keep working and agreed to audition. I liked Ruben a lot and enjoyed our improv reading together, and as luck would have it, I was cast. Although the role was limited, the cast was amazing! Sean Penn was the star, and God knows I had always wanted to work with him. The hunky Ryan Gosling was also in it, as was the lovely Emma Stone.

Gangster Squad told the true story of Mickey Cohen, a Jewish gangster who came to Los Angeles in the early '40s. He was notorious for stepping on the L.A. Mafia's toes and was confronted by the head of that group, Jack Dragna, which was the character I was playing. I didn't physically resemble the real-life Dragna at all, and even though he didn't appear to be the strongest or smartest guy, he looked like he would've held his own in the mob. That's the angle I wanted to emphasize.

As the time for filming approached, I took a seat at a table in a gorgeous restaurant that was once an old Hollywood theater. In the scene, I had a bodyguard standing behind me played by an actor named Sullivan Stapleton. I *loved* this man because he was in a movie called *Animal Kingdom*, which I thought was amazing. He was an Australian who could play the perfect bad guy and I gushed whenever I saw him on the set. Sullivan was a little taken aback by my enthusiasm toward him and he really didn't believe I knew his work until I began to rattle off his list of performances. He began to feel more comfortable and admitted that he wished he had more to do in this scene than simply stand around.

Sean Penn walked onto the set and I could see his Method intensity a mile away. His bodyguard was played by someone I'd known for many years named Holt McCallany, who was a very good actor and a sweetheart. In the scene, Penn denies he's doing anything wrong with how he's conducting his business in L.A., and I tell him he's screwing up by killing people left and right and he's gonna wind up dead because of it. At that point, he explodes in anger and walks out. I must admit Penn was a powerhouse. He was doing way-over-the-top anger and it wasn't what I expected. Stylistically, I was never sure whether the film would work because everybody was doing their scenes one touch larger than necessary, which could be why it wasn't well-reviewed.

As our rehearsal continued, Penn suggested that he should get rid of the bodyguards before we started talking business. He was polite enough to ask for my opinion, which made me like him immediately. "That makes perfect sense," I said. "Whatever you want to do is fine with me." Before we began to rehearse the scene again with this new element, Penn told Ruben he could film it, and that's something exciting because you have the chance to catch magic.

The cameras started to roll and Penn walked up with Emma Stone. As he sat down, he shooed her away and looked up at the bodyguard behind me. Penn said something like, "We don't need any monkeys around," and since it was a rehearsal, Sullivan made a loud comment under his breath. Penn looked at Sullivan like he was going to kill him! He had no idea how to express his absolute rage that a bodyguard would dare speak to him, so he grabbed a glass ashtray and threw it at Sullivan. Thankfully, it missed me, Sullivan, and a few of the background extras as it hit a wall and shattered into a million pieces. I turned to Sullivan and screamed, "Get out of here!" It was partly in character but mostly out of fear that Mr. Method Penn was going to lose it.

Gangster Squad *with Sean Penn*

The tension in the room was palpable. Penn immediately apologized to me and I said, "No, no, I understand what happened." Sullivan, on the other hand, was pissed and looked like he was going to do something about it. We took a break to catch our breaths and clean up the shards of glass, and I approached Sullivan, who was cursing up a storm about Penn's outburst. I tried to calm him down, but it wasn't working. As I walked away, Penn came up to me and started rambling, trying to explain his behavior.

"Sean, I understand," I told him.

"He's mad at me," he responded, pacing nervously back and forth.

"You talked to Sullivan?"

"Yeah, I went up to him and apologized but he's really mad at me." I felt bad for Penn because he'd gotten caught up in the heat of the moment for the good of the movie. This was a brilliant and sensitive actor who crossed the line and he knew it. Despite all the drama, I was silently in awe of him. Even though it was just a rehearsal, his reaction was *exactly* what would've come from the real Mickey Cohen. I knew I was working with a pro; someone who had become this character and was portraying him with an incredible amount of internal rage that I could see from the moment he sat down. That made it easy to play my character because I knew I was dealing with a lunatic.

During breaks, Penn would hang out at the front of the building under the marquee where we were allowed to smoke, and he asked me to join him for a cigarette. He was reaching out and wanted to talk, and I was touched by the gesture. I remember one night when we stopped for lunch, a production assistant delivered food to my trailer. She said, "Mr. Penn would like to know if you'll have lunch with him."

"Really?" I asked, shocked. "Does he do this a lot?"

"He *never* does this."

I grabbed my meal and walked over to his trailer. After thanking him for the invite, I had no idea what to say so I started telling stories about how much I loved working with his late brother, Chris, and his ex-wife, Robin Wright. While he enjoyed my tales, I discovered the real reason for the meeting was to show me videos of his humanitarian efforts, such as helping rebuild villages after earthquakes and other tragedies. He asked if I was able to help and I had to tell him, "I'm unable to help physically in any way, and truth be told, I'm not really financially able to, either. I wish I could because the work you're doing is amazing." It may have sounded like an excuse, but if I had been able to support him in those endeavors, I honestly would have.

At the party after the premiere, Penn was moving across the room surrounded by bodyguards. When he saw me, he broke through his security circle and came over to us. I introduced him to Darryl, and Sean introduced us to his mother and his children. It was a lovely exchange, and he's one of the reasons I have such a great fondness for the film.

Another reason was Ryan Gosling... There were police barricades surrounding the set, keeping back the throngs of women waiting to catch a glimpse of Mr. Gosling. He *is* a sexy motherfucker, but also adorable, sweet, and very pleasant. Between takes he made a point of sitting beside me and talking, which made me feel like a million bucks. On the last night of the shoot, I'd mentioned that one of my cousin's daughters was a big fan of his. "Well, if you want something signed, that's no problem," he said.

When work was finished, I began to pack up my stuff. Ryan still had six more hours to go and was frantically being rushed from scene to scene. Before I left, I went to the makeup trailer where he was getting a touch-up and said, "I'm sorry, I know you don't have the time, but that cousin of mine..."

"Don't be silly," he replied. "I'll do it now." He asked an assistant to go to his trailer and she came back with a poster that Ryan not only autographed, he also added a personal message to my cousin's daughter. It was a classy gesture by a classy guy.

Although I was extremely proud of *Gangster Squad*, it was slaughtered by the critics. *The New York Times* was particularly vicious, and as an online reader of the paper, I decided to respond to its excessively negative reaction. I went back and found the similarly dismissive 1990 review of *Miller's Crossing*. The critic felt Marcia Gay Harden looked silly in her wardrobe and the Coens shouldn't have gone into the mob genre. While I was spoken of kindly, the review overall was bitchy. My response to the critique of *Gangster Squad* was something along the lines of, "This newspaper totally missed the point of this lovely film just as you missed the point years ago with *Miller's Crossing*, which you now call a classic. Critics be damned!" That response went viral, and The Huffington Post wrote about my defense of the movie. Honestly, it was gratifying seeing my name mentioned in something other than an article about cancer, so I was quite pleased.

At the Gangster Squad *premiere*

I love *Gangster Squad*. I'm sorry it wasn't a better movie, but it was one of the most enjoyable moments of my career.

20
HTC and RDJ

"Out of the blue." "It can all change in an instant." "It's just a phone call away." These are verses from the actor's bible that an artist lives by. Sometimes – just sometimes – they turn out to be true.

I received a phone call from Dave Fofi, the head of the Elephant Theatre where we had done the reading of our play, *86'd*. Dave had been talking with a producer/director named Ronnie Marmo, and Ronnie – who ran a small theater of his own – had come into possession of a restaurant set. There were tables, a bar, a back wall, and other furnishings that made it look like a functioning eatery. Ronnie asked Dave, "You wouldn't happen to know of a play that takes place in a diner, do you?"

Ta-da!

Dave told Ronnie about *86'd*, and a meeting was quickly put together. Darryl and I were thrilled at the thought of our work being produced and were even more excited after meeting Ronnie. He was something of a player, rather attractive and a natural born charmer. He had Darryl wrapped around his finger in a matter of seconds! According to the contract, we'd sell the rights to Ronnie's company for a twelve-month period and receive a percentage of the box office. I honestly wasn't expecting much but at least we were going to earn *something* as playwrights, which was pretty damn cool.

After we signed the deal, Darryl began to lose interest but I wanted to know how it was all going to be put together. I went to the first run-through and that's when I discovered just how amateurish the actors were. They were C-list at best but certainly eager. I could see the play would be tough to produce as there was a lot of action. Things had to be solved on stage because, unlike the movie, you couldn't just cut to a different room. We began to figure out how this could be done, and I found myself becoming more and more involved. I was scared since this wasn't really a professional company, but I thought Ronnie was doing a hell of a job directing. There were times when his frustrations would boil over, but I'd step in and we'd come up with a solution.

The 86'd *company*

One of the most problematic elements was the finale. During the climax of the movie *Whiskey Down* – after all the mayhem of people trying to get their hands on the winning lottery ticket – the bag lady eats it, which isn't a surprise because she's been eating paper through the whole film. When I asked other writers for their opinions, that ending was the thing they all hated the most because it seemed incredibly obvious. So, I changed it into something completely off-the-wall. I remembered the film *Being There* and I always loved the fact it closed with Peter Sellers walking on water. It was an absurd move that completely changed the tone of everything that came before it, and I thought I'd try something like that. Instead of concluding the play with her eating the ticket, I had her do a very strange dance that offered no clear answer as to what happened next.

The last week of rehearsals was a whirlwind of excitement, nerves, and changes. A lot of the difficulties were caused by the stage directions Darryl and I wrote. We had made them up as we went along, and although they looked good on paper, they weren't very practical, so I said, "Instead of doing it this way, do it that way." It was all coming together but I was still skeptical because we didn't have professional actors. I couldn't ask them, "What's wrong with this speech? What's wrong with this scene?" because they wouldn't know. Still, we did the best we could, and it was shaping up to be an honest-to-God *real* play.

86'd opened on Sunset Boulevard in a small but lovely theater. Critics from all the major newspapers were there, which was both exciting and scary. Darryl's involvement with the Dan Band and my association with the Coens meant that our names were front and center in the publicity. The first review that came in was from *Backstage*, and it was mediocre at best. The next one was from *The LA Times* – the biggest newspaper in town – and it was great! The critic was David C. Nichols, who emphasized how dark and uncomfortably funny he thought our show was. Another local paper listed it as a "pick of the week," and just like that, we were a hit. It wasn't the same as being in an Off-Broadway success in New York, but it was just as gratifying. Although I'd hoped it would lead to a major run across the country, it never went anywhere else. It's in my library of possibilities for the future, and perhaps I'll get an opportunity to mount it again.

Critics' Choices

86'd Would that all indie films translated to the stage as well as Jon Polito and Darryl Armbruster's dark comedy about collective moral equivalency in a late-night diner. Although director Ronnie Marmo permits his adroit players to risk overkill, it's hard to cavil with the uproarious payoffs. (D.C.N.) Theatre 68, 5419 Sunset Blvd., Suite D, Hollywood. Today, 7 p.m.; Fri.-Sat., 8 p.m.; next Sun., 7 p.m.; ends Dec. 22. $25. (323) 960-5068.

86'd happened at a time when I wasn't necessarily at the edge of the abyss, but I was still on shaky ground, so I'm going to call it one of my unicycles. It fulfilled me artistically, it brought Darryl and I closer together, and one of my dreams came true: I was now a produced playwright with a great review from *The LA Times*. In the grand scheme of things, it was an achievement on a small scale, yet it meant the world to me.

Back East, my family was in chaos. After removing my sister and her negativity from my life, my brother and I made a deal whereby he'd assume the responsibility of looking after our mother. We took control of her accounts, which were really *my* accounts. Dad had passed in 2004 and Mom sold their house, but her money ran out rather quickly, so with Darryl's knowledge and blessing, I was paying for her apartment and putting money into her savings to keep her afloat. My brother and I shared power of attorney duties, but since he lived in Philadelphia and I was in L.A., I thought he should have primary responsibility while I had secondary. It was a decision I would later deeply regret.

On the acting front, things were starting to dry up. I went to see my manager, Maryellen Mulcahy, and asked, "Is this it for me?"

"I'll tell you when you're retired," she replied. That was reassuring, leading me to believe there might be a few more projects in my future. I made up my mind that I wasn't going to turn down any role, no matter how small. If I could rack up enough of them in a year, they'd help me – along with my residuals, social security, and pension – to get by.

One day, Maryellen called. "Jon, are you signed for on-camera commercials?" When I told her I wasn't she said, "Well, a request came in regarding a commercial campaign. Robert Downey Jr. is the spokesman for the HTC One cell phone and they want to see you for it."

"Is that something you can handle?" I asked.

"I know nothing about commercials. What should I do?"

"As far as I know, the only thing you can really negotiate is the pay," I answered. There's scale, which is a rate that everyone is paid, and there's double scale, a rate that no one is paid anymore unless you're *really* lucky. I told her, "Just find out how serious they are about seeing me and we'll go from there." Imagine my complete and utter shock when I learned that Downey Jr. himself requested that I get an audition!

I had Maryellen tell them I'd come in as long as I'd make double scale if I was cast. A few hours later, she called and said they agreed to my terms and wanted me to meet with the director via Skype.

The next morning, Darryl and I started talking about how much of a financial boon it would be if I got this commercial, especially since acting gigs were becoming scarce. We didn't usually get our hopes up when it came to auditions, which is the actor's way. When you don't expect to get the job, sometimes you do; when you think you've got it, you usually don't. Trying to temper my optimism, I went to Santa Monica for the audition. There were four or five other people sitting in the room, and the director – Bryan Buckley, a very successful commercial guy – was on the computer screen with his entourage in the background.

From the beginning, I didn't feel like Bryan was very excited to see me, but despite his lack of enthusiasm, I thought the audition went well. He'd ask me to change something or do it a different way and I followed his instructions to the letter. The lines and the set-up were strangely familiar. I'd seen them before, although I had no idea where. I thought "strange" was going to be the key to this concept, so I was sort of myself with a little more emphasis on my odd and unusual side. When the reading concluded, everyone in the room expressed positive feedback, and I went home to wait for a decision. Ninety minutes after leaving the casting office, Maryellen called. "Jon, I'm sorry, it didn't work out. The director has someone else in mind who he's worked with before."

Darryl was more disappointed than me because I'd learned how to deal with rejection long ago. We went about the rest of our day, and I got another call that evening. "Get ready to fly!" Maryellen exclaimed.

"What the hell are you talking about?" I asked.

"Robert Downey Jr. told HTC's advertising agency he was only going to do the commercial with *you*!"

My mind was blown. It was a huge gesture for him to insist I get an audition, and now he was threatening to walk away unless I was hired?! I'd worked with Robert on *The Singing Detective* about ten years earlier and we got along great, but it wasn't as though we became best friends. His risky insistence was a mystery but learning the reason for it would have to wait. I was booked on a Miami-bound flight the following morning.

After checking into a glamorous oceanfront hotel, I was taken to wardrobe and issued a military outfit. I still couldn't put my finger on why the whole thing seemed so familiar, but most of my thoughts were preoccupied with my physical health. I was recovering from hip replacements, my knee was going out, and I was on medication for cancer. However, I kept quiet about all these ailments, determined to make the best of it.

Downey Jr. had been hired to do a whole campaign for HTC, and this was going to be the first of several commercials. The theme was that the company's initials stood for anything in life that you wanted it to: "Hold This Cat," "Hot Tea Catapult," things like that. It was a huge promotion costing millions and starring the highest-paid actor in the world. When I arrived on the set before dawn on Saturday morning, the director was polite, the HTC people were welcoming, and the head of the advertising agency was a New York gal whom I liked instantly. Robert was filming only on Saturday and Sunday, while the rest of us were staying Monday and Tuesday to do pick-up shots. I was happy to be getting double scale, but at this point I still didn't know why he wanted me there.

HTC commercial with Robert Downey Jr. and Phil LaRocca

The first scene to be shot was the introduction of Robert to a board of directors in a conference room. I was to announce that we had brand new, unconventional concepts and he'd walk in with a briefcase hand-cuffed to his wrist, yet another element that struck me as oddly familiar. The director said, "Robert has ideas for your look."

"Well, I already have my wardrobe," I replied.

"No, no, no, I'm talking about your hairpieces."

This was news to me. Out came a large Afro wig, an ugly curly-topped Italian thing, and a smaller piece that looked absolutely dreadful. I hated all of them, but I was told to try them on because Robert – who was holed up in one of his two massive trailers – wanted to see pictures of what I looked like. I agreed but went to the hair person and said, "Let's put them on badly." Had we put real effort into making any of them work it probably would've appeared okay, but I didn't want any of them, so the photos reflected how ridiculous they were. The images were sent to Robert and we waited for his response.

A while later, the director announced that Mr. Downey Jr. was on his way to the set. I asked, "So, what are we doing with my look?" He explained that Robert had sent him a text that read, "What does Polito want?"

I told him, "Tell Mr. Downey Jr. that Polito wants to use Polito, not hairpieces." The message was sent, and almost immediately Robert texted back, "What Polito wants, we're going with." I couldn't believe it!

Robert walked onto the set and I immediately ran up to him like a deranged fanboy, giving him a big hug and kiss. After exchanging a few pleasantries, he gave me a serious look and said, "How are you at improvisation?"

"I've been doing it for years, darling," I replied. "My whole life is an improvisation."

"Then let's shake up this first scene. Don't just say, 'Hello, workers,' when you enter the conference room. Let's do something different. Got any ideas?"

"In the mood I'm in right now, I'd go with, 'Hello, pumpkins!'"

"I love it! Let's try it," he said.

I marched into the room for the wide shot and barked, "Okay, pumpkins, focus up. Look alive. Tuck in your tailpipes." Robert walked behind me, followed by another actor named Phil LaRocca. I don't think the director was pleased with all the improvising, but I was having a blast. We had other locations to do that day so most of the time was spent covering Robert's stuff, knowing the rest of us were going to be there for a couple of days in case they needed close-ups. After lunch, the production moved to a dock that had a large catamaran covered in foil: "Humongous Tinfoil Catamaran." Sunset was approaching and we were well into overtime, but since Robert was only there for a limited amount of time, we moved on to the next sequence, which was him landing on the roof of a building in a helicopter, jumping out and giving me a high-five.

And that's when it hit me. What I was seeing was the opening of a film called *Putney Swope*, which was directed by Robert Downey Sr. I knew his father socially and thought he was an interesting man, although there were stories that Robert Sr. was the reason his son started doing drugs, giving him a joint when he was eleven or twelve. I wanted to learn more but nobody was speaking directly with Downey Jr. There was a kind of wall between him and everyone else, but being the big goof that I am, I pulled him aside at one point and said, "I know your dad and I have to ask you something. Is this *Putney Swope*?"

"Yes, this is for my father," he answered. "He's going through some treatments."

"Well, if he has cancer I can certainly relate." I told him about my multiple myeloma, and in that moment, I wasn't talking to a movie star or the highest-paid actor in the world; he was just Robert, and he was wonderful. On his new HTC phone, he pulled up the opening scene of his father's movie and we watched it together. Robert was allowed free reign to do whatever he wanted in the commercial, and he had chosen to pay tribute to his dad, which I thought was beautiful.

At nine o'clock that night we moved on to a huge, *Hollywood Squares*-type set with people doing different routines – singing, dancing, fighting, you name it – in their boxes. This was the last scene in the commercial, and as we walked in front of the building with all this crazed activity going on behind us, I say, "What does it all mean?" and Robert answers, "Happy Telephone Company." Then the tag comes at the end: "HTC... Here's To Change."

HTC commercial with Robert Downey Jr.

On Sunday, we had to shoot a scene at a carwash, which was going to be a "Hipster Troll Carwash." There were two little people who were hired to wear large troll heads, and they had to be filmed in several different places so the footage could be digitized to make it look like there was a lot of trolls. The day started out sunny and 110 degrees and transitioned to 98 degrees and rain, which made for a tough set-up for such a simple scene. We were all standing next to a car as a guy was playing music from his HTC phone, and we began to dance. Our moves were improvised, and since I thought my character would be the worst dancer, I just kind of bounced up and down. There were all kinds of delays and technical issues, which meant having less time to film another segment in an art museum later that day. In fact, because of time constraints they had to cut out a planned sequence in which Robert is in a sleeping pod and I wake him up. They'd already built a full set and it was going to go unused.

During one of the breaks, I asked Robert about his son, whom I remembered fondly because he had been guarding his father during *The Singing Detective*. The boy was now a teenager, and Robert talked about his family, which surprised everyone because nobody else really tried to relate to him like I did. At one point I said, "Robert, I have to ask you… Why am I here?"

"Don't be silly; you're Polito," he responded.

"No, seriously… This is a wonderful thing you've done for me and I'd like to know why. Why did you insist on me?"

"Jon, I've been through a lot. I feel like I'm becoming part of the old guard of actors and I think of you as my old guard uncle."

I'm not afraid to admit I teared up after hearing this. I was so touched; it was a beautiful thing for him to say. Whether it was true or not, it was very important to me. All actors like to think they have an impact on an audience, but in that moment I felt my entire body of work had been worth it because I had a fan in Robert.

We finally made it to the museum sequence, which was very complicated. There were a lot of props and extras to deal with and Robert was on a time limit. We shot as quickly and economically as we could, but it still took seven hours to film (and ended up being nine seconds of footage in the finished commercial!). As things were winding down for the day, I was starting to get a little sad. I had no idea if I'd ever get to work with Robert again – hell, I didn't know if I'd ever work again, period! The next two days were just going to be me and Phil LaRocca, which I don't think the crew and director were very excited about.

Robert came up to me as he was about to leave and said, "I can't say goodbye without thanking you for agreeing to do this," and he handed me a gift. I thanked him and he said, "Open it when you get back to the hotel." That night, I opened the box to find a TAG Heuer watch, which I later discovered was worth several thousand dollars. I didn't know what to do with it then and I still don't! I keep it in a guarded area of my house, afraid to wear it while I'm out, frightened that somebody is going to try and rip it off my wrist. Also in the box was a wonderful note from Robert which included his cell phone number, inviting me to get in touch with him whenever I wanted.

The rest of the shoot was uneventful, although I did become friends with the head of the advertising agency. We got along famously, and she said the HTC people were really impressed by my ability to give different performances for different takes. I went back to Los Angeles thinking I was going to be seeing this commercial all the time since it was a full-scale international campaign, but it didn't really play much in America.

However, there were rewards! As a thank you, the HTC people gave me an HTC One phone – which was much more advanced than the flip phone I was using – and the double scale Maryellen had negotiated paid pretty well. As a matter of fact, I made more money on a commercial with Robert Downey Jr. than anything else I had done in my career. It shook up my accountant, who had to rearrange some things because I went from making about $80,000 in most years to almost $250,000 for one week's work. People think actors make that kind of money all the time, but I'm here to tell you it took me thirty-four years to hit a payday like that. I used some of the windfall to buy Darryl a brand-new truck, which he desperately needed, and we put a lot away in savings, continuing to live frugally.

The whole experience was a gift, as was Robert, who to this day still quickly responds to any text I send.

21

Big Eyes
(and an Even Bigger Arm)

The money from the HTC commercial put me in a good financial situation but I still wanted to work as much as possible. I told my manager, "I want to do anything that's out there – anything. I don't want to wait for offers, let me get out there and audition."

There was a half-hour sitcom being produced for ABC called *Saint Francis*. Michael Imperioli was parlaying his success from *The Sopranos* into a starring role as a cop who takes over the family bar. Paget Brewster, whom I liked very much, was cast as his wife, and his mother-in-law was portrayed by Sharon Gless from *Cagney & Lacey*. Spencer Grammer, the daughter of Kelsey Grammer, was playing Michael's sister, which I found fascinating. I knew people who'd worked with her in New York who spoke highly of her, and I thought she was terrific in the role. I remembered her as a child back when Kelsey and I had a wild couple of days doing drugs, and she'd grown into an amazing young woman. It was a great cast and script, and the network had so much faith in the show that James Burrows, one of the best directors in television, was assigned to the pilot of *Saint Francis*.

Mr. Burrows wasn't impressed with me, which may have had something to do with my role. I auditioned for, and won, the small part of the drunk guy at the end of the bar who was going to have one funny scene per episode. It wasn't like Norm from *Cheers*; it was more of a cameo. However, I saw it as an opportunity to turn the appearance into something that would be anticipated every week. Mr. Burrows kept calling me "Joe" instead of "Jon," so I knew he had no idea who I was. I'll admit that was a bit disheartening, as I thought I'd done enough over the years at least to warrant the director using my right name. When we got to my bit, I had a series of lines with the handsome Henry Simmons,

On the set of Saint Francis *with Gianni DeCenzo*

who was a joy. He was nervous and didn't have a lot of experience do-ing comedy, but we played off each other well.

Since there was so much money backing the production, we were able to rehearse for a week. The studio even hired a test audience to sit in on a Thursday rehearsal to see how the pilot would play, and it was playing beautifully. At such an early stage the episode was running long, which is normal. When it came to my intro, the audience laughed, and when I did my exit, they *really* laughed. I thought, *Oh boy, they're laughing a little too long. That's not good.* On Friday morning, I was told my part was getting trimmed a bit in order to get the running time down, and that's when I could see the writing on the wall. The audience reaction to my stuff was so good that the producers were worried it would overshadow the rest of the episode, so their initial instinct was to cut my lines and shorten my appearance.

We were told to be ready for camera blocking on Monday, which meant the script was pretty much locked, with my part being smaller than it was the day before. Tuesday was the actual shooting day, and I was excited because it would be in front of a live audience. We shot the episode and it came in on time, but it didn't quite work like it did before. It felt good but not great, the audience wasn't as engaged, and I think the cuts had removed some of the original script's heart. I'm not going to praise my work with James Burrows – even though I still think he's one of the greatest television directors in the world – but I don't believe he allowed the project to grow as naturally as it could have. Not only that, he basically edited my already-reduced part down to one line. I think I said, "Hello," at which point he cut away from me and I was never seen again. Such was life on *Saint Francis*, but at least I made some money for my efforts.

Darryl and I then went off to Palm Springs for a mini-vacation. At the time, there were news stories about California legalizing gay marriage, and Darryl seemed to be hinting that he'd like to get officially hitched. There's a tram that goes to the highest mountain overlooking Palm Springs, but I'm afraid of heights so I never had any desire to ride it. It was October 16th – we'd met fifteen years earlier on that day – and my idea was to take him to the top of the mountain and propose. We planned to board the first tram ride that morning, but it was having mechanical problems, which did nothing to calm my fears. Darryl said we should skip it, but I suggested we go to breakfast and come back later. He started questioning why I was being so insistent on riding the tram, and I kept telling him it was something I wanted to do. We came back in the afternoon and got on board with a large crowd. The tram started moving slowly and frighteningly up toward the mountain, rotating the entire time and making me nauseous. When we got to the top, I made a beeline for the men's room. After composing myself, I came out, took him onto a balcony and said, "Darryl Armbruster, will you marry me?"

To my surprise, he began to cry. He's a dry German; emotional as can be yet rarely prone to tears. At this moment, though, his eyes were overflowing. He said, "Yes, Jon Polito, I will marry you!" After fifteen years together, we were finally engaged.

In 2014, I was offered a part on the television series *Castle*, which starred Nathan Fillion, Stana Katic, and the great character actress Susan

Sullivan. The episode involves the discovery of a gangster's corpse bur-
ied in concrete after he'd gone missing thirty years earlier. His remains
included a coin from a New York amusement park, which leads the main
characters to investigate his murder. I played Harold Metzger, the con-
sigliere to the deceased gangster who, in his mind, is still living in the
1970s. He wore leisure suits, listened to disco records and was a chau-
vinistic lunatic, all of which was whipped cream to an actor like me. My
character was crazy as a loon – or so one thought – until the final plot
twist when he's shown the coin and begins to cry, revealing that he was
in love with the dead gangster. They were gay at a time when it wasn't
widely accepted and working in a criminal organization that certainly
wouldn't have tolerated it. The role had a lot of color and the director
was John Terlesky, a terrific guy who used to be an actor. His experience
on both sides of the camera helped with my performance, and I was quite
pleased with that episode of *Castle*. I know it doesn't sound like much,
but every guest appearance is a joy when it's like this. It's not often you
get offered a part with some real meat, and I sank my teeth into it.

I then got word I was going to be auditioning for a small role in a
Tim Burton film called *Big Eyes*. I'd worked with the Coens, Ridley

Scott, and some other wonderful directors, but this was Tim Burton! I couldn't wait to read for the part, which was based on a real person named Enrico Banducci. He ran a nightclub in San Francisco and allowed some paintings of little waifs with big eyes to be put up near the bathroom. The artist was Margaret Keane, and what she didn't know was that her husband, Walter, was taking credit for creating them. My character was in only a couple of scenes and there wasn't much to it. The job was to look and act like Banducci did back in the day. I got online and found out he was famous for wearing a French beret, so I bought one and wore it to the audition. The casting lady kept asking me to do less and less, and I did about as much "less" as I possibly could. I really wanted the part and tried to do it exactly as instructed while still trying to get a bit of myself in there.

After I won the role, I was whisked away to Vancouver for ten days of work. I loved it there, and while everyone was staying at the newest and fanciest hotels, I asked to be put up at The Sutton Place. People were shocked I wanted to go to what was, in their words, such an "old and antiquated" establishment, but I wanted to be in an environment that was part of my history. The first day on set, I went in for wardrobe and was told I had to do some promo pictures that were going to be included in the film. Once that was finished, I was taken to meet Tim Burton. He couldn't have been sweeter, and more surprisingly, he couldn't have been more *normal*! I wasn't ready for that; I just thought he was like a vampire because he had this wild hair and always wore black. He was a gentle soul, but during our initial conversation, he implied that the style of the film was going to be more realistic than his other work. I looked at him and said, "Mr. Burton, are you giving me a 'do less' note before I've even done my first take?" His face went blank and he immediately began to apologize, but I told him, "I'm only joking. I'll do whatever you want, however you want it."

Amy Adams, who I think is a powerhouse, was playing Margaret Keane. Cast as Walter Keane was Christoph Waltz, someone I admired and had voted for in Oscar races over the years for his performances in Quentin Tarantino's films. In my first scene I had to introduce a jazz band, walk off stage and be met by Christoph, who was trying to convince me to put up some paintings in the club. Waltz was a lovely man, but truth be told, I couldn't quite understand what he was doing vocally. I finally realized that he was a German who always played a foreigner, but in this movie, he was trying to get his mouth around an American accent and was struggling with it. I felt bad, but I was fighting my own battle, trying my best at being subtle and realistic. I was also determined to play to the center, which is something I believe an actor should always do. In my opinion, a scene shouldn't really focus on one actor or another; it's the exchange between them you want the audience to pay attention to. Acting is like a tennis match and it's the match you watch, not the individual players.

Big Eyes with Christoph Waltz

While things were going well on the set, my multiple myeloma numbers were all over the place and starting to cause some problems. One of the chemotherapy pills was Revlimid, which can cause bouts of neuropathy, an unusual nerve condition in which your brain sends false signals to your limbs. Sometimes I'd have to use a cane because my left knee was in need of being replaced, and walking on my right foot was becoming extremely painful. Since my cancer diagnosis, I was always in fear of what would happen to my body and never quite knew what I would feel like day-to-day.

In my most important scene in *Big Eyes*, I have an altercation with Christoph that was described in the script as an epic brawl. He insults me as I'm standing with two women and I tell him not to speak to me like that in front of the ladies. He swings at me, I swing at him – accidentally hitting one of the girls – and then we run through the club fighting, which comes to an end when he slams a painting over my head. This happened in real life between Enrico Banducci and Walter Keane, so sixty-something Jon Polito had to do another fight sequence while trying to hide his physical limitations.

We rehearsed and blocked the sequence, but I was nervous about throwing my punch because I had to hit the girl next to me. She was a stuntwoman and kept on saying, "Don't be afraid, I know how to do this." On the first take, I tried to do the full swing and it didn't quite work. The stuntwoman felt I could have swung harder to justify her fall, so on the next take I was determined to do it with everything I had. I swung perfectly, she fell perfectly and as I started to run, I slipped across the floor and fell, catching myself with my left arm. People ran to help but I immediately waived them off, insisting I was fine. At this point in my life, I didn't want anything to be reported as a medical problem. Getting a job is hard enough; you don't want to give people another reason *not* to hire you. I jumped up like nothing was wrong and went right back to shoot it again. By the third take, it was in the can and I was proud as a peacock. We followed that with the dolly shot of me running and the bit where I get slammed over the head with a painting. All of it turned out well, and it was a good day's shoot.

As I was getting out of wardrobe, I had a funny feeling in my left arm. I looked at it in the mirror and saw that it was turning purple. Since it wasn't going to be visible under my clothes, I didn't think too much about it. By the time I got back to the hotel, that plum-colored appendage was swelling to Schwarzenegger-like proportions! I took pictures of it with my phone and sent them to Darryl. He said I should go to a doctor right away, but I refused. I wasn't going to turn this into a problem that might affect the shoot, so I took a wait-and-see approach.

The next day, I had to notify wardrobe because the arm had become so enlarged that I couldn't put on my shirt. When those folks saw it, they panicked and asked for the nurse to come take a look. When *she* started to freak out, I knew this injury might cause some difficulties. I tried to convince everyone I was fine and ready to go, but the schedule was changed and scenes were switched around. I now wasn't needed for at least a couple of hours and they urged me to use that time to re-lax and be examined by a doctor. I was getting worried, but instead of a doctor, I asked that they bring someone else in, and the head of the stunt department was brought over. The man said, "Well, it's definitely a contusion but I've never seen this much swelling."

"My only concern is whether this can cause blood clots because I've had heart problems," I explained.

"Yes, it's possible. You really need to see a doctor."

"Okay, but *please* don't tell Mr. Burton. Let's try to get this done quietly."

In less than an hour, a doctor had arrived and was examining my massive purple arm. She asked lots of questions and came to the same conclusion as the stuntman. Although I wasn't in pain, she gave me a couple of pills. Since I didn't want any conflict with the other medications I was taking, I came clean and told her about my cancer treatment and heart issues.

I went on the set about three o'clock that afternoon and the very first person to approach me was Amy Adams, asking if I was okay. I didn't know that other people were aware of the injury, and she couldn't have been kinder or more caring. Sometimes you just fall in love in a second, and I definitely fell for her. From that one interaction, I wanted her to be my nurse for the rest of my life. Mr. Burton came over and asked how I was doing, and I insisted there was no problem that would keep us from moving forward.

I had high hopes for the film. It was based on a true story with great actors and a wonderful director. I was hoping all those ingredients would come together to make a box office hit, and the film's late release in 2014 would put it in a position to get some awards recognition. Christoph and Amy were both nominated for Golden Globes – which Amy won for Best Actress – but *Big Eyes* was another one of my clunkers. Who would've thought a Tim Burton film with this cast could fail? It played for about a week and then disappeared. It'll never be a classic, but it was a labor of love for Mr. Burton and I enjoyed being allowed to participate.

2015 was coming and things were getting progressively worse on the East Coast. The health of my wonderful mentor, Dominic Garvey, had deteriorated so much that the only way to keep him alive was through a series of blood transfusions. Even then, his physician cautioned that the treatment would only buy Dominic another year of life at most. We hadn't spoken *that* much over the years but were now talking on the phone two or three times a week. We'd have very open discussions about what he was going through physically, and he wanted to know everything that had happened to me when I had my death experience.

In an effort to keep things light, I'd try to segue into something we did together or mention a play he turned me on to. By bringing up events when he was at my side or at my lead, I wanted him to know how much my life was changed, influenced and inspired by him.

Dominic wasn't the only one staring into the abyss. My mother was in bad shape, too, and my six phone calls a day were becoming more and more difficult for her. Sometimes she wouldn't answer, and when she did, she was usually disoriented or confused. She was failing and started implying that she wanted me to save her in some way. At one point, she asked if I'd consider moving her from Philadelphia to California to be with Darryl and me. I was shocked that she'd want to leave since my brother and his kids were there, but Mom said, "Jonny, to be truthful, I'd rather die with you guys." That was a major thing to admit,

Jon and his mom

and I didn't take it lightly. I began to investigate all the places around our area and found a good Catholic-based living unit I thought would be ideal.

I was gathering the application papers when I talked to my brother, Jack, about relocating her. Without any hint of consideration, he refused. I told him, "You can't do that. I have power of attorney."

"No, you don't," he replied. "I do." I flashed back to that day a few years earlier when I decided Jack was closer and should have primary power of attorney, and there wasn't a damn thing I could do about it now. He said he was refusing because her family was close by, but the truth was that nobody was visiting her much and nobody was talking to her as often as I was. She was lucky if she saw her grandchildren once every month or two, and my sister was nowhere to be found.

I couldn't understand why Jack was fighting me. He said, "You're in bad health, too. What if something happens to you and she's stuck out there? Is Darryl going to take care of her?" After relaying this concern to Darryl, he vowed that he would, but Jack wouldn't budge. I had the horrible task of telling Mom that although things weren't working out at the moment, I was still going to try and bring her to California.

It was a lie, and I knew it was never going to happen. She was going to die in the assisted living facility in Philadelphia and I was going to be 3,000 miles away when it happened.

22

Reality Check

As conditions intensified back East, they were becoming pretty severe in the West, as well. My multiple myeloma numbers were rising, prompting the medical team to explore the idea of different treatments. I was also having injections in my knees just so I could walk, while my body was going through a rough series of assorted aches and pains. In the meantime, I was trying to keep all of this from my manager and agents, telling them I was ready, willing, and able to work.

I got a call from the folks at *Modern Family*, the fabulous TV show starring Ed O'Neill, Jesse Tyler Ferguson and Ty Burrell. Ed's character runs a closet manufacturing business, and throughout the series he occasionally mentions his hated rival and nemesis, Earl Chambers. As a fan of the show I remembered those references, and as luck would have it, I was cast as Earl! Not only was I featured on one of the top-rated comedies on television, it was a part I absolutely loved. Ed and I got along famously, spending most of our downtime talking about the old Hollywood actors we grew up watching.

Jobs were few and far between at this point, so I thought it was the perfect time to deal with some of my nagging physical ailments. My left knee was long overdue for replacement, but I was warned the recovery would be challenging. Even though I was usually quick to bounce back from injury, this was a completely different animal. I arranged a meeting with a doctor who was supposed to be one of the best knee-replacement guys in the area, and we scheduled the procedure. However, my right foot was also giving me problems, so I had another doctor in the same hospital look at it. He said my foot was filled with horrible arthritis, but it would be an easy fix to relieve the pain. It was a classic catch-22: if I got the knee replaced, recuperation would be heavily dependent on the ability to walk on my right foot. That same foot, though, was causing me extreme discomfort and would be under even more stress after

Modern Family *with Ed O'Neill*

the knee replacement. I consulted a physical therapist and he recommended I get the foot taken care of first. I called the hospital, switched the operations, and on June 5th I went in for a simple foot repair.

When I came out, I had what I referred to as a "stigmata" scar on the middle of the foot where they went in and scraped the arthritis away. About a month after the procedure, we went to David Burke's place in Palm Springs for the Fourth of July weekend, and I noticed my foot wasn't looking particularly good. Not only had the swelling not gone down, it seemed like it was getting worse. I dismissed it as part of the healing process until I woke up in the middle of the night screaming in agony. Pain was nothing new to me, but it honestly felt like my foot was going to explode. Darryl asked, "What can I do?"

"Get me to a hospital!" I pleaded.

We drove around Palm Springs in the wee hours of the morning and couldn't find an emergency room anywhere. With nowhere else to go, we went back to David's house and I took two Norcos, one more than I was supposed to. The doctor had also given me OxyContin in case of major pain, so I popped one of those, but nothing was helping. David was an early riser and as dawn began to break, he heard all the commotion and said, "Dear God, why didn't you tell me? We've got to get you to a hospital!"

"We tried that," I told him.

There was a facility nearby that we missed, but based on its appearance, you'd never know it was a hospital. This place was so run down it should've been condemned. After a brief exam and a battery of tests, a doctor gave me his diagnosis: "You need surgery tomorrow morning. If you don't have it, you could lose your foot or possibly even die."

Naturally, Darryl and I began to freak out! There weren't any surgeons on staff in this shithole, so one was brought in. He was a lovely man, and he sat down with us to shed some light on the problem. "You have an infection in your foot that's going into your bloodstream," he explained. "We have to flush this wound, but the problem is that you have screws in your foot. Even if we eliminate the infection in the rest of your body, those screws might still contain traces of it, so they need to be removed. Do you want me to do it?"

"No," I answered. "I should have this done back in Los Angeles with my own doctor."

"Well, I'll do what I can."

"Please do it and get me the hell out of here!" They gave me some very strong intravenous antibiotics, the doctor flushed the wound, and back to L.A. we went. Upon arrival, we went directly to my foot doctor. He examined the infected appendage and nonchalantly announced he'd remove the screws on Friday. He didn't seem the least bit concerned, making it sound like it was a simple, run-of-the-mill procedure, which put my mind at ease. His only instruction was that I should stay off my feet as much as possible until then, so I got settled in the condo and started making phone calls.

I talked to Dominic on Tuesday and learned his care team had stopped the blood transfusions because they were no longer a viable option for extending his life. "Jon, I'm going to die," he said. "I don't know how much longer I have." I told him I loved him and that I'd call every day. I then got on the phone with my mother, who was completely out of it. I couldn't make any sense of what she was saying, so I talked to a nurse who said Mom was having good days and bad days, but the end was coming. I explained I couldn't travel due to my own medical issues, to which she replied, "Get here as soon as possible."

Two of the most important people in my life were headed for the abyss and I wasn't their unicycle. On Thursday I called Dominic, who was surrounded by nurses and pumped full of morphine. I asked if someone could put the phone to his ear, and after some fumbling and mumbling, I heard him whisper, "Is it Jon? Is it Jon?"

"Dominic, how are you?" I asked.

"I have no idea. I've never been this stoned before." I let him know that I loved him; he murmured something and then passed out.

His nurse said, "That's the clearest he's been since yesterday. I'm surprised he was even able to talk to you."

When I finished that call, I spoke to my mom and gave her the news that I was going in for surgery the next day. She was in a lucid state of mind and asked how I was. I admitted that although I wasn't feeling well, I was making plans to come visit her in a couple of weeks. "I can't wait to see you, Jonny," she said.

I went into the hospital on Friday and that's when all hell broke loose. We got word that Darryl's grandmother had passed away, which was closely followed by news that Dominic had died. We'd lost two people within hours of each other, which I thought was a pretty shitty way to go into the operation. Thankfully, it was minor surgery, and even though I felt fine afterward and was ready to go home, the doctor insisted I stay overnight for monitoring. I wanted to be with Darryl after he lost his grandmother and I wanted to be home so I could mourn Dominic in private, but I was stuck in the hospital.

At two o'clock in the morning, I was awakened by a nurse on duty. "Mr. Polito, you're going through a situation right now. Emergency services are on the way."

"What's the problem?" I asked.

"You're having a heart issue and it could cause a stroke."

I thought, *What the hell is this?* I was moved to another area of the hospital and hooked up to several different machines. With the help of some drugs, my heart settled into a normal rhythm, at which point a specialist came in and said I'd developed a severe new infection and could still lose my foot. This one had to be fought with intravenous antibiotics which were now going to be administered through a chest port. What was supposed to be a simple foot procedure was spiraling out of control! I was told that once I was discharged, I'd need to have a portable suction device attached to my foot to suck out the pus and goo because the foot wasn't healing on its own.

On Sunday morning, Darryl came to visit and brought a wonderful breakfast of lox and bagels from the local deli. He sat with me while I ate, and I could tell by his demeanor that he had bad news to share. "I have to tell you something," he said softly. "Your mom died." I knew this day was coming but it was still a shock, especially after losing his grandmother and Dominic less than forty-eight hours earlier. I made the medical staff aware of my situation and they assured me I'd be released the next day with the additional machinery attached. However, it was made clear that under no circumstances would I be able to fly.

My prediction came true. I was 3,000 miles away when my mom died, and I couldn't even tell her goodbye.

* * *

Darryl went to Chicago for his grandmother's memorial service, and as I sat at home with a tube in my chest filled with antibiotics and another tube coming out of my foot removing infectious liquids, there was a funeral in Philadelphia I wasn't able to attend.

Although it was only a morning viewing and burial, it turned out to be a large event with many more people showing up than we expected. I paid for everything, including an open bar and lots of Italian food. It went off without a hitch, despite an attempt by my sister and niece to sabotage it, and ended up being a lovely tribute to a wonderful woman. As for Dominic, he was cremated, and his ashes were saved for me to scatter.

A few days after my mother's service, I received a call from a man I didn't know. "I'm a friend of Tian King," he said. Tian was a girl I met in college. We did a few plays together and started hanging out, eventually becoming good friends. In my youthful days of sexual experimentation, I was trying everything, and one of the things I tried was Tian. I remember the sex was uncomfortable and awkward, not only because I was gay but because of our friendship. However, she admitted many years later that she always thought of it as a pleasant experience. She was another lifelong friend I didn't want to let go of, and we'd talk every six months or so. When I was getting settled in Los Angeles in the '90s, Tian came out to give acting a try and did some nice work in the theater. Unfortunately, she also got involved with a cokehead "boyfriend" who was using her for money. My own cocaine consumption was extreme during those days and she couldn't handle being surrounded by so much drug abuse, so she moved back to Philadelphia. Around this point – the beginning of the 2000s – I lost her contact information, and this was the first time in fourteen years I'd heard her name. The caller went on to say that Tian had just passed away, but he wanted me to know that she'd always spoken highly of me.

Now there were four deaths, but it wasn't over yet. Five days later, I received a call from my manager, Maryellen. She was sobbing hysterically, and since Maryellen isn't a crier, I immediately feared the worst about her health. "Oh my God, are you okay?" I asked.

"No... Gabrielle Krengel just died."

Gabrielle was the head of my agency, Domain Talent, and a great supporter of mine. I'd been with them for almost ten years, and whenever I had doubts about my work, she always made a point of saying, "You're a feather in our cap." Maryellen and Gabrielle were good friends; in fact, it was Maryellen who convinced Gabrielle to take me on as a client. The three of us often had lunches together and I enjoyed their company very much. It was revealed that Gabrielle had cancer, and since she didn't talk about it publicly, her passing caught us completely off guard.

Fortunately, in the midst of all this death there *was* a bit of a bright spot. A man named Alan K. Rode contacted me, introduced himself as a fan, and wanted to talk about his business, which was organizing events

for film retrospectives and anniversaries. Alan had quite a roster of character actors he worked with, so I agreed to meet and discovered he was an absolute sweetheart. "Let me know what you have in mind," I told him.

"What's on my mind is *Miller's Crossing*," he replied. September of 2015 marked twenty-five years since the movie's premiere at the New York Film Festival, and Alan had arranged a screening at the Palm Springs Film Noir Festival where I was invited to speak. I tried to find some new things to talk about regarding my career, which is when I began to think about compiling these stories into a book.

During this time, my foot was finally in healing mode. The drain had been removed and the stigmata hole left a very nasty scar, but the wound continued leaking fluid every day. That's when a producer for *Modern Family* said I was being brought back for another episode. My character hires Ed O'Neill's son for a job that turns out to be a prank to embarrass them, and a fight ensues. It was a funny scene, but I was worried if I'd be able to do it because my lower back had gone out. Not only did I have a lot of problems physically, I had also gone back to my oncologist and learned that while I was off the chemo meds due to the foot surgery, my multiple myeloma numbers started to rise. I was fighting cancer again, I couldn't walk properly, and the night before I shot the *Family* episode, I had to pop some steroids and put a brace on my back. Fortunately, the footage turned out great and nobody had a clue I was ailing. At the end of filming, I took off my shoe and it was filled with blood and liquid, but I was proud of finishing the job, especially since opportunities for work were becoming scarce.

Earlier in 2015, the Supreme Court ruled that same-sex marriage was now legally recognized all across the country, and after being engaged for a year, Darryl was making it obvious in his not-so-subtle way that it was time to do the deed. On October 16th, 2015, the sixteenth anniversary of our initial meeting, we were the first couple of the day at the Palm Springs courthouse to get hitched. Armbruster and Polito were now bound forever! My cousin hosted a reception for us on the beach, where we were surrounded by friends and family. It was the perfect way to start our lives as a married couple.

Shortly thereafter, I learned that for the first time in thirty-five years, I hadn't made enough money to qualify for Screen Actors Guild health insurance. Even though I had residuals and the *Modern Family* episode, I hadn't done a film. I was facing an uncertain future, not only with my health but also my career. Meetings were held with my agency and manager, and I was basically told, "You're reading for stuff you're not

going to get. Studios want stars, and although you're well-respected, you're not a star."

It was a reality check. The first of many, actually. Christmas was different because my mother was no longer here to join us. My sixty-fifth birthday came on December 29th, and while it was a good one, it also marked the end of a long, great ride of being together with family. To make matters worse, some asshole wrote on Wikipedia that I was a *retired* actor! Thank God I was able to get it changed, but it reinforced the notion that I wasn't working anymore. However, I did get a voiceover gig for *American Dad*, and the wonderful *Modern Family* producer called and said Earl Chambers was being written into yet another episode, allowing me to antagonize Ed O'Neill again.

I managed to get an audition for a show called *Major Crimes*. Tony Denison is the lead and he's been a lasting friend ever since the *Crime*

Story days. We've known each other for thirty years and I'll always love him. When I went into the reading, I was having problems with my balance, so I used a cane to get myself there and back. I didn't want the casting people to see me like this, so I left it in the hallway and walked into the room with as much panache as I could muster, standing straight as an arrow and hoping I looked great. The casting woman took one look and said, "My God! Jon Polito, you haven't aged a bit since *Push, Nevada!*" Considering that show was shot almost fifteen years ago, I took it as a huge compliment. I had a terrific audition and walked out of that room thinking, *You know what? I can still do this. All I need is a chance or a little bit of luck to come my way.*

Major Crimes *with Katherine Narducci*

Amid all these events and changes, I've been sensing recently that Maryellen has been pushing me off to another person in her office, probably because I'm not bringing in the bucks as I'd been doing. We lunched recently and I could tell something wasn't quite right. Domain Talent is in a state of flux due to the passing of its head, Gabrielle Krengel. It's trying to regroup and I'm not sure where they stand, or where I stand with them.

I'd been unicycling at the edge of the abyss at many different points in my life, but right now I don't see an abyss lying ahead. I see a desert, and I think about how difficult it is to ride a unicycle in the sand.

I don't know what the future has in store, of course. So, I simply go along, awaiting life's next chapter.

Epilogue

Jon Polito began dictating this memoir on Sept 25th, 2014. About a year earlier, I'd interviewed him for the second volume of my book series, *Character Kings: Hollywood's Familiar Faces Discuss the Art & Business of Acting*. Upon its publication, I'd arranged a signing event at Dark Delicacies in Burbank, CA where Jon and several other actors sat alongside me and autographed copies for patrons. It was an enjoyable afternoon that was highlighted by his jovial attitude and good-natured sparring with fans. A few days later, he asked if I'd be interested in working with him on his autobiography. I couldn't say "Yes" fast enough!

Countless hours of phone conversations, transcribing, organizing and rough edits later, a first draft was ready in August 2016. We talked about my coming to L.A. to work on the editing. However, his cancer had other plans. On September 1ˢᵗ, Jon succumbed to the disease.

A memorial service was held in the Theatre Arts building at L.A. Community College (since he'd come of age in the theater, it was only appropriate he should be remembered in a theater). It was the perfect venue to honor a man whose presence and personality were larger than life and played to the back of the house. Several people took to the stage and shared their stories about Jon, including Ethan Coen, Marcia Gay Harden, Derek Cecil, David J. Burke and Ed Begley, Jr. Their recollections were hilarious and mostly R-rated. This was not a solemn, reverent event; these were tales of a man told as wildly as they were lived. At times it was more of a roast than a farewell, but that was by design. When his friends spoke of Jon, they did so with a laugh and a smile. Grief had been checked at the door.

During our two years of collaboration, Jon had transformed from a celebrity I admired from afar into a beloved friend, and I treasure the brief time we shared. I'm also eternally grateful to his husband, Darryl Armbruster, for his unwavering support and confidence in my ability to deliver Jon's life story.

I hope you enjoyed it.

— Scott Voisin

Alysia and Scott Voisin with Jon and Darryl in Chicago on February 14th, 2015

Afterword

Jon was, and still is, the most honestly unfiltered person I have ever known. You may have guessed that after reading the previous pages, and I'd like to include one more anecdote along those lines. We were at a Hollywood party years ago with mostly unknown actors, writers and directors. They were charming people at a lovely gathering where Jon was holding court as only he could. The topic of tattoos came up in conversation, and someone asked Jon if he had any. Without missing a beat, he responded, "I don't need tattoos, darling, I have talent!"

The place instantly fell silent as he had, of course, insulted every tattooed Hollywood hipster in the room. And it was genius. Not cruel to anyone in particular, just honestly unfiltered. I had the sense that more than a few people were quietly using their phones to search Google for tattoo removal services. That is just one of hundreds of examples of his non-existent filtering system, and it's one of the things I loved most about him.

Jon Polito was my life partner for seventeen years and he remains the love of my life. Scott Voisin has captured his spirit in these pages, and for that I am deeply grateful. Thank you, Scott.

And thanks to all who read this book.

— Darryl Armbruster

Index